Architecture in Practice

Design-Build

Published in Great Britain in 2006 by Wiley-Academy,
a division of John Wiley & Sons Ltd

Copyright © 2006 John Wiley & Sons Ltd, The Atrium,
Southern Gate, Chichester, West Sussex PO19 8SQ, England
Telephone (+44) 1243 779777

Email (for orders & customer service enquiries): cs-books@wiley.co.uk
Visit our Home Page on www.wiley.com

Other Wiley Editorial Offices

John Wiley & Sons Inc., 111 River Street,
Hoboken, NJ 07030, USA

Jossey-Bass, 989 Market Street,
San Francisco, CA 94103-1741, USA

Wiley-VCH Verlag GmbH, Boschstr. 12,
D-69469 Weinheim, Germany

John Wiley & Sons Australia Ltd, 42 McDougall Street,
Milton, Queensland 4064, Australia

John Wiley & Sons (Asia) Pte Ltd, 2 Clementi Loop #02-01,
Jin Xing Distripark, Singapore 129809

John Wiley & Sons Canada Ltd, 22 Worcester Road,
Etobicoke, Ontario, Canada M9W 1L1

ISBN 13: 978-0-470-01446-2
ISBN 10: 0-470-01446-6

Series designer: Christian Küsters, CHK Design, London
Layout and prepress: Artmedia Press, London
Printed and bound in Great Britain by
TJ International Ltd, Padstow, Cornwall

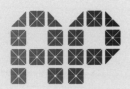

Architecture in Practice

Design-Build

Andrew Thomas

WILEY-ACADEMY

CONTENTS

Introduction

Elevation of Arup's Broadgate,
was this the start of a new era?

Reading a newspaper or magazine, or watching or listening to the news, many of the leading stories will be about international events. We talk of a global economy; currency exchange rates between the pound and the dollar or euro are quoted every day.

With multinational companies, international travel, the global transfer of data, was it possible that the foreign influence was not going to affect the way we do things in Britain? Was it really possible that there would not be a form of global harmonisation towards something as simple as procuring a building? Over the last 25 years there has been a dramatic acceleration of different management techniques, each challenging, pushing and refining established procedures.

Sir Michael Latham captured this change in a recent quotation:[1]

Let's recall some industry features we take for granted which were unknown in 1993/4, when I was doing my research for Constructing the Team, let alone 1980. No constructors or designers talked about benchmarking, which was regarded as impossible. Every job was different, bespoke, architect or engineer designed, often involving nominated subcontractors and with a transient workforce. How could you compare one project's performance with another? Nobody talked supply chain management, either. The client, who was advised by the architect, chose the contractor competitively. The subcontractors were chosen by the main contractor, usually from a long list of tenderers, or else were nominated. There was no clear link of contractual or management responsibility.

Other terms considered normal nowadays but unknown or barely understood in 1980 were project management, design-and-build, construction management, adjudication, best practice and above all, partnering.

In the early 1980s, the nature and quality of British architecture was under scrutiny. One of the most vocal critics of the current architectural style was the Prince of Wales, who spearheaded an attack on architects and developers in 1984–5. Fashions among building professionals and clients were also changing; the raw concrete and modernistic styles were falling out of favour.

Two new trends in design were emerging, 'high-tech' and 'post-modern'; the change in architectural fashion saw a swift demise of the tall and plain curtain-wall tower block. The deregulation of the City of London led to a major building boom in the mid to late 1980s, and although the effects of the boom go far beyond the square mile, it was in the square mile that the change started.

Following on from the success of Cutlers Gardens, Stuart Lipton (Greycoat) and Geoffrey Bradman (Rosehaugh) were responsible for the introduction of the American style fast-track construction techniques into Britain. Projects like Cutlers Court, 1 Finsbury Avenue and Broadgate made use of this new management style. These new 'fast-track' construction techniques clashed with the requirements of the London Building Acts, but these were the 'Thatcher' years where state monopolies, regulations and restrictions were being lifted by radical conservative governments in many different areas of public and business life. The London Building Acts were duly redrafted in keeping with the era.

America is often cited as the major influence behind the uptake of design-build project delivery, but even there it has not had the smoothest of journeys. In Britain, by the end of the 1970s, there was sufficient pressure to allow contractors to control all or part of the design, and Britain produced its first design-build contract.

The Joint Contracts Tribunal (JCT) publish a form of contract that has been developed by the various parties involved, contractors, architects, surveyors etc. Although there are other types of contract, engineering forms and even client specific forms, this JCT contract is always referred to as the standard form. The original 'standard form' is the basis of the 'traditional form' of procurement.

'Traditional' is an interesting term, it is used to describe the design-bid-build procurement route. However, if you delve back into history, the builders were master craftsmen, people who designed and then constructed. Design-build is actually closer to how the master builder performed.

Contracts evolve; they are corrected and amended over a period of time. A form of contract could have many revisions before it is so dramatically changed from the original concept that it has actually become a new form of contract.

JCT 63 (first issued in 1963) is often referred to as the original 'traditional' contract; many of the methods and systems used today were developed for and used with this contract. There was a contract administrator, almost inevitably the architect, and the contractor simply followed instructions. The contractor was responsible for the provision of the work, of the required quality in the required time, but the responsibility for the provision of and quality of the design remained completely with the client and his team. It should be noted that although this original concept is now over 40 years old, it still forms the basis of architectural and quantity surveying contract education.

If something in the design did not work, it would be corrected at the client's expense. If the contractor were delayed through lack of information, then the client would fund the delay. The contractor did not share in the responsibility for the design, design delivery or design development process. Although there are ways of bringing in specialist designing subcontractors, perhaps through nomination, this form of contract does not really make use of the contractor's knowledge on build-ability and available products etc. If a contractor is not free to choose the product, it is unlikely that he will be able to use any of his influence and buying power; as a result it is probable that the project may be more expensive than it could have been. This type of contract maintains design control, there should be no possibility of a contractor substituting a lower standard of product and increasing his profit at the client and project's expense.

In fact, in the mid 1970s, The Department of the Environment asked the Royal Instiute of British Architects (RIBA) to raise with the JCT the need for a standard form under which, for a lump sum, a contractor would design and construct the works to the employer's stated requirements. By this time there were several types of contract for private use but no form existed for use by local authorities or the private sector that fairly apportioned the responsibilities, obligations and risks of the parties. Clearly a new form was needed which would deal with the situation where the appointment of neither an architect nor a quantity surveyor was envisaged.

Design-build was becoming established, and some architects had realised that it would create opportunity. In 1978 David Hutchison gave a talk[2] to about 400 guests at the RIBA Florence Hall; his talk centred on the analogy that Chippendale had designed and made beautiful furniture so why could we not do this with buildings?

In 1980–1, a whole series of JCT contracts were reissued. The traditional contract of the administrator type was refined and amended and became the first major reissue since 1963. A brand new variation of the contract was also introduced, still by the JCT, and became a variation of the standard form. This new type of contract, for the first time made the contractor responsible for all (or a portion) of the design.

JCT 81 with contractor design (JCT 81 WCD) became known as the 'design and build' contract. Although not entirely new, design-build began to gain in popularity. What was new was that this type of building procurement was now available using a set of standard conditions of contract. The new standard form was not simply a redraft; it completely changed fundamental roles. The architect as designer now reported to the contractor and there was a new role, the 'employer's agent', which was normally undertaken by a quantity surveyor.

Although some specialist companies appeared in the early 1980s, it took a long time before the main contractors were fully familiar with 'design-build'. The more enlightened companies, realising the significant differences, set up specialist departments including recruiting new skills to administer the new system.

Will Hughes[3] prepared a paper in 2003 based on the British construction industry, called 'Comparative costs of the commercial process in different construction procurement methods' for delivery to an International Symposium in Singapore. For the paper he had researched the construction industry and produced some very significant findings:

Procurement method	Amount		%
Design-build (pure)	£	863 099 810	20
Design-build (novated)	£	1 101 205 275	26
General contracting	£	1 584 080 930	37
Management contracting	£	229 488 535	5
Construction management	£	515 766 540	12
Nonproject supplies	£	19 342 930	0
Other	£	962 500	0
Total construction turnover attributed	£	4 313 946 520	

The figures indicate that 46 % of British construction turnover comes from projects delivered through design-build. Personally I suspect that the actual figure would be significantly higher if all of the Private Finance Initiative/Public Private Partnership (PFI/PPP) projects were included in these figures, but I can produce no data to substantiate this.

Moss Construction, part of Kier Regional, specializes in design and build, with a dedicated department and director. They have been prepared to share figures[4] that demonstrate the percentage of turnover that is attributable to design and build.

In 1991 Moss had only one design-build project, with a contract value of £1.8 million in a turnover of £22 milion. Figures for more recent years are as follows:

Year	Percentage of turnover
1999	52.3
2000	66.2
2001	71.8
2002	64.1
2003	57.1
2004	53.8

It is interesting that at the peak (2001) nearly three-quarters of a £90 million turnover was generated from design-build projects. This would appear to be in conflict with architectural media, although no examples are to be presented here.

Robin Butler, managing director of Moss Construction, stated[4] that the reason for the decline in percentage of turnover since 2001 highlighted in the Moss figures is simply that they have been successful in the traditional market place: 'The drop in D&B percentage over the last two years does not relate to a perceived drop in popularity of D&B but more to one or two significant non-design-build projects being secured – such as Cheltenham Racecourse at £18m.'

However, I suspect that this is not the whole story. Arlington are one of Moss' main clients for speculative office space. I am not aware of many new projects on either of the Arlington business parks within the Moss region, in the relevant timescale. It appears that Moss have simply diversified during this temporary blip in the speculative office market.

Figures from other companies seem to support the higher than envisaged percentage of turnover attributable to design and build project delivery. RG Carter Construction Ltd[5] confirm that in a turnover of £175 million, £50 million is attributed to design and build.

John Turner, technical services director of Moss Construction, described the Moss attitude towards design and build[6]:

'In these early days, design-build had a reputation of being high risk but potentially high profit. The idea that the 'buck stops' with the contractor was difficult for Moss to come to terms with. Around this time Moss were given an opportunity to become involved in a major project to design and build a motorway services facility on the M25. Accepting the challenge, the project gave Moss the opportunity of expanding its design-build team of design co-ordinators who were site trained but had an engineering background.

Important policies developed quickly as more design-build work was now usually in tender. Firstly it was that a specialist design co-ordinator should be employed to focus on the design solution, in terms of its timing for procurement and construction, technical detail, complication with budget and employer's requirements. To leave all this to the site manager would distract 'the builder'.

Within eight years 50 % of Moss turnover was design-build and employers responded to Moss' ability to respond technically and to contribute to the design and cost process much earlier in the overall project development. The second policy therefore was to try wherever possible to create a 'cradle to grave' approach, ie continuity from early involvement through to completion. This continuity of relationship and knowledge is invaluable, as set out in both Latham and Egan statements.

As design-build became more accepted within the company, Moss became more aware of the risks in building services, structure and some architectural specifications. With the previous overseas experience of the design-build manager, and the ongoing needs to reduce risk, it was decided to employ professionally qualified staff in the form of an architect, a structural engineer, and a building services engineer. Whilst not designing for Moss, they provided technical knowledge to help Moss understand the risk and opportunities present in a design-build project.

Today Moss has fourteen design managers covering most professional disciplines.

As the capability has increased, so clients have responded and Moss are now involved in design management and cost planning on a mix of very prestigious projects. They have built a reputation of proactive problem solving and 'construction with co-operation' which led to them being one of the top three most successful Kier companies as a leader in the design-build process.

Whilst there are clear unavoidable risks in the design-build method of procurement, Moss' structure is designed to focus on the risks, and manage them through the process.

Design-build has enabled Moss to move into a collaborative working arrangement with their clients much earlier in the project development process and to understand and manage risks in a more controlled manner. As clients have seen the benefits of the approach (more time and cost predictability, single point responsibility etc), Moss has benefited in a higher volume of repeat business and better margins.

We are therefore more than happy to undertake design-build projects in any sector of the market.

The change to procurement processes can happen for many reasons. One of these reasons could be that the government may influence change either directly or indirectly. Over the last decade, the government has commissioned a series of reports. The first was in 1994 and is called the Latham report. Sir Michael Latham was Chairman of the Construction Industry Training Board (CITB) when he produced his report called *Constructing the Team*.[7] He was keen to use what he saw as the advantages of construction management, linked with providing suitable advice for inexperienced clients. He noted that clients' wishes 'must be paramount for all construction participants – subject only to planning and development control and the wider public interest'.

The role of 'lead designer' was introduced, and to achieve quality architects were to sign off building stages as they were achieved. It was also noted that change was a major problem, and the report highlighted the fact that the project should take all reasonable steps to avoid changes to preplanned works information. However, where variations do occur, they should be priced in advance, with provision for independent adjudication if agreement cannot be reached. It is now normal practice in a design-build contract for the contractor to engage the architect as 'lead designer'.

The Latham report was followed in 1998 by a report by Sir John Egan, who had a background in the motor industry before he became chairman of the British Airports

Authority. This clearly influenced *Rethinking Construction*,[8] a report of the construction industry taskforce.

The report set the industry a series of targets, notably:

- Reductions in capital cost and construction time of 10 %.
- Reduction in defects and accidents of 20 %.
- Increase in project predictability of 20 %.
- Increase in productivity and profitability of 10%.

'The parallel is not with building cars on the production line, it is with designing and planning the production of a new car model.' The report was based on a 5:4:7 formula or drivers, processes and targets, but when the construction industry had not been transformed, in April 2003 the Government asked Sir John to have a further look.

This time the report was called *Accelerating Change* and his conclusions were different; he advanced the idea of a therapeutic perspective covering respect for people, consensus, health, safety, training, skills, teamwork and an increase in self-esteem in the building industry. The other idea was that of the natural perspective, focusing on sustainable communities and buildings.

In his foreword to the report, Brian Wilson MP[9] said:

> To become world class the industry must invest in training, in the development of new skills, and in research and development to make the best of new materials and new technologies. Even more importantly it must change its culture and the way that it does business, by working more effectively together in a partnership to meet – and exceed – its clients expectations.

It will take time for the influence of these reports to become clear, but there are already signs of influence. Latham's wish to use construction management has translated into a greater use of the contractor's knowledge. Moss Construction recently provided a construction orientated design manager to help the client's design team on a traditional JCT project.

Design-build delivery systems have gone some way to achieving Egan's targets, even if this is only guaranteeing the final outcome. This presents a saving on potential cost overruns. I think that it will take more time for the impact of Egan's second report to be seen. I also think that he missed an opportunity. Egan specifically said that he did not see an analogy with the motor industry, but surely construction can only benefit from increased prefabrication. One of the uncertainties of construction is the weather; prefabrication could decrease the influence of bad weather, increasing the predictability that he was striving for earlier.

The RIBA produced *Constructive Change* containing proposals for action as a response to *Rethinking Construction*. This document accepted change and advised architects to be involved in the change. The following is taken from the report:[10]

> Large sections of the profession have suffered economically as a result of the marginalisation of the architect's role in the last 25 years. *Rethinking Construction*

can be read to suggest further such marginalisation. Indeed there are many in the industry which would favour it. However, no acceptable case against this can be made on any basis resembling self-preservation. Our duty as a body of 27 000 people in the UK who spend a large part of their lives thinking about the nature of the built environment is to promote vigorously change which improves its quality and resist that which does not. Our focus all the while must be on benefit for society and not, except perhaps in consequence, the profession.

It is vital that architects engage closely in the challenge of *Rethinking Construction* to promote the core values widely shared by architects and non-architects. This will not be achieved by the RIBA simply producing a policy document in response to *Rethinking Construction* .... Far better to get all architects re-thinking for themselves in all their myriad circumstances and methods of practice how to improve quality of design and, crucially, the delivery of the built environment for the benefit of the user – our customers.

Performance measurement is a cornerstone of *Rethinking Construction*, and a set of key performance indicators has been established to measure this performance improvement.

Although not directly a part of *Rethinking Construction*, the government have contributed to the design quality debate through the Construction Industry Council. The result of this contribution is a piece of web-based software called 'Design Quality Indicators'[11] that is now available, making it possible to measure design quality. The intent behind the software is that you visit the questionnaire three times during the project, design, construction and completion. The software then compares how the project has lived up to your perceptions. Input is required from many people from both the client and contractor functions, and the software produces an average response as well as allowing 'design quality' to be quantified.

Once made, changes to procurement and associated attitudes are irrevocable; these will only be altered or directed through development and popular requirement. The significance of JCT is that it comprises all sections of the construction industry; it is not simply the outlet for one blinkered minority, and in its own way it represents construction democracy.

The current release of standard forms of contract come under the title of JCT 98. These include not only a revised 'traditional' form, but also a revised 'with contractor's design' form. Also of interest is the fact that you can now use a traditional form but include within that contract an element of contractor's design responsibility. It appears that making the contractor responsible for the design is here to stay.

Architectural education contains an element of contractual administration, but quantity surveying education examines this in much more detail. This procurement and contractual administration education tends to be limited to the traditional forms of contract. The idea that the traditional forms of contract are the 'proper forms' is thus reinforced by education. Architectural education provides little insight into the working of a design and build contract, which tends to add support to the profession's concerns 'that this is not the proper way to procure buildings'.

Although this is how I perceived my own architectural education, and have not read or heard anything since that would change my mind, it appears that the official view of the RIBA may have moved. Richard Brindley RIBA, director of practice at the RIBA, said:[12]

> Design-build is a popular and valuable form of procurement, particularly with clients who are seeking transfer of the design risk and responsibilities to the contractor. However, Design & Build is only suitable to certain types of buildings and client requirements where the Client's design specification and building outputs are clearly known and described. To benefit fully from a design-build delivery system, the Client should also give the Contractor, with their architects and design team, the opportunity to develop the design and to produce a building solution that utilises their specific skills and resources.

Generally little prestige is given to design-build contracts, with a feeling in architectural circles that 'quality' cannot be achieved by using a design-build form of procurement. This is disappointing because not only may design-build be the most appropriate procurement route but also there are now many examples of superb buildings procured in this manner.

However, there are project types and circumstances that make a design-build route totally unsuitable. A balanced knowledge of all contract types will help to aid selection of the most appropriate form of contract.

Kevin Merris, Faithful & Gould:[13]

> Whilst I believe that the chosen method (design-build) was suitable for the Dean Close School project it is important that each project is reviewed on its merits.
>
> Furthermore, if the level/quality of design and information, design team, contractors is of a poor standard then whatever the form of contract it will be difficult to produce a satisfactory product.

John Christophers, Associated Architects:[14]

> Design-build seems much more appropriate for some types of project than for others. The risk is that, if cost is fixed before quality is fully defined, then quality may suffer. It is also sometimes difficult for architects, with or without a 'retained duty', to act in the client's best long term interests when employed through the contractor.

Steve Andrews, principal, Gensler London:[15]

> Design-build whilst laudable in its intent to make things easier for the end user, with a single point of contact, has hugely variable outputs. In its most raw form, quality can suffer hugely as the drive for cost savings vastly outweighs aspirations. At its best, the process is easy, the client gets exactly what he wants at the price he wants to pay. Ultimately the difference between success and failure comes down to one of attitude and people. Get it right at day 1, with the right team and it works. This has the obvious constraint that most of the team should already know each other, should

preferably have worked together and everyone should be vigilant in ensuring that quality of product and service is not compromised. Do it right and you will do more together, just like any other contract.

There are advantages to each type of contract. 'JCT 98 with Contractors Design' gives the contractor certainty, he has control over change. This allows the tender to be fixed or become a guaranteed maximum price (GMP). This fixed price gives the client certainty, he knows how much his building is really going to cost and can have confidence in his cost planning, which in turn can help to reduce the cost of borrowing.

It must be noted that although the contract can be the sum of a GMP, the overall project costs are not necessarily lower. The burden of risk has shifted to the contractor and this will attract a premium. Why take risk for no reward? On many occasions this additional premium will be more than offset by other cost reductions. This is supported by the Royal Institute of Chartered Surveyors (RICS). Ed Badke, Director of RICS stated:[16]

> The design-build procurement route has grown considerably in recent years. It has the attraction of offering clients a single point of contact with a fixed price and programme. However, as with all forms of contract, it is incumbent on the design team to provide a clear and concise brief, which accurately reflects the client's requirements. This publication provides an excellent insight into this form of procurement.

The use of a design-build contract means that certain architectural and other design team services are no longer required, e.g. contract administration. This has the effect of reducing the project consultancy fees, again an element much appreciated by the client. The client has a single contract for the procurement of the building. All contact goes through the contractor (who may have additional contracts with the employer's agent, quantity surveyor (QS), services consultant etc) so this single point responsibility is of benefit to the client.

The Egan report discussed earlier suggested that building procurement costs should be reduced by about 10 %. The 'JCT 98 with Contractors Design' alone will not achieve this figure, but it is a start. As cost certainty is very attractive to the client, the culmination of a reduced and guaranteed contract sum will surely increase the use of design-build. One of the major advantages of design-build is being able to use the contractor's buying abilities. He will have discount arrangements with certain suppliers and bulk buying arrangements with others.

Most domestic commercial retailers have some form of price promise, 'double the difference if bought cheaper locally' or 'not knowingly undercut'. What the retailers are doing is using their commercial muscle to buy the goods at a reduced rate in the first place, which allows part of the reduction to be passed on. The consumer benefits from a reduction in the price of the goods, the retailer benefits from an increased profit margin, due to an increase in turnover. Therefore, why can this principle not be used in construction? The retailer is the large contractor, with national purchasing agreements to drive down prices. The contradiction is that the contractor is rarely in a position to pass these buying savings on to the customer (client). With the specification being set in the name of quality, there is little opportunity to pass on or fully utilise these buying agreements, thus keeping the cost of construction inflated.

Prefabrication is another method that produces a reduction in the cost of the finished component, and so it is easy to make the case that prefabrication increases quality. As prefabrication takes place in a controlled environment, it is possible to achieve certainty of outcome, increase the finished standard or quality and increase the rate of production. These parameters are surely of interest to everybody: the client likes the reduction in cost and certainty of outcome, the architect likes the increase in quality or certainty of defined finish and the contractor likes the certainty that prefabrication brings to the operation, defined costs, less risk on programme and a predetermined quality of finish. So why is prefabrication not used more?

Building procurement has traditionally been treated as a unique event, something special that the everyday rules do not apply to, it is variable and prices are not fixed. Management is by the 'professional' consultants and there is little effort to involve the contractor.

Traditional forms of procurement had an independently appointed architect designing and administering a contract. He rarely liaised with the specialist designers and suppliers, with the idea of maintaining quality, specified products and standards, and had little knowledge of market forces and availability. This almost certainly resulted in the client paying more than could have been necessary.

Design development is an interesting concept, covering both omissions and mistakes on the part of the designers. Traditional contracts require that the client sets aside a sum of money (up to 5 % of the contract sum) to cover these errors. This figure is referred to as the contingency sum. Part of the evolvement process is to provide a 'better deal' for the client. A design-build delivery system is not the whole answer, but it does limit the risk to the employer, perhaps this is the first step to the 'better deal'. The ideal solution will be the integration of the consultant's design skills with the contractor's buying power and practical management skills. With this amalgamation we can achieve quality design constructed in an economical manner.

Whereas efforts have been made to achieve this sort of integration on several larger projects, the construction industry has a long way to go until this is a common approach on all projects. Most current 'design-build' contracts involve the contractor far too late in the process; at this late stage too much is already fixed and the contractor cannot offer many real savings. Design-build type contracts are accounting for a larger proportion of contractor's turnovers. While this remains the case, the industry will put effort into further developing the process.

While I am a true believer that design-build is the way forward, I am aware that several contractors consider it as an opportunity to increase profit at the client's expense. Although such stories do exist, a 'catch 22' situation is created: clients will look for greater protection from the contract, which in turn will lead to the contractor having less influence in obtaining materials at an economically advantageous price.

Traditional procurement involved the architect in the full spectrum of activities that make up 'project managing' a project, including of course the design, selection of contractor and subcontractors, and then the management or administration of the contract. Perhaps it could be argued that, since an architect is primarily a designer, the loss of the administrative function in a design-build contract could actually be good, leaving the architect more time to design.

Jo Wright, Feilden Clegg Bradley team leader of the National Trust Central Office, stated:[17]

> The construction process at the National Trust's Central Office has been a delight. The employer's requirements for the shell and core were extremely tightly defined and, based on design to RIBA stage D together with exhaustive environmental modelling, left very little scope for change.
>
> Since the appointment of the contractor the whole team has focused energy on achieving the best possible solution, unhindered by the energy-sapping exchange of contractual correspondence, which so often distracts from the primary task in traditional procurement.
>
> The building demonstrates that design-build can result in high quality, highly sustainable, cost effective buildings.

Various British governments have promoted the various forms of design/build/operate; the initial obvious advantage is that the facility is made available without the large capital outlay. The building is even maintained for the period of the concession before it is handed back. Contractors have embraced this type of project and most large contractors now have their own facilities management companies for operating such ventures. These projects are referred to as Private Finance Initiative (PFI) or Public Private Partnership (PPP).

Both PFI and PPP projects all use a form of design-build. The consortium will be the client or employer for the contractor. The contractor will employ the design team. It is not unusual for the business function user to have some input into the design development and actually be involved in the approval/acceptance of the design.

This introduction opened by suggesting that the design-build market blossomed in the early 1980s as a result of an American influence in the late 1970s/early 1980s. America was clearly using design-build significantly in the 1970s, but it was Britain that adopted the first industry standard form of contract in 1981, some four years ahead of the Americans.

Britain has a blossoming design/build/operate culture that covers most if not all significant use sectors. In America, only about one-third of states are allowed to use design-build delivery systems for schools and education buildings, while Britain's global figures suggest that design-build equates to only about 44 %[3] of construction turnover.

The Office of Government Commerce (OGC) produces a series of guides in the series *Achieving Excellence in Construction*. Guide 06, *Procurement and Contract Strategies* has a section called 'Preferred integrated procurement routes' which stated:

> Since April 2000, government policy has been that projects should be procured by one of three recommended procurement routes (PFI, Prime Contracting or Design-Build). Before concluding the preferred integrated procurement route, Departments should consider the HMT report 'PFI: meeting the investment challenge'. This suggests that construction projects whose capital cost does not exceed £20m are not likely to achieve value for money under the PFI route. Traditional procurement routes should only be used if they demonstrably add value in comparison to the three

recommended routes. Assessing value for money is a central process in procurement. For PFI projects the government will institute a new assessment of potential value for money procurement options when overall investment decisions are made; reform the Public Sector Comparator (PSC) (alternative route may still be chosen); and set up a final assessment of competitive interest in a project.

The new Achieving Excellence targets, agreed by Ministers in December 2002, require projects to demonstrate a significant improvement in performance against quality, cost and time targets. In order to achieve these, it is essential that all procuring bodies move towards proper integration of the design, construction and operation functions. This will require a move to fully integrated teams, early supply team involvement, incentivised payment mechanisms, continuous improvement processes and joint commitment to achieving best whole-life value. These requirements are applicable whichever of the three preferred procurement routes is selected. Framework arrangements may also add value.

The OGC literature carries the following endorsement:[18]

> The National Audit Office recognise that proactive client leadership and robust project management are prerequisites to the successful delivery of construction procurement.
> They consider that procurement of construction should be on the basis of whole-life value for money and endorse the use of the good practice promoted by this suite of guides. They may investigate whether this good practice is applied in practice in any future examination.

The objective of this text is to explain all of the components of this type of 'design-build' procurement and to try to remove some of the mysteries and misinformation commonly propagated. By providing an understanding of everybody's role, it should allow people to clearly focus on their responsibility, in the end fostering better working relationships between the design team and the contractor.

I think that this introduction can be summed up by Chris Johnson, managing director, Gensler, London:[19]

> While most architects hold reservations with regard to working in the design-build environment, I personally enjoy the closer relationships between the architects and the builder contractors which over time develops into mutual trust as opposed to the antagonistic behaviour more common in the contracting environment.

Great buildings are built by great teams, any process which encourages the development of that teamwork is welcome. Design-build can do this if given the chance.

Towards the end of the book are a number of case studies. While these have been selected to demonstrate how design-build has dealt with different challenges, each should begin to show that there is nothing inherent in design-build that prevents good architecture. Design-build procurement is not limited to Britain and the United States, but is thriving internationally.

Europe

Europe covers such a large number of different countries that it is difficult to form a meaningful group to discuss trends.

France is considered in isolation because its traditional procurement method can be considered as a form of design-build. Although it is a design-bid-build process, the design is developed to approximately 50 % complete, sufficient to clearly define the basic design intent and standards required. Post bidding process, the contractor completes the design.

Austria, Belgium, Finland, Ireland and Italy do not have a standard design-build contract and probably as a result the design-build market equates to approximately 10 % for both public and private sectors.

Greece and Spain distort the contract assumption, although they do not have standard contracts. In Greece design-build equates to 50 % of private and 70 % of public markets. Spain similarly has 30 % and 10 % respectively.

Denmark, Germany, Norway, Russia and Sweden do have specific design-build contracts and approximately 50 % of private and 20 % of public sectors are procured in this way.

Pacific

The World Trade Organisation's 'Government Procurement Agreement' opened up the Asian markets by allowing equal opportunity to participate in bidding for the public works worth more than a specified sum. American and Australian construction companies have taken advantage of the opportunity, with many companies opening Asian offices. Influence from these Western partners has increased the use of design-build procurement.

China and its neighbours in Southeast and Southern Asia together account for over half of the world's population. This population requires urban infrastructure, leading to many large construction projects, including 61 nuclear power plants.

China

In late 2004, the Ministry of Construction introduced Provisional Measures on Construction Project Management. In an effort to speed change in the construction market, these measures encouraged the use of external project management. This added greater momentum to the number of overseas construction companies working in China.

Despite this external influence, design-build only accounts for 5 % of the private and 1 % of the public sectors. The Chinese construction industry remains organised in the traditional manner, with the design institutes on one side and contractors on the other.

China is moving its population, increasing the urban population by 29 % by 2020. This will produce a colossal scale of urban construction, unparalleled in modern history. Linked with this is the preparation for the 2008 Olympic Games in Beijing. This massive construction market will surely provide increasing opportunity for design-build.

Japan

In an attempt to reduce government expenditure, many countries are using a build-operate-transfer system for their major power and infrastructure projects. Japan in particular has modelled itself on the UK PFI system.

The American influence has led to widespread use of the 'bridging' type arrangement. This works particularly well in the Japanese private sector where many construction companies have an in-house design team who specialise in the production of construction information; 70 % of projects are procured in this way.

The Japanese public sector requires that design and construction must be purchased separately, although design-build is now tentatively proposed.

India

A large infrastructure programme is being funded through private sector involvement, as opposed to the traditional funding through sovereign debt. To attract the private sector further, restrictive regulations are being revised or eliminated. The percentage use of design-build is increasing.

Australia

Construction procurement in Australia has tended to mirror UK procurement, probably because of the

Commonwealth links. Design-build is currently accounting for up to 40 % of the private and 30 % of the public sectors.

The National Public Works Conference 1990 and the Construction Industry Development Agency 1993 and 1995 have both urged everyone in the construction industry to modify their performance by achieving higher levels of productivity and efficiency. The manufacturing industry has influenced the construction industry with trends towards best practice, benchmarking, quality assurance and re-engineering.

The Australian government is following the UK in developing Public Private Partnerships (PPP), which generally follow the PFI route of the 1990s. The existence of multiple jurisdictions or regional governments with different PPP policies is acting as a significant impediment to the formation of a national PPP market. Victoria published its policy in 2000 and projects include Spencer Street Station redevelopment and Beswick Hospital. New South Wales published its policy in 2001, projects include major infrastructure as well as schools. Queensland also published its policy in 2001 and A$2 billion of construction has already been assessed. South Australia followed by publishing its policy in 2002.

The Australian public seem to have accepted PPP procurement for major infrastructure projects but remain divided over social infrastructure including schools and hospitals.

Americas
The American continent splits conveniently into North and South.

United States of America
Like the UK, American buildings were produced by 'master craftsmen', companies that could design and then manufacture or construct the product or building. However, this was seen not to be the best route for procuring buildings and so the design and trade disciplines were split. By 1909, the American Institute of Architects (AIA) had prohibited its members from engaging in building contracting.

Since the 1940s, the private sector was successfully using design-build for a range of projects including industrial plant, hospitals, office buildings, retail centres and hotels, but the public sector resisted the design-build route. Many states had a statute that prohibited the use of design-build by specifically requiring the design-bid-build route.

Seeing the change coming, in 1978 the AIA reversed its decision not to participate with a building contractor and in 1985 published a recommended design-build contract. In 1987 the Department of Defense received authorisation to use design-build through the Military Construction Act of 1986, although this limited the use to three projects per year. This numerical limit was lifted in 1993. The American Institute of Architects (AIA) in 1996 and the Associated General Contractors of America (AGC) in 1999 produced standard forms of contract for use in design-build projects. In 2001, 40 % of the project delivery market for the private sector was taken by design-build, with many industry analysts forecasting that this will be 50 % by 2010. These figures show that the 1977 predictions were wildly optimistic.

Federal and Local governments have been slow to take up the new procurement route. Currently only one-third of states allow design-build to be used for schools and education buildings.

The massive reconstruction needs in Afghanistan and Iraq will provide a positive overseas market. Congress has already earmarked $18.4 billion for infrastructure projects. American companies either have overseas offices or joint venture with overseas companies. This gives them access to Asian and European markets and, further promotes design-build procurement.

Canada
Design-build is widely used in the Canadian private and public sectors. Many construction companies have either joint ventures or have offices established in Asia to take advantage of the new markets.

Brazil
Design-build accounts for approximately 30 % of the private sector, but regulations mean that its use in the public sector is not feasible.

Mexico
Design-build accounts for 60 % of the private and 40 % of the public sector construction projects.

Mailbox, Birmingham

The Mailbox in Birmingham was the biggest multiuse development in Europe at the time of construction. It is an innovative mixed-use development that has seen the existing Royal Mail building, a 1960s concrete monolith, transformed into a distinctive landmark building. The development includes 200 000 square feet of office space, 200 apartments, two new hotels, 40 designer shops and 15 waterside restaurants, cafes and bars. The upper levels of the building provide office and residential accommodation. The site also has 900 secure parking spaces.

The project involved major structural changes to the original building. Carillion's innovative procedures for the sequencing of demolition works allowed them to work from the top down to create the 'street', and simultaneously from the bottom up to build the car parking in the basement.

The concept behind the mailbox scheme was to use contemporary architecture to change the character of Birmingham city centre. The prominence of the scheme, its importance as an extension of the city centre and its potential for regeneration on a large scale meant that the local planning authority was involved in the project at an early stage.

The architects have grafted a contemporary design on to an old monolithic structure and have introduced landscaped public spaces that effectively link the site to the city centre and the canal system. The building is dramatically lit at night so is a prominent feature on the city skyline. It is already an icon for Birmingham city centre, attracting visitors itself.

The quality of the finished project is excellent, and the letting agents have managed to attract some very prestigious tenants, including: Auberge, BBC, Christian Lacroix, Crosby Homes, Fish!, Harvey Nicholls, Iceberg, Mailmaison, Premier Hotels, Railtrack, Shogan Sushi and Noodle Bar, Society Cocktail Bar, Zizzi, Emporio Armani, DKNY and Thomas Pink.

The concept for the project was designed by Associated Architects and constructed by Weedon Partnership/Carillion Building, with completion in December 2000.

Right
Front elevation

Below left and right
Interior

Procurement Route

(The Client Choices)

Kingsmead Citiplex
View of atrium under
construction

THE SUBJECT OF THIS BOOK IS DESIGN-BUILD, SO THE PROCUREMENT ROUTE AND PROCEDURE WILL FOCUS ON THIS ROUTE. THE PROCUREMENT ROUTE IS EXPLAINED BY COMPARISON WITH A TRADITIONAL (DESIGN-BID-BUILD) PROCUREMENT ROUTE, COMPARING EACH TYPE'S EFFECT ON CONSTRUCTION PROGRAMME, GLOBAL PROJECT COSTS, QUALITY OF THE DESIGN AND FINISHED CONSTRUCTION. ALTHOUGH THE BOOK CENTRES ON DESIGN-BUILD, IT MUST BE NOTED THAT THIS PROCUREMENT ROUTE IS NOT RECOMMENDED FOR ALL CLIENTS OR PROJECT TYPES.

When commissioning a building, the client is faced with a whole array of different procurement routes and contract types. The construction market will provide a variety of options ranging from a complete turnkey package (the client arrives at the finished project and simply turns the key, to enter the fitted-out building) through a very complex bespoke project, where each element is carefully designed, many components being provided by exceptionally specialist suppliers or craftsmen, to the other extreme, where a very simple shell is provided for fitting-out by others.

To evaluate the benefits of the different procurement options, it helps to define what is wanted in the complete project. In simple terms a project can be considered to have three parameters, time, cost and quality. Although it is easy to claim that all parameters are important, one of the parameters will be more important to the client in producing a successful project. By selecting the most important option the most appropriate procurement route will follow.

Time is the length of time the project will take from start to finish; this is for the whole project not just the construction phase. Time is important; buildings are constructed for a reason, mostly with a commercial basis. Until the building is open and functioning, the commercial activity will not produce income. Consider something like a North Sea oil-drilling platform. The income from one day's operation will be a significant amount of the construction costs. The effect of a construction delay could be devastating. The client may be happy to increase the construction cost or downgrade the quality if that guaranteed delivery on time.

Cost is the total project cost including all construction, design and management costs. Many clients will need to arrange funding for the project; to arrange funding the total cost needs to be known. It can be more than a little inconvenient if the amount to be borrowed needs to be increased, let alone increased several times. Being able to fix the cost may become more important than either time or quality.

Quality is slightly harder to define. It includes both the complexity and suitability of the design as well as the standard of materials to be used on the project. Using a high standard of materials alone may not produce the desired requirements if the detailed design is not to the same standard.

It is conceivable that the complexity of the design will require a specialist designer to be used for individual or specific parts. This could be done either in conjunction with the building designer or as an independent portion, which is integrated into the whole package. The client will want to keep total control over the design development of this portion, which may be considered as more important than both time and cost.

If everything went exactly to plan, the choice of the appropriate form of contract would not be so important. Most people will know of at least one project that finished on time, the construction cost was on budget and the delivered design and specified materials were all as anticipated. Unfortunately, such projects are generally considered to be a minority.

The reality is that the project is at the mercy of several uncontrollable elements, the weather and people being just two. If the weather was unnaturally cold or wet, then it is possible that construction could be delayed. People make errors! They could be design errors that need correcting, perhaps specifying incompatible elements, omitting elements or the contractor's team may have failed to procure materials on time, or procured an element that is not as specified, or worse still, misunderstood the construction information and produced an element of the building incorrectly. Whatever the mistake, it will lead to pressure being placed on one of the parameters discussed above. If the client team has selected an appropriate procurement route, then the client should be insulated against change in the parameter that is most important.

The parameters are now considered again, but this time suggesting how a particular procurement route might allow control. If time is considered, remember that the project flows from inception to completion; in other words, time includes the design from concept, through scheme design, to detailed design and into production information. It also includes the construction activities required to complete the project. There is a very significant hold point in any project. Planning permission is inevitably required. It is probably better to consider the project post planning permission when the concept and scheme design stages are complete.

Consider the risks to the project programme. Design and construction are separate activities, so delays in design will delay construction. Delays in feedback from the construction could delay further design, which of course could then delay construction. How can we prevent one delaying the other and resulting in a delay to the project?

One answer might be to give the responsibility for the design and construction to the same person. If there is clear responsibility for both operations and that responsibility lies with the same person, then if a delay should occur it is not unreasonable to expect the client to be compensated.

A design-build contract does what it says; the contract is for the design and the construction, so if the contract lies with one person, there is single point responsibility. The contractor engages a design team, which completes the detailed design and then produces the construction information. Since the contractor manages design and construction, it is common for construction to start without the design being completed. Information is provided to the contractor as it becomes available and delivery stays ahead of the construction programme.

There is a significant drawback to this approach. If there is little time available between the contractor receiving the information and then needing it for construction, there is little time to carry out value engineering, verify the design or even check the market for the best value materials or products.

If time is the most important parameter, allowing the design to be managed by the contractor will prevent design delays and problems from impacting on the construction programme, and consequently remove the risk of design delivery delaying construction. A design-build form of contract gives the contractor control of the design delivery and so is probably the optimum route.

As far as cost is concerned, if nothing changes then it is not unreasonable to expect that the cost should be the same as stated in the contract at the outset. Unfortunately, change occurs all too often. Change is good news for the contractor as it normally means more money, so he will be looking for any little irregularity or error in the contract documentation. To control cost, the contract type must be a 'fixed price lump sum'. It is also possible to obtain a guaranteed maximum price (GMP), which is what it says: the price is fixed, provided nothing changes! Please note that alterations or changes are not the same as irregularities. In a GMP situation, the contractor takes responsibility for the detailed design and construction information and must correct any irregularities or errors in the documentation, without amending the price.

For a GMP to work, the contractor must have control of the preparation of the detailed design and construction information; in a design-build contract, the contractor has control of the design development. If a fixed cost is the most important parameter, then a design-build form of contract with a GMP is probably the optimum route.

It has just been stated that changes or alterations are not irregularities in the contract documentation; they are instructed changes to the contract. This instruction could be the addition or omission of some requirement. Please note that even in a GMP situation, this instruction will vary the contract sum.

It has been suggested that the contractor is responsible for any irregularities in the contract documentation. If the contractor finds conflicting requirements, he will ensure that it is the cheaper requirement that is contained in his proposal. Under these circumstances, if the client actually wanted the other requirement, then this would need to be instructed. Such an instruction would of course vary the contract sum.

With regard to quality, if a specific standard of material is required, this could be specified and become part of the contract. As part of the contract, such standards would be delivered regardless of route. However, the more the materials are specified and fixed, the less a contractor can use buying power, the fewer buying discounts are available to a contractor and thus the more expensive a design-build contract would become. If quality reflects the complexity of the design, then it is probably important that the client retains full control of the design development. The client retaining full control of the design is not a design-build situation. If the design is complex and the client wishes to retain control of the design, it is probable that some form of traditional remeasurement contract will be the optimum route.

Traditional Procurement

Various forms of media may have created the impression that it is only the architect that likes a traditional contract; this is far from the truth. The main contractor very much likes traditional forms as they carry minimal risk from his point of view. Most people involved in the construction industry favour the traditional form of contract. The architect will be paid the full-scale fee, the contractor carries no risk and the person procuring the building carries all the risk and pays all the costs.

The contractor can expect to receive all of the relevant information in adequate time and in a suitable form to allow the procurement and construction of the works. If the information is incorrect, late or deficient, then he can expect to be compensated. Compensation would come from the client, even though it is possible that he was not a party to the delay.

There should be few unknowns and, the design should be well coordinated, specified and billed. In a tender situation the contractor knows that his opposition has exactly the same information and he does not have to worry about omissions in his own bills of quantities; if there are any omissions then they are common to all! However, this goes deeper. If there is an omission in the bills of quantities; the contractor will expect this to be corrected, and of course the correction will come from a contingency fund, funded by the building procurer.

Tendering traditional procurement is a much faster and cheaper operation. The contractor does not have to produce a design or compile his own bills of quantities, which saves the cost of employing a bills of quantities production service and can save weeks on the tender period.

The architectural profession likes this form of procurement because of a perceived gain in quality. During the design the exact requirements can be specified and during the construction phase, standards of materials and workmanship can be enforced. This perceived gain in quality refers to the standard of design as well as the standard of the materials used. To achieve the higher standard of design will involve considerably more design time and the associated higher architectural fee. If both the architect and contractor like this traditional form of procurement, why are there alternative forms of contract anyway? The answer is simply because clients deserve a better deal! Why should the client carry the risk for the construction? Why is construction considered such an unknown that it cannot be tied to a fixed price? Once a design-build route had offered this concept to the market, there was no going back.

In the 21st century, how realistic is it to expect a client to pay an unknown amount for his building and, within this unknown amount, include a contingency figure to pay for the mistakes of, or omissions by, his professional team? It may be unfair to say unknown amount because, after all, the contract has been tendered and then awarded to the successful tenderer. The type of contract could be a remeasurement contract, where at completion the whole process is audited and the contractor paid for what he actually did. There is the possibility that this has significantly varied from what was included at the tender stage.

At least the contingency figure is in the open, it is disclosed in the contract sum analysis, and the contractor does not need to include for risk or elements of design development within his tender figure. The risk is declared in a single place; others involved in the contract do not include monies to cover risk.

The main drawbacks to the traditional forms of building procurement are:

- Because of remeasurement and responsibility for risk, the final cost is unknown.
- There is a certain amount of duplication of services required, resulting in an increase in the total project consultancy fees. The contractor is still providing many of the services that the client's team provide.
- The contractor has access to national buying agreements, but only for certain products. A specification compiled by the architect will not, or is highly unlikely to, take full advantage of these deals.
- Advantage is seldom taken of the contractor's knowledge of 'build-ability' or indeed

other construction or programming advice.
- The construction information is not tailored to the contractor's requirements, potentially resulting in delays, lack of information or simply confusion.
- While there are drawbacks to the traditional forms of building procurement, it still has the advantage that if the design is really complex, there may be no other real alternative procurement route.

'Design-build' Procurement

'Design-build' is what it says, the same point of responsibility for both design and construction. Since it is relatively rare for a contractor to have in-house design consultants (architects, engineers, landscape architects), this normally means that the contractor appoints the independent consultants.

The design in the 'design' part of the contract can vary quite significantly. At one extreme, it could simply be a requirement for an area of use class, eg 50 000 square feet of warehouse, which then requires the contractor's team to supply a complete design. At the other extreme, the requirement could be to complete a fully designed and specified building, in reality not much for the contractor's team to do in completing the design (although the contractor will still take responsibility for the whole design). The typical contract will lie between the two extremes, a design developed in sufficient detail to obtain planning permission and be adequate as a vehicle for tendering and beginning to procure the project. The greater the amount of design pre-contract, the lower the cost savings that can be achieved by this route. In fact, if it is a fully designed building, the cost of this route can be more expensive than using another or traditional route.

Using a design-build contract with an Employer's Requirement (ER) that includes a full design and specification is simply risk-shifting. The contractor carries the risk and is totally responsible for the design, even though he now has no influence over it. The contractor will simply price the risk.

In a like for like situation a design-build contract should deliver the finished building at a lower capital cost as the contractor can take advantage of market forces on material and subcontract procurement and can control the design. However, if the controls are taken away from the contractor, he will simply price the risk. This may be acceptable to the employer; he still gets cost certainty, no instruction and no change to the contract sum!

Even on a fully designed and specified project, the tender documents are unlikely to include the bills of quantities. Since this bill is required for the pricing exercise, the contractor will still have to purchase the 'take off' service. This service varies in price with the size of the contract, but should be expected to cost several thousand pounds. This fee is payable whether the contract is won or lost, but some 'take off' quantity surveyors will offer a reduced fee with enhancement if the contractor is successful.

From a contractor's point of view, one of the major drawbacks to tendering a design-build project is the cost of the bill production. On some projects it might be possible for two or more competing contractors to share a bill, but this is rare. It also provides difficulties when trying to price 'bright ideas'.

There would appear to be a conundrum surrounding building procurement: the contractor would like control, but there are limits to this. If the control is absolute then there will be no design in the ER; the contractor would have to provide his own design before it could be billed and priced. The contractor is typically very poor at leading the design on cost grounds and very good at complaining that others cannot design to a cost – and still very uneasy when given the ultimate control.

If you cannot give the contractor ultimate control, then you at least need to provide the flexibility to allow market forces and buying power to be used. In this way the employer can receive a building of equal quality but at a lower capital cost – a lower capital cost because the contractor will pass on some of the saving as part of the winning tender.

The Future

Building procurement will evolve until all parties consider that it is both fair and the optimum route for achieving the agreed result. Latham and Egan will continue to have a major influence on the development of the British construction industry. With a design-build contract the contractor carries the risk and the employer pays for offloading the risk, but at least the price is fixed.

Allowing the contractor some element of control should allow greater degrees of prefabrication to be used. Prefabrication has many advantages, including:

* Achieving uniform factory production standards.
* Less reliance on the weather to allow trades to progress.
* Greater financial certainty over the cost of a major element.

The future of building procurement must surely take advantage of the best parts of the current procurement process and try to lose the less successful elements. This could include:

* Using the contractor's buying power.
* Greater use of prefabrication.
* Reducing tendering costs (overheads) by providing a common bill of quantities or negotiating the project cost.

Kingsmead Citiplex, Bath

Aaron Evans Architects have designed Bath's first multiplex cinema and leisure complex. It is a contemporary building and the first in a World Heritage site, inspired by the proportions of a Georgian terrace. A curving structural glass façade forms the entrance, flanked on either side with elevations in natural stone, creating a new street elevation of over 50 metres long. Entering the building the visitor finds a central full-height glass atrium rising to a roof five storeys overhead. This atrium gives the feel of an open courtyard, with restaurants visible through the transparent walls. A feature staircase gives access to the first floor restaurants; on the lower ground floor is a health club with a 20 metre swimming pool. A glass-sided lift connects the floors, giving views out over the city.

The project for Deeley Freed Estates was constructed by Warings.

Below
Elevation detail

Bottom
Upward view of atrium

'Design-Build'

Gloucestershire College of Arts and Technology, Cheltenham
Elevation showing curtain wall and external columns with overhanging roof

'Design-build' is a common or popular term; it can be used to describe construction projects ranging from a small domestic kitchen extension up to the largest PFI projects. In each case, the same authority holds responsibility for both the design and the construction of the project.

Design-build is quite a simple operation. The employer defines his requirements, and the contractor offers his proposals, the two should match and be the basis of the contract. It is common for the contractor to be responsible for the design and construction; the contractor has always been responsible for the construction. He now takes responsibility for the design by employing the designers. I am unable to quote any examples of where a designer has employed the contractor.

By becoming responsible for the design the contractor removes one of the variables that can disrupt a project; it also helps to make this form of procurement more flexible. The contractor can be responsible for all design development from an outline planning permission, or he can simply be responsible for a certain element or detail. In the latter case, the design has already been completed and would have been available at tender stage.

The question of planning permission is important. It is highly unlikely that a contractor would be prepared to tender for the construction of a project that does not have planning permission. Tendering is an expensive business; it could involve the preparation of the design, production of bills of quantities, all the estimation research and finally the document preparation. It is also unlikely that a client would be prepared to fund the complete design process if this design process was speculative.

It is a fair assumption that the start of the process is the planning permission. It is worth giving a lot of thought to the format and content of the planning application. If too much is specified and included in the planning application, then this will greatly limit the options available to the contractor.

The level of detail contained in the planning permission will form the basis of the Employer's Requirements. If an economical solution to a simple building is required, then it would be unwise to handicap the contractor by specifying all materials in the planning permission. Planning permissions can contain conditions on materials along with the other standard conditions. It is quite normal to make the contractor responsible for discharging the conditions.

If a proportion of the design is going to be determined by the planning permission, the concept of scheme design is complete. This leaves the detailed design and production information phases to be completed. Perhaps this is not often discussed, but these are the stages that contain risk. Errors here generally cost more to correct.

The actual mechanics of tendering are covered later, but it is interesting to consider the design information required for a tender. A contractor needs to be able to price bills of quantities or a schedule of work. For either of these documents to be produced, there needs to be some design information in place.

To price the tender, if there is not a detailed specification, the contractor will need to produce one. If this specification is produced in isolation from the other tenderers, then it will form part of the Contractor's Proposals and reflect the standard of design and materials that are going to be offered or used.

In most projects, the contractor will be left to develop or finish the design and then produce the production or construction information. Since this information controls how the project will be constructed, the contractor will need to control this phase to be able to offer a fixed price. Even if not purported to be a guaranteed maximum price (GMP), a design-build contract is a fixed price.

It is of benefit to both the employer and the contractor to have the contractor control the production or construction information stage. This is the stage where inaccuracy or other errors result in additional costs. If the contractor is in control then the cost is his and not the employer's. It has long been a criticism of architects that they lack an understanding of build-ability; some would suggest, perhaps unfairly, that architects do not actually know how to build. With the contractor controlling this phase, that statement should not be made. The contractor has every opportunity to contribute to the methodology of the design.

The contractor is responsible for the design, but how much control over the design does he have? This will depend on how much of the design is included within the Employer's Requirements. It is common for the design and planning permission stage to be included within the contract, but also to require the contractor to engage the same design team to complete the design. It is often felt by the employer's team that this continuity will ensure the desired result.

The requirement for the contractor to engage the design team responsible for the previous design stage is called novation (bridging in America). Contractually it should not make any difference as to who is in the design team; the contractor employs them all. However, this is not always the case in reality. Many consultants think that they still have a duty of care to the original employer or client, or that they know the design intent – whatever is or is not contained in the Employer's Requirements.

Successful projects hit the middle ground, with the contractor appreciating that the design is the architect's, he is liable for the design and will need to defend many design decisions in the future. The architect also has to accept that there may be other equally adequate construction methods and materials. The ideal is for the contractor and design team to produce the defined building, a building that either through design or construction they can be proud of.

Pressure will be placed on the project by money. If the consultants misjudge or accept an inadequate fee there will be a temptation to try to limit time expenditure on the project, which may affect the quality of production information. If the construction information produces questions, the design team will need to answer the questions. If time is being constrained, this may cause a delay in answering, if answered at all. Once a relationship becomes strained, it is very hard to correct.

If the contractor has made an error in the tender, he will try to recover the monies lost by substituting materials or trying to omit work altogether. This will have an effect on the design, which again will cause a strain in the relationships.

A professional being employed by the contractor is relatively new and still creates misunderstandings on both sides. The consultants must realise that their client is the contractor and that reporting to the employer (original client) is wrong. The contractor must also realise that he has engaged the professionals for a reason; he must give serious thought to the consequences before he goes against their advice.

One of the main benefits of design-build is that it avoids a split in responsibility between design and construction. This single responsibility avoids conflicts, omissions and general noncompatibility, or rather it does not, they still occur, but in this form of procurement the costs of such conflicts, omissions and general noncompatibility are not passed on to the client.

Conflicts, omissions and general noncompatibility in the design information constitute risk from the contractor's point of view, and since it is normal for the contractor to hold the single point responsibility he needs to offset this risk. The contractor's tender figure for the project will include two elements to offset this risk: the first is a sum of money to cover design development, the second is a sum of money to cover contingency. At first sight it may appear that both elements are the same, but they are different.

The design development figure is used to cover elements that had not been foreseen and consequently measured during the bill preparation for this tender. The figure is not for the architect to change his design! Contingency is there to cover genuine mistakes or errors as the tender has been partly based on bills of quantities. If the design information offered at the tender stage was not clear, these bills could contain inaccuracies and under-measures.

Both the design development and contingency figures could be viewed by the client as a sort of insurance policy. If insufficient monies have been allowed for the design development process, the contractor is not entitled to ask the client for more money and the client's liability is limited to the tender figure. If the costs exceed the allowances that the contractor has in place, then the profit figure will diminish. If, however, the allowances exceed the actual costs, the contractor benefits!

When set up properly, a design-build project is a very simple contractual relationship. There are only two parties, the employer (client) and the contractor. There are no mediating consultants involved in the contract, although the employer will normally act through his agent.

The post-contract design consultants are the responsibility of the contractor and the contractor must carefully control the direction of design development. A lack of control will very quickly result in spending all of the design development allowance. To help in the control of design development, larger contractors now embrace design management and will employ individuals to manage the design process. These design managers or coordinators will be the point of contact for the design team, and normally the contact with the client or employer.

Because in a design-build situation the client is not employing the consultants, the client tends to communicate directly with the contractor. This is a major difference from more traditional forms of contract, where mediating consultants are placed between the contractor and the client. In reality, it is more likely that the client contact is actually the employer's agent, but even so this is the client authority. With closer interaction between the client and the contractor, it is possible to surmise that fewer misunderstandings will occur. Both parties are in contact and should be able to communicate any concerns. We have already begun to discuss the single point responsibility. If there is a problem, then it is the contractor's problem and he must resolve it.

Another advantage of design-build is the speed that the project can be brought to site. Although the actual tender period will be longer for a design-build project, because the contractor is in control he will be able to start on site with considerably less design information.

A fixed price is an advantage, but the price remains fixed only while nothing changes. Change is good for the contractor; he can recover or increase profit when change occurs. Any QS working for the client will have so little information on the contractor's price build-up that costing a variation will be very difficult. If work is omitted, the full value is never returned; it is not uncommon for only 60 % to be returned. However, before this gives an impression of a deceitful contractor, the overheads have been based on the total contract price, the overheads will be fixed, so if the contract price is reduced, the overheads increase as a percentage. To maintain the same profit margin, the full value of the omission cannot be fully returned. Design-build is not a contract for change. If change is likely then this is probably the wrong procurement route.

A design-build approach can be very flexible on the amount of design the contractor is responsible for. Indeed, the design-build setup will need to establish exactly what will be the extent of the contractor's design. This could start with everything; perhaps there is a requirement for a given area of warehousing and everything else would be left to the contractor's design. Actually, this is probably not a very good example, for the project to be 'real' planning permission will have been achieved and so this will be the base of the design. It may not be a lot but it will establish the concept.

The contractor's design element could be limited to a small specific area; perhaps the warehouse discussed above has been designed but the contractor is left to design the portal truss. Consideration needs to be given to the amount of design that the contractor is going to take responsibility for. If the contractor is unconstrained in terms of design output, the solution may be very economical but it is unlikely to win any design awards. Most design-build contracts have the design already completed up to scheme design (RIBA stage D), leaving the contractor the responsibility of developing the design through detailed design and the production information stages (RIBA stages E, F and G).

It is possible to include within the design an element that is designed by either the employer or his consultants. This may be a small but significant piece, such as a work of art, or more fundamentally could be a specific area, such as the fit-out of a certain space. All these are possible, but must be clearly defined and included in the tender documentation. To try to introduce such areas of employer's design once the contract has come into being would constitute a change, and as discussed above change can be expensive!

One of the major selling points of design-build is design economy. However, you need to be careful; the contract figure includes amounts to cover design development and contingency. If the contractor is not able to bring economies to the project, it will cost more than the same project procured by traditional means. Even though the project has cost more, the fact that the final figure is guaranteed may be a sufficient reason for the employer to pay more.

The contractor should be able to add economies by buying savings; eg knowing a particularly good value product, savings should be available. Allowing the contractor to work with the consultants should produce a more efficient result. The contractor is exposed to market forces and is aware of economies of using various materials or products. This should lead to design economy which is often stated as one of the benefits of design-build.

The tie-up between design and construction should produce value for money. This value can be derived from either the contractor's practical experience or through the market forces arrangement. Such arrangements will include buying savings and loyalty schemes.

For the design and construction partnership to produce rewards, both parties will need to be fully committed. If one of the parties is not sufficiently interested in the relationship then it is unlikely that the union will produce the desired results.

Economies produced through the design are to the benefit of all involved in the project. Interestingly, if design consultants are going to use their experience to reduce the capital costs, it then seems unfair to penalise them by agreeing a fee based on capital cost alone. Consultants should be aware that this design development process will happen and perhaps try to fix their fee on the first cost estimate or gain some of the reward from the saving produced.

When selecting parties or possible parties for the contract, consideration should be given to past experience. People who have completed similar projects should have learnt from their previous mistakes and provided construction methods that have been as economical as expected.

If efficiency can be introduced into both the design and construction processes, then financial reward will follow. It should be possible for the contractor to reduce overheads and for the designer to produce designs with a lower resource cost than anticipated, in both cases giving increased profit. If the employer also gains from the added efficiency, then all parties will win. As with experience, repetition will produce rewards, provided both the contractor and the designer are prepared to learn from mistakes or opportunities provided by the repetition.

Expensive elements or items can be packaged together. This may reduce the interface risks for the contractor (aligning various parties practically and contractually to carry out the work) or allow a buying saving generated by the bulk purchase.

Gloucestershire College of Arts and Technology, Cheltenham
View of building massing from within the site

Gloucestershire College of Arts and Technology, Cheltenham

Atkins Walter Webster created the competition winning design for the project. The brief was for 12 700 square metres of naturally ventilated campus for 2000 sixth form and further education students. The building was designed for a long life, loose fit, low energy and low maintenance. Further complexity was added by the requirement for 2000 PCs located in high densities.

The uppermost level of the structure is a braced steelwork frame. In this area thermal mass is not required. Ihis solution provided rapid speed of construction. The reinforced concrete staircase cores provide stability, with the stairs themselves being precast concrete.

The exposed concrete floor slabs absorb heat emitted from the occupants and computers, store it within the structure and are cooled naturally overnight to reduce temperatures the following day. This reduces the need for mechanical cooling systems. The dense IT zones are grouped together within the central spine of the building and are provided with chilled slab cooling and displacement ventilation to deal with the exceptional heat loads. The chilled slab cooling system incorporates embedded cooling pipes located within the exposed concrete soffit.

To soften the acoustic environment and reduce reverberation times, absorbent rafts are suspended clear of the exposed soffit and provide attenuation both from direct noise striking their under side and reflected noise on their upper side.

Artificial lighting is linked to a presence detection system, which adjusts the lighting level at the working plane. This system coupled with high efficiency lamps will produce a significant saving in electricity consumption.

The building is heated through a combination of perimeter radiators to the highly insulated envelope and limited underfloor heating zones. The boilers are modulating fully condensing units. The heating system uses the concrete frame's thermal mass to balance heating demands over a 24-hour cycle.

Bovis Lend Lease constructed the project for Gloucestershire Education Authority, handing it over in June 2002 to allow it to be fitted out in time for the start of the new term in September.

Right
Elevation showing mix of
block and render finishes
Below
Entrance corner viewed from
road approach

Opposite
The internal dining area
showing open spaces and
natural roof finish

Below
View of the foyer from upper
level

The Contract Documents (ER/CP)

CONTRACT DOCUMENTS DEFINE THE AGREEMENT BETWEEN THE CONTRACTING PARTIES, THE EMPLOYER AND THE CONTRACTOR. EVERY TYPE OF CONTRACT CONTAINS SOMETHING THAT SETS OUT THE PARAMETERS OF THE AGREEMENT; CONSTRUCTION IS NO DIFFERENT. A STANDARD DESIGN-BUILD CONTRACT REQUIRES THREE DOCUMENTS TO BE BROUGHT TOGETHER TO DEFINE THE REQUIREMENTS: IN SIMPLE TERMS, WHAT THE CLIENT WANTS, WHAT THE CONTRACTOR IS PREPARED TO OFFER AND A SCHEDULE OF COSTS.

THE DOCUMENTS ACTUALLY HAVE MORE ELEGANT NAMES: THE EMPLOYER'S REQUIREMENTS, THE CONTRACTOR'S PROPOSALS AND THE CONTRACT SUM ANALYSIS. TOGETHER WITH THE STANDARD CONDITIONS OF CONTRACT, THESE DOCUMENTS DEFINE THE PROJECT.

Documents required to form the legal agreement between the parties, the employer and the contractor, are referred to as the contract documents. These are legal documents and need to be carefully retained for use during the construction and then stored and retained for the specific periods beyond the completion of the construction works. The documents are generally the terms of the contract (JCT form) plus the various other requirements, design, cost and programme.

In addition to the standard form of contract published by the JCT and the various sections that need to be completed, the contract documents consist of three distinct sections:

- The Employer's Requirements (ER).
- The Contractor's Proposals (CP).
- The Contract Sum Analysis (CSA).

All three documents are referenced and required by the standard conditions of contract.

Unfortunately, part of the Employer's Requirements will probably be a schedule of modifications to the contract conditions. Therefore the 'standard form of contract' is no longer the standard form but a bespoke model that is actually the employer's contract.

The Employer's Requirements

The Employer's Requirements can be as simple or comprehensive as required, which perhaps demonstrates some of the flexibility associated with a design-build contract. This can vary from a simple statement, ie 50 000 square feet of B2 class enclosure, to a very complex design and schedule of deliverables. In the case of the simple statement, the contractor will include the design, specification, construction programme and CSA in his proposal.

The more complex Employer's Requirements will involve a completed design and specification, which will include all design drawings, architectural specification, structural specification, mechanical and electrical specification and a very comprehensive set of preambles. In this case, the Contractor's Proposals need simply be an acknowledgment that all requirements of the ER are included in the CP.

It is interesting to consider that neither of the above situations genuinely suits the contractor. The first case would allow the contractor to use all his strengths, market forces could be used to determine the best economies for the materials to be used and the most efficient structural solutions could be applied. However, in general, the contractor will have difficulty with this approach. Design management is generally still not very good within the contracting organisation and the contractor is used to dealing with given constraints and not being the team leader. Without the design and specification, what are the estimating department going to measure, quantify and derive the cost from? The contractor relies on making small changes to the design; wholesale control is a little alien and not handled well.

To take the project any further the contractor would need to commission a design. This could then be priced and would form the basis of his proposal to meet the ER. The contractor is not a designer; he will price the design. As stated above, the contractor is not good at design management, and so will rely on the abilities of his selected team. It is essential that the team are selected for innovation and designing to economies. If simply selected on price it is highly likely that the contractor will regret his decision.

The second case referred to above (complete design and specification) is simply a risk-shifting exercise and almost certainly using the wrong form of contract. If the design is complete why not have the bill of quantities prepared and use a 'traditional' JCT 98 with quantities? The answer is simple, because in that case the employer will take responsibility for the design, and should there prove to be any inadequacies in the design, then the employer is financially responsible.

In practice, what tends to happen is that the scheme is predesigned, there is an outline specification, a comprehensive preambles section, and the conditions of contract will be amended (even if only slightly). The Contractor's Proposals will clarify or qualify the offer and the contractor's efforts will be to reduce the risk.

The standard form of contract states that the Contractor's Proposals take precedence over the Employer's Requirements. This makes some sense as the CP are a response to the ER and it would not be fair for a contractor to make a series of qualifications only for them to be ignored in the contract. However, the Employer is also wary of the ER being ignored. The typical result is that the conditions of contract are amended to make the ER take precedence over the CP. In such circumstances it is essential that the contractor ensures that each of his qualifications is addressed, either by the risk being covered financially or by the qualification being incorporated into the final contract.

If the ER take precedence over the CP, then the ER need to be amended to include all the requirements of the CP before the contract documents are ready. In fact, with the CP absorbed into the ER, in theory there is no need for a CP as a contract document, but that is not what the conditions of contract require.

The Contractor's Proposals

These are basically a response to the Employer's Requirements. If the ER were very basic then these contain the design that the contractor is offering to meet the requirements of the ER. If the ER were quite comprehensive, then they are the contractor's opportunity to offer alternative methods or materials and to clarify or qualify the proposal.

It is never easy to know whether the document should be written in a positive or negative style. The positive could be 'we have included for the use of polished plaster in the reception' or even more specifically 'our proposal included 10 square metres of polished plaster in the reception area.' The negative is 'we have not included polished plaster in our proposal'.

As a response to less than clear ER, it is easy to compile pages of negative responses; this could be viewed as minimising risk. However, it should be remembered that the first function of the CP is to sell the contractor to the client. A negative CP may not be achieving this.

The employer's agent will compile a comparison of the proposals received. You need to assume that you will not be penalised by a positive CP and that all the proposals from the tendering contractors will be reduced to a 'level field'. If all are level, a positive CP still has a nice feel about it and may be acting as a marketing document.

If the tender documentation omits the design, the CP need to include the design. Presentation of the design requires some thought. Should the design drawings be bound into the CP, perhaps integrated into the text, or should they be sent as A1 production type drawings in a box? Perhaps the answer is a combination of both. There is no reason why the tender return could not be a multimedia presentation, unless the preambles section of the ER defines the format of the CP.

It is important that the CP defines the design. If there is any ambiguity this is likely to cause problems or disappointment later on. As an absolute minimum the design must define the overall size and specific areas together with a statement of material quality, perhaps an NBS type specification.

The Contract Sum Analysis

It is usual for the format of the CSA to be provided with the tender documentation. The CSA simply breaks the building down into component parts. The contractor completes the value of each part.

One of the component parts will be the preliminaries section. Care must be taken when comparing preliminaries since no two contractors calculate their preliminary costs in exactly the same way. One contractor may include an item in the preliminaries while another may divide the figure among various rates for work.

The CSA provides a way for the employer's agents to get a feel for how the tender has been priced. It is not normal for a priced bill of quantities to be submitted but the CSA will be the only help when trying to value any variations required later on.

General

It will normally be necessary to provide at least two sets of documents, one for each party. Both parties sign each set. However, if the client is a developer, a fund and perhaps a fund surveyor may be involved. These will all want copies of the proposals. The Employer's Requirements should define what is required.

Vivekananda Bridge Tollway, between Kolkata and Howrah, India

The project is the largest (total project cost of US$147 million) transportation project in eastern India being undertaken by a public-private partnership, using a design-build-operate-transfer delivery system. A multinational team of designers are engineering the project's infrastructure for the consortium of infrastructure development, investment, engineering and construction firms from the US, the Philippines, Malaysia and India.

The 6.1 kilometre (3.8 mile), six-lane tollway under construction will link the twin cities of Kolkata (formerly known as Calcutta) and Howrah, and will include the second Vivekananda Bridge – the world's first multispan, single-plane cable-supported bridge with short pylons.

The bridge will be located 50 metres (164 feet) downstream from an existing rail-cum-road truss bridge built in 1931, crossing the River Hooghly and connecting five national highways, a historic temple site, an airport, several industrial zones and residential/commercial townships under development.

The project forms the critical eastern link of the $10+ billion Golden Quadrilateral Program under implementation by the National Highways Authority of India. That programme will link the four cities of India, New Delhi, Mumbai (Bombay), Chennai (Madras) and Kolkata (Calcutta). The agency works as an autonomous body under the Ministry of Road Transport and Highways (MORTH).

Under a loan agreement, a consortium of 14 commercial banks led by the State Bank of India is providing project financing of US $91 million. During the three-year construction period and for 27 years after completion, SVBTC will operate the revenue-producing bridge and tollway before it is handed over to the Indian government.

Traffic in the first year of operation is projected to include 20 000 commercial vehicles (trucks) on an average annual daily basis. The bridge is expected to serve as a preferred crossing for the long-haul trucks using the national highway network of eastern India. These trucks will be prohibited, beginning in 2007, from using the existing rail-cum-road bridge.

All bridge work is being done using the precast segmental construction technology, which will result in a functional, cost-effective and aesthetic toll facility serving as a national landmark for the Indian subcontinent.

Engineers for the project are Parsons Brinkerhoff

Above
Artistic view of the six-lane highway approaching the start of the bridge

Below
Artist's aerial view showing the support towers

Tendering

Bluewater, Kent
Evening view of walkways,
lake and entrances

TENDERING IS THE TERM USED TO DESCRIBE HOW A CONTRACTOR COSTS OR PRICES A PROJECT, USUALLY IN COMPETITION WITH OTHER CONTRACTORS. TENDERING IS NOT GUESSING; IT IS ACCURATELY BUILDING UP A COST OF A PROJECT. WHY THEN DO TENDERS VARY? BECAUSE EACH TENDER REQUIRES CERTAIN ASSUMPTIONS TO BE MADE. THESE ASSUMPTIONS MAY HAVE A SIGNIFICANT INFLUENCE ON THE PERCEPTION OF RISK AND ULTIMATELY THE COST!

Most consultants have a good knowledge of most aspects of the construction process, but tendering is given little thought and remains a bit mystical. How a contractor actually arrives at a financial figure is not completely understood. The following is intended to provide an insight into the tender process.

It is probably true of all tender situations that to achieve competitive tenders you have to invite people who actually want to tender. There are many reasons for a contractor not wanting to tender. It may be that the tender period coincides with staff holidays and that the tender could not be adequately resourced, perhaps the risk is unacceptable, particularly in the case of existing buildings, or there may be something in the contract preliminaries that is unacceptable to the contractor, parent company or insurance company. Perhaps the contractor does not want to work with the client, but would still like to work with the employer's agent or quantity surveyor. Perhaps the contractor does not want to work with the employer's agent but would still like to work with the client. The contractor may not be able to undertake the construction work within the given timescale, but still wants to work with the client and employer's agent in the future.

There are many reasons why the contractor does not actually want to tender, but because of a public relation image does not want to be seen to decline the opportunity to tender. In these circumstances, it used to be common practice to take a 'cover'. A cover simply involves contacting one of the other tenderers and asking for the 'cover', a guide price for the tender. This guide will not be so extreme to leave the contractor embarrassed, but will achieve the goal of ensuring that the contractor submitting the tender will not be awarded the contract. What happens if four contractors have accepted the invitation to tender, but then three take a cover? The result is unlikely to be quite as competitive as assumed. The simple answer would be to increase the number of tenderers, but one of the criteria used to judge whether a contractor will tender is the number of tenderers; if too high he will decline or take a cover.

In June 2003, new legislation was introduced – the Enterprise and Competition Acts came into force. There is no doubt that the cover process outlined above is uncompetitive and against both the spirit and wording of the legislation. The financial penalties imposed by this legislation are so severe that a single infringement will liquidate most companies. It will be interesting to see how tendering changes and whether contractors decline more tenders. It will lead to an interesting situation. Suppose five contractors are approached and two or three decline, presumably the employer will want to make up the numbers. The new tenderer will require the same amount of time as the previous group; as a result the tender period could be significantly extended.

The most important aspect of compiling the tender list is to consider the contractor's abilities when compared to the type of project and standard of information produced. A contractor who has a limited design capability may be very pleased to receive a project with very limited design information, but when receiving a design that is fully designed and specified, may feel that he can add little value, and so may be considerably less competitive.

In considering whether a contractor is likely to submit a competitive tender, the following points may be relevant:

- Is the project of a similar size to others that this contractor has bid or completed competitively?
- Is the project of a similar type to the contractor's normal work?
- Does the contractor appear exceptionally busy?

One of the benefits of design-build should be design economy. The contractor is exposed to market forces and is aware of economies of using various materials or products and should be able to bring these supply chain advantages to the bid. Design and build provides the opportunity to deliver value for money, this being derived from either the contractor's practical experience or through the market forces arrangement. Such arrangements will include buying savings and loyalty schemes.

The person compiling the tender list will need to determine how proactive you want the contracting organisation to be. It may be possible that the employer organisation would be pleased to be offered various alternative materials or products, driving down the overall cost of the project. It is also possible that the employer organisation has a finalised design and specification, in which case the contractor offering alternatives is just causing more work and slowing down general progress.

When compiling the tender list, it is worth considering previous experience, particularly if it includes elements of repetition. A contractor who has performed well previously could be expected to perform well again, although this is of course not always the case.

Tendering, the ability to place a value on a description of requirements, is how a contractor procures workload. The actual mechanics of tendering are rarely covered in architectural education, but it is helpful to know how a contractor builds up the tender figure as this may help when determining timescales and documentation requirements.

The second element that is given little consideration is exactly how a contractor wins a tender, or arrives at a competitive tender figure. This is a little more complex than simply cutting the profit margin. On very small projects, a main or regional contractor may prove uncompetitive, simply because he will have clearly established overheads which will include welfare standards. By cutting these standards, the preliminaries figure is reduced and so the tender becomes more competitive. You will need to determine your client's and your own feelings to a low tender, which may not provide adequate facilities for the workforce.

There are very few ways in which a contractor can develop a lead or produce a very competitive tender, although these are discussed throughout this section and are summarised at the end.

There are many misunderstandings of competitive tendering, the first being that it is 'secret'. Within a few days the contractor will be aware of his competitors. There is nothing devious or subversive in this; it is simply that within a given project area, the contractors are likely to approach common suppliers or subcontractors. This stage highlights a weakness in 'design and build' tendering. Because the design information varies in quality and amount, and because each contractor will have a different 'take off' quantity surveyor producing the bills of quantities, the subcontractors will often highlight the differences in the bills of quantities. It is interesting to find that a piling subcontractor may have been asked to price half the amount of piles, for the same building!

Fixed Price Competitive Tender

This is the full title of what is commonly called tendering. The contractor receives the Employer's Requirements and has a specific time period in which to submit a fixed price tender figure to a nominated agent. The Employer's Requirements will normally consist of a contractual preliminaries section, an indication of the design required or design parameters and some form of specification or quality indicator. The design information can vary from a limited concept to a full package of production information. Similarly, the specification can vary from a few words to a fully comprehensive NBS (National Building Specification).

Once the documents have been received and recorded or registered, they need to be copied. The estimator, planner, design manager and 'take-off' quantity surveyor all need copies of the documentation. Tender periods are generally not generous on time. It is important that the process starts as quickly as possible. It is always a good idea to warn and then confirm to the contractor exactly when the documents are going to be despatched.

Many projects have a design completed to quite an advanced stage, perhaps even including an NBS type specification. Although this gives the contractor less opportunity for change, at least it is a base for the schedule of work and bills of quantities.

The quantity surveyor will need to measure something – no measure, no tender! If the design is not included in the tender in sufficient detail to allow meaningful bills of quantities to be prepared, then the contractor will need to procure the design. The length of time it takes to produce the design will of course depend upon the size, value and complexity of the project, but, either way, the tender process cannot really start until there is a design available.

The bills of quantities preparation now commences. This element dissembles the building and identifies each area of work and material. It is an essential requirement, allowing the contractor to price such elements as bricklaying and plastering.

In parallel with this process, either the estimator or design manager will compile a list of subcontractors to receive the more specific enquiries. These enquiries will include elements such as steel frame, cladding, windows, mechanical and electrical services. The list is project specific.

The length of time required for any element is directly related to the complexity and size of the project, but it is not unreasonable to be expecting the return of sections of the bills of quantities to be happening towards the end of the second week. The time taken to get input from specialist manufactures/suppliers/subcontractors unfortunately has further complications in the form of time of year, how many staff are on summer holidays and the general state of the construction industry. When very buoyant it can be very hard to get the information simply because the subcontractors are too busy to price enquiries.

It is not hard to appreciate the magnitude of work an electrical or mechanical subcontractor will have to perform to be able to give the main contractor an accurate fixed price. Large elements of the design must be produced to allow accuracy and certainty of pricing; the main contractor will not take a risk and will require the subcontractor to provide fixed price quotations. A heavily qualified subcontract quotation, or one that is reliant upon provisional sums, serves to pass the risk for the specific element back to the main contractor, which is ironic, because the only reason that the specific enquiry has been placed with the subcontractor is to remove the element of risk from the main contractor.

It should be noticed that both of the above procedures involve people external to the contractor; the contractor cannot totally control the work or input of others. By reducing a tender period too much, the number of external subcontract quotations will be reduced. This will probably have an effect on the competitiveness of the tenders received for the project.

While the bills of quantities are being prepared and all necessary subcontract enquiries have been issued, the main contractor will now review the project. The purpose of this review is to try to find a reason that will allow the contractor to appear more competitive. This reason could be one or a combination of many factors, including programme change, altering phasing which could have implications on preliminary costs, amending the structural design, a steel frame may be more competitive than an RC frame or there may be more efficient ways of forming the slabs. Reviewing all elements of the design may produce time/cost benefits. It may be that a subcontractor can offer an alternative product that will equal or better the quality specified, but this product will again produce time/cost benefits.

The results of this review will allow the contractor to consider how he is going to respond to the tender enquiry. He will need to consider if any of the modifications are going to render the bid noncompliant. If the bid will be non-compliant, what is the likely effect of such an approach? The contractor may choose to submit a compliant bid but offer the alternative as an option or he may choose to simply submit the non-compliant bid and allow the client to make the next move.

Submitting a compliant bid with a 'shopping list' of options is unlikely to be a successful approach. The client/employer's agent is more likely to supply the list of options for pricing to the two or three most competitive tenderers. This leaves the author of the list without any advantage from compiling the list.

The review must also consider 'build-ability' and health and safety considerations. The pre-tender health and safety plan should identify all the hazards, but inevitably there will be more. The contractor should compile a list of elements that cause concern; these could include blocks that are too heavy (even a 140 millimetre DCM block weighs more than allowed by the manual handling regulations), trenches that are deeper than they are required to be (a trench deeper than head height requires additional side protection) and even hazardous chemicals (resinous floor finishes will require operatives to wear respirators). The list is by no means exhaustive and identifies just a few examples, but all of these examples could easily be designed out.

CDM 94 requires the designer to design out risks to health and safety. When the design is not included as part of the ER, the contractor will need to compile the pre-tender health and safety plan.

The 'take off' quantity surveyor will have been submitting questions from receipt of the documents. It is important that the design manager and estimator answer these questions. The questions will be flagging up holes in the tender information, so it is important that the answers to these questions serve to drive the bill preparation in the correct direction. Following the review, the design manager may choose to meet the quantity surveyor and review the preparation progress. It may be that the project review has determined an approach that will require an addendum bill being produced. This addendum bill can then be used to compare the costs involved with the two approaches.

Whatever the result of the review, the next stage is to calculate the fixed costs associated with the project. Fixed costs include staff costs as well as hire of all equipment required. The equipment required is comprehensive and will include everything from the amount of scaffolding for the building to the site setup, including electricity, water, and telephones. These costs are called the preliminary costs, or prelims. Although they are going to be project specific they will amount to close to 10 % of the total project.

The construction programme drives the preliminary costs. It is the project planner who will perform most of the base work, including obtaining scaffolding quotations, defining what cranage is required and obtaining quotes and arranging for the temporary electricity supply. Working with the estimator, a schedule of preliminary costs will be produced. The schedule is a very comprehensive document and includes all items that need to be provided for the successful completion of the project.

The bills of quantities are now arriving, either in sections or as a complete bill(s). The estimator can now quickly review all the enquiries sent out to subcontractors on a plan and specification basis. The review is to determine if forwarding the relevant section of the bills could help any of the enquiries. The fact that a specialist subcontract enquiry has been made suggests that the element in question is complex and unlikely to have been measured in detail, normally appearing as an 'item'. The mechanical and electrical works will not have been measured; this is a very specific discipline.

The main purpose of the bills of quantities is to allow the estimator to determine the costs for a large part of the building. The bills describe and measure the works connected with all elements of the building. This essential document is used as the basis of enquires for all the construction type elements including groundworks, brickwork, plastering, external surfing and the like. The list is not exhaustive and will include most sections in the CI/SFB (Construction Index/Samanbetskommitten for Byggnadsfragon).

The accuracy of the bill will have a direct effect on the competitiveness of the tender. Without the bills, the contractor will not be able to submit a tender! Measuring the design produces bills. Design information is conveyed in the plans and specification submitted with the tender documentation. If there is not a design or sufficient design information contained in the tender documents, then the contractor is going to have to produce the design information before the bill preparation can commence. To provide this information the contractor is going to have to engage an architect or designer, since this information must be produced prior to bill preparation. If the tender documentation does not include a design and design information (specification) then this needs to be considered when establishing the tender period. The contractor will need to produce his own information.

Enquiries are now made for all the trades that make up the project. The enquiry will consist of sending the design information, specification and relevant bills of quantities pages to the subcontractor. The subcontractor will then price the bill pages. More complex subcontracts could involve design work. It is important that professional indemnity (PI) limits comply with the requirements defined in the Employer's Requirements. However, it is equally important that the ER are sensible with the PI requirements. Specifying a PI figure, which is completely out of proportion to the package value, could leave the contractor with a very limited choice of subcontractors, or having to provide the PI in some other way. It should be noted that some types of subcontractors do not carry PI; eg it is rare to finds a lift manufacturer who can provide PI cover. If the contractor is to engage his own consultants, again the employer's PI and warranty requirements may limit the choice. Setting an artificially high PI limit makes little sense.

The estimator will transfer the bills of quantities to a specific estimating software package, with the estimating software ready; the subcontract figures can be 'plugged in' as they arrive. It is important to try to obtain a range of figures for each element; this then shows where each received figure stands. A figure that is far too low compared to others might be the subject of a mistake, misunderstanding or omission. By being able to compare the figure, the contractor can make further investigations into the validity of the figure. If only one figure is received for an element, the contractor must determine the risk associated with this figure and amend the figure accordingly.

The preliminaries will be scheduled in the estimating software package. These are then priced in the same manner as subcontracts and materials. With all the figures determined, there is actually very little that can be adjusted within the tender. The tender team must determine if any of the elements or assumptions creates a risk; eg an exceedingly low tender figure from a subcontractor could create major problems if the low figure was the result of an omission, qualification or error. The team must determine the likelihood of the subcontractor carrying out the subcontract for the tendered sum. In such circumstances it is probably wiser to use the second lowest figure, or at least adjust the subcontract figure upwards to arrive at a figure with which there is some confidence that if the element was put back out to the market, it could be procured for.

With the risk determined, the margin or profit percentage can be adjusted. Because this adjustment is likely to be in the region of 0.5 %, the figure may not be particularly big.

The final adjustment that can be made is an assumption of the amount of buying gains that the quantity surveyor will make. A proportion of this figure can then be subtracted from the tender figure to provide a 'keener' price. The buying savings assume that the quantity surveyor will be able to procure the subcontracts and materials at a discounted price. Should circumstances arise in which these discounts are not available, and then this figure will contribute to a much lower profit margin.

The profit margin included in the tender figure is typically around 5 %, but, if the project goes well and the quantity surveyor manages to procure the subcontracts and materials at a discounted rate, this profit margin could rise to a figure more in the region of 10–12 %.

Two-Stage Guaranteed Maximum Price
This form of tendering is becoming more common. A contractor is selected for a project on the basis of a presentation and a guaranteed maximum price (GMP). The employer and his agent and/or advisers select a series of contractors to form an initial list. The contractors on the list are then invited to perform a presentation, demonstrating their suitability for the specific project. The presentation should certainly include examples of similar work, but the contractor may wish to describe clearly the systems that are in place to deliver the project

and explain how the employer's team will be integrated into the project.

It may be a requirement that the contractor's team are introduced; this may create a few difficulties. The contractor will not know which personnel are going to perform the various functions required until the project moves from tender to contract. At that point resources will be appointed. At the interview the contractor will simply use people who perform well at interview, developing reasons for personnel changes later.

The employer may be interested in the construction programme, sequence and method statements, provided there is sufficient design information available. This is possible and may be quite useful to determine the different approaches to the project.

From the interview, and any subsequent questions, a contractor is selected to go on to the next stage. The preferred contractor will now be invited to develop a cost plan jointly. If there is failure to agree the cost plan, the preferred status will be removed and another contractor from the initial list will be promoted. It is possible that there is not another suitable contractor, in which case wider enquiries will be made.

To develop a cost plan, the design has to be advanced to a standard that can be measured (bills of quantities produced). This may take some time, but the costs of this stage are underwritten by the employer; this is not a speculative stage.

The cost plan will be made as accurate as possible, using real subcontract/supplier quotations. The contractor will try to remove all guesses, estimates and assumptions. Since subcontract/supplier quotations are very easy to verify (simply by looking at the written quotation!), the main areas of disagreement will be the profit margin and preliminaries. Profit margins are ridiculously low in the construction industry, a figure of 5 % being fairly common. Even the 5 % margin is not what it appears, a contractor may add a lower figure to the tender sum, assuming that he will make further savings later by getting better subcontract or material prices. If the profit margin is only 5 %, it is not difficult to see how a few simple mistakes can wipe out the profit completely, putting the contractor into a loss-making situation.

With the agreed cost plan available, the other contract documents are added, ie the Employer's Requirements and the Contractor's Proposals. To be able to guarantee the price, the contractor includes various contingency monies. The employer must determine if cost certainty is a real advantage, as he will certainly pay for it! Cost certainty to the employer means that the risk is with the contractor; he will have priced this risk.

Negotiated Tender

This is a refinement on the two-stage tender described previously. The client will normally have experience of the contractor and simply invite costed proposals for the provision of his requirements. When the contractor's cost proposals are in agreement with the client's financial adviser's proposals, there is the basis for a contract and the project proceeds.

With the contract documents in place, the contractor proceeds as with the other types of tender, using discounts on material and subcontract procurement to boost the profit margin.

Partnering or 'Open Book'

This is an interesting situation, if used properly. It is completely alien to the quantity surveyor's normal role. To work, it relies on complete honesty and each party must have faith in the other.

There are probably differing degrees of 'partnering'. Should it just be between the employer and contractor or is the contractor expected to have partnering arrangements with his whole supply chain?

The first difficult part to accept by the employer is the profit margin. There are not going to be any subcontract or material procurement discounts, or if there are, they will reduce the contract sum, so the employer must pay a realistic profit margin up front. In simple terms the arrangement is a 'cost plus' one, in other words the contractor will receive all of his direct costs, plus a figure to cover indirect costs and profit. In return the contractor will manage the project to achieve the best financial reward for the employer.

Each subcontract can be reviewed and adjusted by the commercial team, comprising both the employer's and contractor's cost consultants. The contractor can help to drive down costs by using any 'bright ideas'. To bring the best out of the contractor it is probably better to offer some form of incentive, with the contractor receiving a percentage of the saving.

It is important to consider where the risk lies, because if it is all with the employer, the contractor will not need to include sums to cover contingency, design development and fixed price. If nothing goes wrong, there could be a significant saving to the employer.

If the 'partnering' is to be with the whole of the contractor's supply chain, it is probable that very few contractors are in a position to offer this. The idea of 'partnering' or 'open book' does not sit easily with the traditional contractor. It is not unheard of for a contractor to actually get two tenders from various subcontractors, showing the higher one to the employer and placing the subcontract on the lower one.

If the idea of partnering were to be taken seriously, then the contractor could really work with the supply chain, helping to drive down universal costs through benchmarking and other modern management techniques promoted by the government (Department of Trade and Industry (DTI)).

Type and Complexity of Tender Information

The quantity and quality of information contained in the tender documentation must relate to how the contract is being set up. If the employer's requirement is simply for 50 000 square feet of B2 class accommodation then all that is really required in the tender documentation is the planning permission (probably outline), the location of the site, together with any available plans or other design drawings, any available information on existing services or contamination, the ground investigation report (if available) and the health and safety plan completed to date.

In this case the length of the tender period is already quite long and the contractor is going to have to prepare a design before he can cost it. The design and cost are then presented as the proposal.

If there is not a site survey, the contractor will need to commission the survey. This is a significant cost and would make sense if several of the tendering contractors got together and shared the cost. The output of the survey should be in electronic form to allow the designers to start using it immediately.

If no ground investigation is available, then the contractors can either commission one or simply qualify their proposals. Qualifying the proposals is not really an option; the foundations and frame are such major parts of the design that leaving them as unknowns to be confirmed later will almost certainly slow down the design process.

The health and safety plan is quite interesting. The employer's team are supposed to identify the risks, which are certain to include services and contamination. If it is possible for the contractor to find this information, then it is also possible for the employer's team to find the information. Certain contamination elements carry mandatory requirements; if there are existing buildings, then an asbestos survey is mandatory, with the employer carrying the risk for any omissions in the survey. When the employer's team has completed the design, this asbestos survey will be included in or be part of the design. Where there are omissions in the design, the contractor carries the risk since he is contracted to complete the design.

Conflicts in the design are more interesting. The contract ensures that the contractor will not suffer financial loss as a result of resolving the conflict. However, this is a clause that is often changed to allow the employer to resolve the conflict at no cost to himself. From a contractor's point of view this does not normally cause a problem. He simply states what he is doing and, if the employer's preference is to use the alternative that caused the conflict, the contractor requests a change instruction. (The change entitles the contractor to payment and so an amicable agreement can now be reached.)

Whatever information is included in the tender documentation, care needs to be taken to ensure that it is accurate and correct. This information is almost certainly going to form a large part of the employer's requirements. If errors, inaccuracies and omissions can be resolved during the tender period, then the costs of such correction are included in the contract sum. If left until post-contract, there will inevitably be pressure for a cost adjustment.

How to Win the Tender
The 'first past the post' tender system that we employ leaves the tendering contractor to determine one question, what contract sum will win the tender? Having determined the figure that will in all probability win the tender, the contractor now needs to establish a method of being able to offer that figure, while still making a profit. The contractor can consider the following areas to reduce the costs.

Preliminaries
Preliminaries are the contractor's internal costs. They are applied as a weekly charge. These costs include staff wages as well as scaffolding, cranes and equipment hire. To remain competitive wages must be kept in line or slightly below competitors, or equipment and site establishment must be cut to a minimum. Downgrading the calibre of staff can reduce the preliminaries, ie instead of using an experienced project manager a site agent could be used, by reducing the time that the members of staff will spend on the project or reducing the length of the project.

Paying wages below the average will cause staff to migrate; indeed, to attract the best staff the wages will need to be above the average. Minimal equipment may prejudice the efficient running of the project, which could increase the project length, which in itself will increase the preliminary costs. Reducing the length of time that people will spend on the project tends to be a paper exercise; people will normally stay as long as they are required.

The major benefit can be achieved by planning the project to be completed in as short a time as possible. Once the critical path is established then acceleration costs can be considered for elements or stages that will allow the whole project to be completed much faster. The project duration is normally dictated by the Employer's Requirements and the commencement and completion dates are normally predetermined.

Buying savings

Buying savings are the discounts that the contractor can expect through national agreements and bulk buying. Other buying discounts arise from simply driving the costs on a 'take it or leave it' basis. Some reductions can be based on such incentives as a 2.5 % discount for prompt payment.

The contractor will sometimes predict the total figure that he can expect from the savings. He can then offset part of this figure against the tender figure. It has to be remembered that if for some reason the quantity survey is unable to realise these savings, then the assumed amount is a simple loss. Many projects start with a significant negative margin that is only turned positive towards the end of the project.

Part of the buying saving ethos stems from the belief that the contractor will have been unable to collate the most competitive bids during the tender period. Indeed, once the tender has been placed it is normal practice for most of the subcontractors and suppliers who tendered for the other contractors to offer their figures to the successful contractor (if not done previously!).

It is an interesting thought that, to enable a contractor to offer the most competitive tender, he must be doing something right, and that includes having several of the most competitive subcontract and supplier quotations. In certain circumstances, it is quite possible for the contractor to have given away more than he will recover.

Margin

This is the amount of profit applied to the project and is normally around 5 %. It should be considered that a regional contractor would have to pay an amount from each project to the main company or head office. This amount could be significant, averaging around the 2.5 % mark. This actually leaves the regional contractor little scope for a major adjustment of the profit margin.

Tighter bill

The bills of quantities are the pricing documents. Even if they are totally wrong, that is the document that will be priced. There are various procedures in place to try to remove errors and incorrect assumptions, attempting to make the bills more accurate and so provide a tender figure that directly relates to the work required.

One of the common problems with the bills of quantities is that if the 'take off' quantity surveyor is not sure of an element, rather than include the breakdown it is simply measured as an item. The contractor still has to put a figure on this item, but without the build-up information. This figure could prove to be very inaccurate, either way!

Paying an additional premium to a 'take off' quantity surveyor who is known for accuracy or spending longer periods with the quantity surveyor to determine that the bills of quantities build-up reflects the method statement for construction could have significant rewards.

Bright ideas, design changes

Most contractors' preliminary costs should be similar; the costs may be derived and accounted in different ways, but as a total percentage of the final figure they should all be very similar. Wages are similar, standards of welfare provision are required by law, unions etc, so the preliminaries should be similar.

There might be subcontract or supply costs that are significantly lower than others, but if that is the case, why or how is it that much lower? What risks are involved? In many cases on design and build contracts, it will be 'bright ideas' or design changes that can provide a significant advantage.

The tender documents will normally include a fairly specific design, but it is quite possible that there may be more economical ways of achieving the same requirement. The first place to look will be the structure; is it economical and are there more economical ways of achieving the same thing?

The envelope can then be questioned, especially if there are named products. One recent tender required a unitised curtain walling system. A unitised system is a very economical option where you do not need scaffolding and the whole façade can simply be craned into position. In this example the scaffolding to the elevations was required to fit the panelling designed to go between the unitised glazing. A unitised system in comparison to a traditional stick curtain walling system carries an astounding premium. Changing to the stick system and qualifying the change in the Contractor's Proposals removed a significant sum from the tender.

All elements of the building will be questioned and checked. It is common for contractors to offer alternative materials, but fairly rare for wholesale design changes to be put forward. The project above was for a fairly standard speculative nine-storey office design (450 millimetre access floor, 2 700 millimetre floor to ceiling and 600 millimetre service and lighting zone). By changing the air conditioning system to one that used the floor zone, omitting the 600 millimetre service zone, changing the structure to a flat slab concrete system and, enhancing all finishes and services, it was possible to provide the spatial requirements of the nine-storey building in the construction height of an eight-storey building. Although it would equate to a 5–7 % saving in construction costs, this option was considered as a 'change too many' and was never offered to the employer.

Ground

The one area where whole-scale design changes are often offered is in the ground. As a civil exercise, the ground can account for a significant percentage of the whole construction figure. Contractors appear to be currently ahead of consultants, particularly if the following fields:

- Contamination works.

- Ground levels and ground modelling with the use of complex software.
- Ground stabilisation and enhancement.

Contamination is very important. There are significant tipping costs that need to be included. Contractors often carry the risk for the ground and so have become very informed on the options available.

It is a sad irony that when you need topsoil, there is none around, when you have topsoil to spare, there is no buyer. Tipping spoil, even clean topsoil, is expensive. It may be possible to adjust the site levels so there is in fact a cut and fill balance on the site.

If the ground California Bearing Ratio (CBR) is low, the design may include a significant depth of hardcore or sub-base. To import clean material is expensive and it may be possible to use a ground remediation technique such as lime stabilisation. Such techniques virtually turn the soil to concrete, reducing or omitting the need for hardcore.

Bluewater, Kent

Bluewater is a regional shopping and leisure destination, conceived by American civic architect Eric Kuhne. Its distinctive modern style is heavily influenced by English culture, local folklore and the Kentish environment.

Bluewater's malls are styled like balconied streets with ornamental balustrades on two floors and topped with glass-sided domed roofs, which let natural light flood in. The amount of natural light varies in each of the three malls, creating a different mood. Fresh air is brought into the malls through rotating aluminium vents on the roofs, a unique design based on traditional Kent Oast house roofs. Each of the three malls has a different design, and many of the retailers have created new store concepts and flagship stores to reflect Bluewater's innovative architecture.

The project was constructed in a 100 hectare former chalk quarry and sits on a class 1 aquifer, which supplies drinking water to southeast London.

Approximately 2.7 million cubic metres of Thanet sand was brought into Bluewater from the adjacent Eastern quarry to reconfigure the lakes and create the building platform. The Thanet sand was dynamically compacted to provide a suitable sub-base for roads and car parks.

Building structures, which are a combination of reinforced concrete and structural steelworks, are supported on approximately 14 000 precast concrete piles, which are driven down to a firm footing in the chalk substrata. The buildings are clad with a combination of precast concrete, blockwork and specialist curtain walling. This work was scheduled to follow on close behind the structure, providing progressively watertight areas for internal finishes. The cladding took over a year to complete.

The project was constructed by Bovis Lend Lease.

Iconic view of the 'Oast house' imagery

Left
View of the entire
development from the air

Below
View of Bluewater across the
lake

Opposite
Internal view of one of the
malls

The Project

**Faber Maunsell's South Plaza
in Bristol**

Below left
Internal view of atrium

Below right
Entrance approach

After the feverish activity of the tender, the commencement of the project is a bit of an anticlimax. Following on from the tender activities and post tender clarification interviews, the contract is awarded to the contractor who would appear to be offering the best value for money.

The value aspect can be viewed in many different ways. If the design was complete in the tender documentation the best value might simply be the cheapest price. Even if the design was complete, one contractor may be able to offer a significantly faster programme, offering utilization of the finished project at a much earlier time. If the tender included the provision of a design, then the best value could be a combination of the design quality, time and cost. Either way, the employing team have now selected their preferred contractor and the contract has been awarded.

There now follows a period of time called the mobilisation period. As the name suggests, this is the period of time for the contractor to get his act together and start the project. The contractor has many things to do in this period.

The project needs to be staffed. The contractor's construction team is selected and brought together for a briefing. Included in the briefing is a 'handover' from the estimating function or department to the construction team. It is possible that nobody from the estimating team will actually be in the construction team; the estimators need to explain to the project surveyors exactly how the tender figure was arrived at. This gives the project surveyor the information to organise and place the subcontracts. There is little time; the first subcontracts for groundworks, demolition or enabling works are needed immediately. This tender figure, when broken down, becomes the cost plan, which will form the financial milestones for the project.

The project will probably need accommodation on the site. Temporary site accommodation needs to be arranged and planned to be located on site. Utilities need to be connected, normally electricity, telephone, water and sewerage.

The project may need special plant, eg a tower crane. The exact location will need to be determined and, unless owned, such plant will need to be hired. If plant like a tower crane is going to be used, then a foundation must be designed. The foundation will be mass concrete. This is very expensive to remove upon project completion, so the contractor will try to arrange for the base to be left in, perhaps at a level that will go below a road. The crane is needed at an early stage and the drainage and service routes need to be known, together with the foundations and piling layout. It is no good if the crane base obstructs some of the works. The contractor needs to consider the spread of the crane, ensuring that all positions that will require cranage can be covered. This coverage will determine how many cranes are required. The position of the crane can influence construction methods. If the unloading location was at the extremity of the crane's reach. then the weight that can be lifted will be limited. Limiting the unloading weight, could make the use of certain materials, like pre-cast concrete panels, inefficient.

Tower cranes are expensive and will only be used if they can be fully justified. The cranes are rented by the week and so, when justified, will only be on site for the minimum period. The contractor will consider whether there are alternative ways of construction that would avoid the tower crane. If the design suggested that a tower crane would be needed for one elevation of curtain walling or cladding, the contractor may consider upgrading to a unitised system and installing from a mobile crane. Even with the construction of the access area for the mobile crane, this is probably a more economic option.

It is easy to think of the design as simply being the building, but the contractor needs to carry out a temporary works design. He needs to consider how materials will be delivered, if any mobile cranes are required and if any special plant is needed for the groundworks. At this stage it may be necessary to put down a capping layer of stone, attempting to stop the early plant from sinking! An alternative to the capping layer is some form of ground stabilisation, whether by lime or cement. This may have been offered in the tender, the raised CBR of the stabilised layer reducing the base requirements for roads and hardstanding as well as providing a much more usable site. This temporary works design is very important and needs to be undertaken by competent people; scaffolding collapsing would be a disaster for the project and even if nobody were hurt would lead to investigation by the Health and Safety Executive (HSE).

Temporary works are particularly relevant to groundworks. Deep trenching will require a temporary works solution to provide a safe method of working. The contractor could be helped by the Construction Design and Management Regulations (1994), which are quite specific in attempting to design out risk. If temporary works are required, then risk is involved. The contractor will look at every alternative to try to avoid the requirement for a temporary works design, but if the designers have done their job, there will be no acceptable alternative and the temporary works design will proceed.

It is important that the temporary works design is understood by the site management team, as they will need to ensure that site activities have been catered for in the design. Mobile cranes with different lifting abilities will have different footprints. If a much heavier crane is substituted for the anticipated crane, it is possible that the crane's stabilisation will fall outside the area of prepared ground. If this lands in the soft ground it is possible that the crane could tip.

The earliest packages will need to be procured; one of the earliest will be the ground worker, or piling subcontractor. During the compilation of the tender, competitive bids will have been received for these elements and so the project quantity surveyor (PQS) can quickly let the subcontracts.

The PQS and the buyer will compile a schedule of materials and subcontracts that will need to be procured, some of which will be needed very early on. In this way quotations used for the tender will be utilised. There is one big assumption here. It is assumed that the contractor has some design information to work from. If the Employer's Requirements did not include a design, then it is essential that the contractor's design team produce the information as soon as possible.

The minimum requirements for a start on site are the structural grid, foundation design and foul and storm drainage design. This information is predominantly from the engineer, but the engineer cannot start work until he has the agreed design from the architect.

Planning permission would cause a major delay at this point. Most projects already have planning permission, even if a large number of reserved matters need to be resolved by the contractor.

Even if the actual piling operation is still a few weeks away, a pile needs to be constructed and tested, the test results being used to confirm the assumptions used in the pile design. The pile design will have been based on the detailed ground investigation report. If such a report was not available in the tender documentation, the contractor will need to commission his own report. The lack of a ground investigation report will have two drawbacks for the employer's team:

- The fact that an investigation now has to be commissioned and carried out will inevitably add a little time to the process, even if only a few days.
- If there is no information on ground conditions, the contractor is unlikely to have accepted this risk and so will have qualified this point in the CP.

The results of the test pile are very important and will need to be submitted to Building Control. They will either achieve the necessary loading or they will not. If they fail to achieve the design loading, the employer's structural engineer can re-look at the loading requirements (there may be more information about the whole building now) or even the required safety factors, but it is more likely that the pile design will need to be modified. Inevitably the initial pile is the smallest pile that the piling subcontractor thought would work. Any redesign will involve deeper or larger diameter piles. This is an additional cost against whoever carries the risk for the ground conditions.

On most contracts, detailed planning permission has already been obtained. This allows the employer to have confidence that he knows what the finished project will look like, and also the knowledge that planning will not delay the construction programme. A design that is acceptable for planning is not necessarily in sufficient detail for building. As stated above, the first things needed are the structural grid, foundation design and foul and storm drainage design. These are not required as part of the planning application and so may not exist prior to the appointment of the contractor. If these basic design drawings are not available, then the novated or newly appointed design team will need to produce them very quickly. Time is money! The contractor then has a few health and safety issues to settle, ie issuing the F10 form to the HSE, which gives notification that the project is in progress.

Contained in the contract documents is the contract programme. The construction target programme now replaces this contract programme. The contractor needs to build in some time contingency and so this target programme will be ahead of the contract programme. All subcontract and short-term programmes will now be based on the target programme. The contractor's internal reporting will be against the target programme.

This is now an interesting point; almost certainly the contractor will report to the employer against the contract programme. If the target programme begins to move significantly ahead of the contract programme, this may cause problems for the employer. All cash flow forecasts will have been against the contract programme, as the target moves ahead, then so monthly valuations will also move ahead of the cash flow forecast. This may cause financial difficulties for the employer and his funding agents.

We now enter a period of design development and production of the construction information. Exactly what is involved in this phase is dependent on how advanced the design was in the Employer's Requirements and to some extent how large the project is.

From the contractor's side, the design manager manages this phase. He will be trying to ensure that any development is in line with the requirements of the ER and CP.

The design will be progressed by a series of design meetings. These could involve the design team and various subcontractors, rationalising, developing and monitoring progress.

On larger projects some of these design meetings might take the form of a workshop, perhaps without the contractor, the purpose of the workshop being to resolve any design issues and allow smooth progress in the production of the construction information. If workshop type meetings are to be used, it is normal to run these in parallel with a high-level management design team meeting.

The employer will want to be kept informed of progress, which is normally done through a monthly meeting. The employer's agent will run through a set agenda, but since the meeting is on site progress or problems can be viewed directly. It is important that the employer's team monitor the progress carefully. It is not unusual to find a contractor reporting to be on programme and then at the next meeting reporting to be a month behind. No progress in the month?

In a design-build contract the quality of the design and the constructed work is the responsibility of the contractor. However, the employer's agent will need to satisfy himself that all is in accordance with the contract documents before agreeing to the monthly valuation.

Since most parties are represented at the monthly client progress meeting, this is a good time to check the valuation and quality of work through a site inspection. The contractor's quantity surveyor will normally fall into this routine, ensuring that the valuation has been issued in sufficient time for consideration.

The tone of the various site meetings generally reflects the progress and success of the project. It will be hard for the employer to be relaxed if the project is behind programme or the quality of design or constructed work is poor. Likewise, if the design information is late or the contractor is not achieving the anticipated profit margins, pressure will show on the contractor's side.

It may be worth considering that many problems or difficulties are simply there because of poor communication or misunderstanding.

South East Essex College, Southend

South East Essex College is a £39 million PFI project to co-locate and consolidate further education in Southend. The development provides 26 125 square metres of floor area over eight storeys, in an 'L' shape on the 2.4 acre congested inner city site.

The structure is steel, stabilised by *in situ* concrete stair towers with precast concrete floors. The mass of the building is actively used by the 'Thermodeck' heating and ventilation system, which has its plant rooms split between the basement and the roof.

The envelope consists mainly of curtain wall and panelised cladding, the atrium to the south is formed from steel arches infilled with ETFE inflated cushions.

Designed by KSS Architects Ltd and constructed by Laing O'Rourke for the client, Equion plc.

Right
View of the brightly coloured auditorium in the atrium.

Below left
External night-time view of entrance

Below right
View of seating zones within the atrium

Consultant Appointment

CONSULTANT APPOINTMENT DOCUMENTATION MUST BE TAILORED FOR USE WITH SPECIFIC CONTRACTS. THE USE OF AN APPOINTMENT NOT WRITTEN FOR THE MAIN BUILDING CONTRACT HAS THE POTENTIAL TO CAUSE PROBLEMS OR FRUSTRATION WITH THE LACK OF CLARITY OVER SOME UNFORESEEN EVENT.
DESIGN-BUILD IS A DIFFERENT SITUATION AGAIN; THE CONSULTANT IS EMPLOYED BY THE CONTRACTOR. THE CONTRACTOR WILL NOT WANT TO USE A STANDARD CONSULTANT APPOINTMENT, PREFERRING TO USE HIS OWN FORMAT. HE WILL ALSO NEED TO "STEP DOWN" ANY ONEROUS REQUIREMENTS, SO THAT THE CONSULTANTS PICK UP RESPONSIBILITY FOR HIS COMPLIANCE WITH THE MAIN BUILDING CONTRACT BETWEEN HIMSELF AND THE EMPLOYER.

When the JCT produced JCT 81 WCD, the RIBA envisaged that it would be mainly used for housing and office schemes. The architect appointment document available at that time was the RIBA Conditions of Engagement, which was published in 1971. This was replaced by the Architect's Appointment in 1982. Although this appointment document was published after the JCT 81 WCD, it had obvious shortcomings when applied to design-build. In 1992, the RIBA produced the Standard Form of Appointment (SFA/92). The design and build version of this document has been specifically devised and drafted to cater for the architect's involvement in design-build.

For projects where the architect is appointed by the employer to develop the scheme to the tender stage, this type of appointment is adequate. If the consultant is then transferred to the employment of the contractor, (novation or bridging) the contractor will try to protect himself further by writing in additional clauses or making some of the existing clauses more onerous. If the consultant works directly for the contractor, as in PFI procurement, then a different type of appointment is used. Most contractors will have their own form of appointment.

Design-build introduces the concept of 'novation or bridging'. This is where a consultant starts working for one employer and then, at a given time, is transferred or novated to another; ie the consultant starts working for the client and then switches to the employ of the contractor for finishing the project.

The consultant normally works for the employer in developing the scheme, achieving planning permission and producing sufficient information to allow the scheme to be tendered. When the contract is awarded to the successful contractor, he inherits the novated consultants.

It is not uncommon for one of the consultants not to be novated, but retained to advise the employer. This helps to provide a balanced view of what was intended in the pre-contract design, and gives a sort of benchmark for the design development. Of course, this can lead to difficulty when the original intent has clearly not been translated into the tender documentation; it is unlikely that the contractor's cost plan will reflect everything that was wanted.

A similar situation arises when one of the consultants feels that he knows what was the original intent of the employer's wishes and leads the design development towards this goal, even though it is not reflected in the original Employer's Requirements or tender documentation.

There are also situations where the consultant is novated to the contractor, but retains some reporting duties to the employer. I have to admit to being uneasy about this last arrangement and cannot help but feel that it is contrary to the professional code of conduct. How can a consultant work for two people at the same time?

In a novation situation, the consultant appointment is defined in advance. The appointment document is part of the tender documents. This allows the contractor to see the terms of engagement and to see how any onerous terms in the main contract have been stepped down. In a novation situation, it is unlikely that the employer's legal team will have stepped down any onerous terms in the main contract into the novated consultant contract, and so the contractor must price this additional risk.

The consultant will have agreed his fee with the employer. This fee is part of the appointment and cannot be varied by the contractor. There are many variations covering the amount of pre-contract work and the residual amount of fee. It is not uncommon for the consultant to have received very little of his fee prior to novation, which presumably helps the employer's cash flow. The fee is often broken down into monthly payments, allowing all parties to understand the cash flow commitments. It is also possible that the fee is paid in stages or at completion milestones, but the latter is much more rare.

In situations where there is not an appointment contained in the novation agreement, the contractor will seek to use his own appointment documentation. In a recent court case, Blythe & Blythe, the consultant made an error in the design work produced pre-tender for the employer. The design and consultant were novated. The contractor entered into litigation against the consultant. It was argued that since the error caused no harm to the employer, it was immaterial. The court found in favour of the consultant. As a result of this case, the contractor will try to ensure that all consultant appointments now contain sufficient additional clauses to ensure that the consultant maintains responsibility for the design, even though it was produced for another employer and before the current appointment was executed.

The contractor's consultant appointment will basically comprise an appointment letter plus a series of conditions. As a contract it is considerably more complex than the RIBA basic contract. The letter of appointment will provide some basic information, including:

- The trading name and address of the contractor.
- The trading name and address of the architect.
- The contract title.
- Description of the works.
- The schedule of services required, often provided as a separate document.
- The design programme or information release schedule (IRS).
- The fee/schedule of rates, again often a separate document.
- Details of other designers engaged on the project.
- Details of the PI cover required.
- Details of the contractor's policy on deleterious materials could be a separate document.
- Details of the contractor's quality system or design management plan.
- Details of the novation agreement.
- Details of any confidentiality agreement.
- Details of adjudication rules.
- Whether the appointment is executed as a deed.

The conditions that the appointment will be based on can be varied by project and amended to ensure that any liability in the main contract is distributed down to consultants. The design liability will need to reflect that to which the contractor is subject under the main contract.

There will often be a clause about performance of duties in line with the agreed design programmes as adjusted from time to time by the procedure for amendment set out in the design management plan. The conditions will start off being fairly generic, but they will then move to being highly specific. At this stage they will include a schedule of services, schedule of deliverables and an information release schedule (design programme). The IRS is very important and is used to measure performance. Falling behind the dates in the IRS will initially mean a reduction in the cash flow, but more seriously could evoke an acceleration clause.

The Schedule of deliverables (scope and completeness checklist) tends to be a generic document. Elements that are not included in the project can be removed from the schedule. The same schedule is used in all consultants' appointments in order to clarify exactly who is responsible for what. The following is a small section taken from the schedule. A more comprehensive schedule may also specify the format of the deliverables.

Item	Contractor	Arch	Civil and Structural Engineering	Mechanical	Electrical	Other	Special Suppliers
1.0 General							
Acoustic design/advice		•					
Alterations/adaptations to existing		•	•				
Attend meetings		•	•	•	•		
Checking subcontract drawings and calculations		•	•				
Design coordination		•					
Energy efficiency evaluation				•			
Fire engineering						•	
Interior design/space planning		•				•	
IT design					•	•	
Presentation and sample boards		•					
Room data sheets		•		•	•		
Services coordination				•	•		
Services design				•	•		
Specialist design Items						•	
Specifications		•	•	•	•		
U values/condensation calculations		•					

The contractor will have his own environmental policies. The employer may have included some of his policies within the Employer's Requirements. These will need to be included in the consultant's appointment to ensure that the requirements of the contract are cascaded down. Such requirements could include a list of deleterious materials that are not to be used and requirements for the sourcing of materials including timber and many others.

NV Buildings, Dock 9, Salford Quays, Manchester

Broadway Malyan has designed the prestigious residential development of three 18-storey towers each containing 82 apartments, situated on the waterfront. The construction is a reinforced concrete frame, with glass and Sto render cladding.

The project for Countryside Properties was constructed by Carillion plc.

Artist's impression of the
finished buildings

The Construction Contract

As discussed in the introduction, the mid 1970s were a time of popular enthusiasm for
industrialised approaches to building and contractor-led design and build became
established as an important method of building procurement. Design-build can have many
variations, but a set of 'rules' is required so that all parties can understand their respective
roles and responsibilities. These rules are referred to as the contract.

The design-build industry needed a standard form of contract; the Joint Contracts
Tribunal was asked to create one. The Joint Contracts Tribunal was established in 1931
and has for over 70 years produced standard forms of contracts, guidance notes and other
standard documentation for use in the construction industry. In 1998 the Joint Contracts
Tribunal became incorporated as a company limited by guarantee. The company is
responsible for producing suites of contract documents and in operating the JCT Council.

The JCT has the following members:

- Association of Consulting Engineers
- British Property Federation
- Construction Confederation
- Local Government Association
- National Specialist Contractors Council
- Royal Institute of British Architects
- Royal Institution of Chartered Surveyors
- Scottish Building Contract Committee Limited

and includes the following colleges:

- Construction Clients
- Consultants' College
- Construction Confederation
- National Specialist Contractors Council
- Scottish Building Contract Committee

The term 'contract' is commonly used within the industry, but what is really meant
by the term is the conditions of contract. These conditions of contract are produced by
the Joint Contracts Tribunal Limited. The 'Standard Form of Building Contract with
Contractor's Design 1998 Edition' is affectionately described as the 'design and build
contract'. Sadly, the standard conditions rarely remain as that, the employer's agent
alters or amends the conditions thinking that this will offer better protection. This is
rarely the case; altering one clause will often unbalance the contract allowing another
clause to have increased meaning.

Although the Joint Contract Tribunal Limited 'Standard Form of Building Contract with
Contractor's Design 1998 Edition' (JCT 98 WCD) is referred to as the design-build
standard form, there are several other types of contract in general use. These include the

JCT's 'Standard Form of Building Contract with Quantities 1998 Edition Contractor's Designed Portion Supplement 1998', the Institute of Civil Engineers 'ICE Design and Construct Conditions of Contract Second Edition' (2001), The Stationery Office 'GC/Works/1 Single Stage Design and Build' (1998) and GC/Works/1 'Two Stage Design and Build' (1998).

JCT 98 WCD
Stanley Cox and Hugh Clamp stated:[20]

> It is intended for use where the Contractor is to accept responsibility for the design of the works to a greater or lesser extent as the Employer requires, although completion of the design is a stated obligation. The Contractor is to use reasonable skill and care in achieving this (i.e. not a fitness for purpose warranty), and the form does not require the Contractor to hold professional indemnity insurance. The more the Contractor is responsible for the design, the clearer the boundaries of design responsibility become. Whilst at first sight, this contract has many similarities with JCT 98, a fundamental difference is the absence of any provision for a Contract Administrator or quantity surveyor to act on the Employer's behalf. The form is for use in England and Wales.
>
> The Employer's Requirements and Contractor's Proposals are the core of this contract and it is important that they are in harmony. The Contract Sum Analysis should be adequately detailed in coverage. Completing the form requires care, particularly because of the number of Appendices and supplemental and supplementary provisions available.
>
> The Employer would be well advised to consider incorporating the optional supplementary provisions, particularly those relating to contractor's submission of drawings, named person in the Employer's Requirements, and submission of estimates by the Contractor relating to the valuation of changes and loss and expense.
>
> If acting as Employer's Agent, any limits to authority should be clarified, and a clear understanding reached on what is empowered by the Employer under the contract. If acting as consultant advising the Employer, care is needed to stay strictly within the limits of the appointment especially once work starts on site. If acting for the contractor under a novation agreement, accountability should be clearly established and respected.
>
> This was the first agreed standard form exclusively for design and build, obviously adapted from JCT 98 and with the same lack of logical structure. The wording is for the most part familiar, and care is needed not to overlook important differences in some provisions. However, the form appears to have worked well enough in practice, and given the current enthusiasm for design and build procurement its popularity will undoubtedly continue.

Highlights of the contract are as follows:

- The contractor is obliged to carry out and complete the works referred to in the

Employer's Requirements, the Contractor's Proposals and the printed conditions. There is express reference to completing the design for the works, and to reliance upon the contractor for materials, goods and workmanship otherwise necessary but not referred to in the documents.

- The Contractor's Proposals are to be accompanied by a Contract Sum Analysis; the assumption is that the employer has examined both carefully.
- Where a discrepancy is found within the ER, the CP prevails. Where there is a discrepancy within the CP, the employer is to be notified and will make a decision about the discrepancy and the proposed amendment. *This might result in a change!*
- The contractor is liable for his own design work, but limited to 'reasonable skill and care'. *This is the same as an independent architect.*
- The employer is to be supplied with copies of drawings and other documents prepared by the contractor. *Note that design responsibility lies with the contractor; the employer does not have right of approval or even the right to comment (provided the drawings are compliant with the ER/CP).*
- There is provision for partial possession and sectional completion. *This is missing in the previous version of the contract.*
- There is no facility for naming or nominating subcontractors or suppliers in the conditions, but named subcontractors may be included in the ER under supplementary provision S4. *Does this include specifying proprietary products?*
- The contract requires all work to be carried out in a proper and workmanlike manner, and in accordance with the Health and Safety Plan. *Conditions of contract are now coordinated with CDM 94.*
- The contractor is required to provide priced statements. There are strict timescales to aid cash flow and nonpayment to time can be a valid reason for suspending work.
- Where provisional sums have been included in the ER, instructions must be given about their expenditure.
- The contractor must comply with all statutory requirements and give all notices required by the statute, except where the ER states that these are in compliance. Any consent or permission obtained must be passed to the employer.
- The contractor is to notify the employer if he finds any divergence between the statutory requirements and either the ER or CP. The employer's consent is required to any necessary amendments. *What happens if consent is withheld?*
- If amendments to the CP become necessary due to changes in the statutory requirements after the base date, this would constitute a change unless this is expressly precluded in the ER. *In which case the contractor should have priced the risk.*
- There is no requirement for the contractor to take out insurance against the risk of his designers becoming liable for negligence – but the ER can require it. This is professional indemnity insurance and does not cover defective workmanship or materials.
- The employer is wholly responsible for defining the boundaries of the site for the contractor. *Party Wall Act 1996?*
- A headnote to the agreement clearly indicates that the form is not suitable for use

where drawings, specifications and bills of quantities have been prepared by the employer's architect, nor where the employer wishes to appoint a contract administrator. *Does this apply to a novated design team?*

- Where variations or changes of a major nature have been issued by the employer, the contractor may be required to submit estimates of the anticipated effects in terms of cost, extensions of time and consequential expense, before the work is authorised. If there is no agreement over terms, then the instruction may be withdrawn, or the matter referred to adjudication.

Contractor's Designed Portion Supplement 1998

The supplement is for use with JCT 98 by which design responsibility for certain defined areas of work can be placed with the main contractor. This supplement is only for use with JCT 98, and is available in a with quantities or without quantities version.

Stanley Cox and Hugh Clamp stated:[20]

It is intended for use only with JCT 98 in the With Quantities and Without Quantities versions. It is available as a separate Supplement, or as a composite Supplement, which also includes for sectional completion. It does not make JCT 98 suitable for design and build, but it makes the Contractor responsible for the design of an identified portion of the Works. It was not intended as a means of placing design responsibility on the Contractor for work subcontracted under JCT 98 clause 19.3.

The Supplement introduces substitute Articles, Modifications and a Supplementary Appendix. Limits of responsibility need to be defined. It is important to remember that the Architect is still responsible for the integration of any Contractor's Designed Portion work into the overall design and must issue empowered instructions as necessary in order to achieve this.

The fundamental difference between a contract modified by CDPS and a With Contractor's Design contract is that in the former control still rests largely with the Employer through his appointed Contract Administrator and quantity surveyor. These persons are not present under the terms of most design and build contracts. Design may be introduced into JCT 98 by means of nominated sub-contract work, which usually has some element of design; or by means of CDPS. Which option is likely to prove more appropriate for a given situation will depend on the circumstances, and a decision requires careful thought.

Highlights of the contract are as follows:

- While the architect can notify the contractor of anything in the design that 'appears' to be defective, even if no such notice is given, it does not relieve the contractor of his obligations to prepare and complete the design.
- While the architect has the power to issue directions to the contractor to make certain that his designed portion can be integrated into the design of the works as a whole, the contractor has the right to object if he considers that this would affect the efficacy of his own design.

- In response to the Employer's Requirements the contractor is obliged to supply Contractor's Proposals and a Contract Sum Analysis relating to the Contractor's design portion.
- The Contractor's Designed Portion Supplement (CDPS) is to be incorporated into the Standard Form of Building Contract (JCT 98).
- The additional obligation on the contractor to complete the design is restricted to the part of the works identified. The integration of this design with the design for the works as a whole is the responsibility of the architect.
- The Employer's Requirements may include drawings and bills of quantities and other documents.
- The provision found in JCT 98 for dealing with a discrepancy or divergence is extended to include the Employer's Requirements, Contractor's Proposals and the Contract Sum Analysis.
- The contractor's liability for design is limited to 'reasonable skill and care'.
- The contractor must be notified if the architect detects a defect in the contractor's design and the architect must be notified if the contractor considers that his design will be adversely affected by an architect's instruction.

ICE Design and Construct Conditions of Contract Second Edition (2001)

Stanley Cox and Hugh Clamp stated:[20]

> This form is intended for design and build by the Contractor. It is primarily for use with civil engineering work. It may be for a lump sum or measurement. The Employer is required to appoint an Employer's Representative to act as contract administrator.
>
> The key features are the Employer's Requirements, and the Contractor's submission. Unlike JCT WCD 98, in the event of any conflict, it is the Employer's Requirements which take precedence. The onus is on the Contractor to check design information supplied as part of the Employer's Requirements. Drawings originating from the Contractor's designers must be approved by the Employer's Representative before work is commenced, but this in no way reduces the Contractor's liability.
>
> This is a welcome and significant design and build contract. For civil engineers, the change from traditional role to Employer's Representative is likely to be much easier than facing architects under the Conditions of the JCT WCD 98 contract.

Highlights of the contract are as follows:

- The contractor undertakes to design, construct and complete the works, including providing all design services, labour and materials.
- The contractor is to institute a quality assurance scheme, which must be approved by the employer, before commencement of design and construction stages.
- The contractor must submit all necessary design drawings to the employer's representative and consent must be obtained before construction work is undertaken.
- The contractor must first obtain consent from the employer before making any change of the contractor's designer from the person named in the Appendix to the Form of Tender.

GC/Works/1 Design-Build

Stanley Cox and Hugh Clamp stated:[20]

> Although there is a Contractor's design provision in the traditional GC/Works/1, this is the true design and build version. Depending largely on the design information contained in the Employer's Requirements, a choice between single stage or two stage tendering will determine which version of the design and build form is the most applicable.
>
> The now defunct National Joint Consultative Committee, and the present Construction Industry Board, have both produced excellent Codes for the selection of design and build contractors. Both advocate that design and build tendering is best achieved through the two stage process, and state that single stage tendering will be suitable only where the Employer's Requirements are for a well defined design with little or no risk of further modification.
>
> When completing the contract details in the GC/Works forms, the Abstract of Particulars is a key document. If any special supplementary conditions are incorporated, then in the event of conflict these prevail over the printed conditions. This, of course, is the reverse of the position with the JCT contracts.
>
> The wording of the conditions is clear and well presented. There are alternatives for design liability depending on whether this is for the professional duty to use reasonable care and skill, or for an absolute fitness for purpose.
>
> Contract administration should be relatively straightforward and there is the customary GC/Works provision for progress meetings in Condition 35. The Model Forms are published in a separate supporting document and must be used. There are eight documents collateral to the contract, and a further 13 administrative forms.
>
> The government has recently set departments targets to become best practice clients. These cover the notions of integrated supply chain routes such as design and build, and value for money, taking into account whole life costing and value management. These 'Achieving Excellence' targets may be progressed by incorporating amendment 1 into the Abstract of Particulars for GC/Works/1 Design and Build contracts.
>
> This form will appeal most to those with experience of GC/Works/1, for the terminology and procedures will be familiar. It is particularly interesting because it seems to give the Employer and the Project Manager a degree of control over the Contractor not usually found with design and build contracts.

Highlights of the contract are as follows:

- The fair dealing and team-working obligation extends to the project team, including those responsible for design and costs.
- In the event of a discrepancy between the ER and CP, it is the ER, which prevails. *This is the reverse of JCT contracts*.
- Professional indemnity requirements are specified.

Beetham Landmark, Liverpool

Aedas AHR Architects Ltd have designed the 10-storey 200-bed hotel and adjacent 29-storey apartment building. The project also included a health club facility, a selection of bars, restaurants, conference rooms and two levels of basement car parking. The tower is the tallest residential tower in Liverpool.

The contractor helped achieve the budget by changing from a terracotta and brick façade to the white look-alike Portland stone precast panels, which were quicker to erect. The bathrooms were all installed as prefinished 'pods'. The construction was optimised by using scaffold-less construction, mastic seals being applied to the outside from a cradle hung from the roof. Using a jump form of shuttering system for the core and a prefabricated flat pack system for the rooms, the contractor was finishing one floor per week.

The project for Beetham Organisation Ltd was constructed by Carillion plc.

Opposite
Nightshot of hotel with tower
beyond

Right
View of interior reception
space

Below
View of balustrades

Opposite
View of 29-storey tower

Below left
View showing the three
buildings in the project

Below right
View of atrium

The Consultant's Role

THE CONSULTANT, WHETHER ARCHITECT, STRUCTURAL ENGINEER, CIVIL ENGINEER OR MECHANICAL AND ELECTRICAL ENGINEER, STILL HAS A VERY SIGNIFICANT AND IMPORTANT ROLE WITHIN A DESIGN-BUILD PROJECT. THE ROLES CAN BE SIGNIFICANTLY DIFFERENT DEPENDING ON WHETHER THE CONSULTANT IS EMPLOYED BY THE EMPLOYER OR BY THE CONTRACTOR. CONSIDERATION IS GIVEN TO SPECIFICATION – SPECIFICALLY WHAT TO SPECIFY AND ADVANTAGES FROM NOT SPECIFYING. THE CONTRACTOR WILL ENGAGE ONE OF THE CONSULTANTS, NORMALLY THE ARCHITECT, AS THE LEAD CONSULTANT. THIS IS A NEW ENHANCED ROLE AND HAS ITS OWN RESPONSIBILITIES.

This section will cover the consultant's role, both pre- and post-contract. The text is written for the architect, but the same applies to other disciplines. Although the implication would be that the same architect carries out both the pre- and post-contract work, this does not necessarily need to be the case.

Pre-Contract

The terms client and employer are interchangeable in this section, and the architect is engaged by the client (eventual employer under the contract for the construction of the building). Any work done during this phase will be included in the Employer's Requirements to clarify the design intent. It will be the Employer's Requirements and will be the basis of the design contained in the contract. This statement is significant, for whatever the level of design information, it must be correct! One of the main reasons for employers choosing to use a design-build form of contract is cost certainty; ie the cost is fixed and will not change or fluctuate. However, this is unlikely to be true if the employer's Requirements contain errors that will need to be corrected by instructing a change.

As designer you will need to consider how you are going to communicate the intent behind the employer's brief. If you are too specific then you will not be able to take advantage of other ideas or available trade discounts. However, if you go to the other extreme, you may not be able to control the direction of design development, and the outcome of the project could be some distance from the original intent. Determine what is important to the project and yourself and be prepared to clearly define and specify those elements within the Employer's Requirements.

The building will probably require planning permission. At this stage the employer will need a design to ensure that his briefing represented his requirements. The design can be passed to the employer's cost consultant for a budgetary check and to ensure that adequate funding will be available to meet the anticipated cash flow. This suggests that a lot of the early design work will have been completed without input from the contractor. This of course does not have to be the case; in two-stage or negotiated tendering it is possible to bring the contractor into the design team following his selection.

To obtain planning permission, information must be conveyed to the local authority. This might include the building's location on the site, the arrangements for external landscaping, car parking, the general form of the building including plan shape and number of storeys, an indication of the elevation treatments and a description of the basic materials.

Since the planning permission will form part of the Employer's Requirements, it will act as a constraint on design development, both in terms of the contract between the employer and contractor and enforcement from the local authority. The design, which has received planning permission, could be the design content of the ER. This might be an appropriate strategy for a simple building, where the client's brief is not particularly complex, eg a single warehouse building.

With a simple building and little information contained in the Employer's Requirements, the contractor's team must determine the design of the foundations, structural frame, drainage, cladding, door and window specifications. While the architect and employer would have little or no control over the detailed design, the employer will receive the lowest possible construction cost for achieving his minimum requirement. That is probably a good enough reason for using this level of detail on simple buildings.

In practice, most buildings are a little more complex, and the employer's team would like more control over the outcome. The following might be worth some consideration:

Location on the site:

* Is the location of the building the optimum solution for ease of construction, ie will the contractor have to include expensive cranage or plant?
* Are the car parks positioned such that the contractor could make use of them? If the contractor can build the car parks early and then make use of them, this could provide a saving on the preliminary costs.
* Will temporary and permanent entrances be in different places? Why pay for two entrances?

Foundation and slab design:

* Are you confident that the reported CBR reading is the same across the whole site? Design assumptions could be wrong if the CBR drops by too much.
* Does the amount of sub-base need to be specified? You could be excluding modern soil remediation techniques such as lime stabilisation.

Drainage design:

* Is the design efficient? The contractor will try to use the minimum number of manholes and lengths of pipe. The installation of the drainage will be carefully monitored by building control, so why pay for more than you may need?
* Cast iron? It might sound a nice specification, but is it really required? Will the contractor be limited on choice of subcontractor because of unfamiliarity with the material?
* Even gradient to the final connection? If the trenches become too deep then health and safety will become an issue. The contractor will probably prefer to use a back-drop manhole for the final connection. This will allow the trench depths to be reduced. If building control accept the back-drop manhole on an adopted system, why pay for the additional excavation?

Frame design:

* Set the structural grid? Large spans over open-plan offices are considered to be flexible. Spans over 9 metres begin to become very inefficient. In reality columns rarely get in the way.

Design-Build

- Provide a steel frame design? This will allow the contractor to proceed with procurement of the steel much faster, but the subcontract design is likely to be more efficient, ie less steel and cost!

External wall:

- Specify the brick? If the planning permission required the specification of a specific brick as apposed to a colour and type, then it should be specified. Providing a specification that will allow competition between suppliers could produce rewards. Specify the range so the contractor includes the cost, but then stipulate that the brick is to be selected from samples derived from the range by the employer. If unable to determine the brick to be used at this stage, stipulate the cost per thousand bricks to be included in the tender. This will provide the opportunity to select the brick at a later date without introducing any cost penalties.

Roofing:

- Should we specify the slate/tile? What is the availability, what happens if the specified product is not available?
- Tac tray? The Tac tray type of products produces a more expensive type of roofing, but the building will be watertight several weeks earlier. This may reduce the overall length of the construction programme and produce a saving in the preliminary costs.
- Standing seam metal roof? Can you see the roof? Why pay extra for something that cannot be seen?
- Standing seam metal roof in a complex shape? A standing seam metal roof becomes very expensive when used in complex shapes and junctions with other materials become complex and prone to failure.

Working for the Contractor

We have considered the consultants being employed by the employer, but there are situations when the tendering information is so vague that the contractor will need to engage various consultants in order to develop the design to a stage where it can be priced. This will be a very intensive stage. You will need to take the information provided by the Employer and develop this quickly into a scheme design. If the tender information does not include a design, it is unlikely that planning permission has been achieved, or at best the permission will be in outline only. It is always worth trying to have a meeting with the Local Planning Officer to judge the authority's likely response to various proposals.

It is possible that a Contractor's Proposal which demonstrates liaison with the local planning authority may be much more attractive to the employer than one which has a cheaper tender figure. The design, which takes on board the planning comments, could be considered as having a high probability of swift progression.

When designing for the contractor, it is important that you liaise with various contacts within the contracting organisation. The design manager is probably coordinating the tender, but working with the estimator will help. It will also be useful if you can make contact with the contractor's supply chain. The procurement function will advise what materials are to be used to gain the maximum use of trade discounts.

Post-Contract

Whether the consultant has been novated by the employer or was directly engaged by the contractor, the post-contract service is to provide the production or construction information. This stage tends to attract a low fee, often in the region of 2.5 %. The low fee makes it quite difficult for a practice to make a profit out of this stage. The RIBA fee build-up tends to reinforce this. The implication of this statement is that there is a tendency to use younger (cheaper!) employees on this phase. The whole exercise is treated as a learning curve, but this tends to be at the contractor's expense!

Production or construction information is a specialism and it needs developed skills and understanding. One of the difficulties of this stage occurs when the consultant is employed by the contractor. He is going to expect you to thoroughly understand the workings of his construction team and is not going to accept errors or mistakes.

Part of the architect's team is going to need to be a gifted communicator. There will be many instances when you are waiting for information. The production of the 'whole' information involves the integration of all the information from the architect, engineer and designing subcontractors. There will also be many stages when you are waiting for information produced by others; equally there will be times when others are waiting for your information. Efficient management of this communication process will help everyone.

The design-build contract has changed the whole ethos of the interaction between members of the construction team. It is this change that needs to be understood before considering how to programme the development of the construction information.

In a traditional contract, the architect and other members of the design team produced the information. Significantly the contractor was not part of this design team and the contractor did not have a right to question the information. In the design-build arrangement the contractor will question many design decisions. You also need to be ready for the contractor to be slightly behind the pace of the design development. This will be because the contractor may be slightly removed from the design process and design meetings or workshops, but mainly because it takes time to build up accurate costings for various design decisions. This slight delay may result in the contractor requiring changes of detail or material long after they have been integrated.

It is highly probable that the contracting organisation will control the status of various drawings, only awarding 'construction issue' when totally happy that not only is the information correct but that all economies have been considered. The contractor will constrain the design development, the first constraint being the cost. It is important to the contractor that the cost of each element must not exceed the allowance contained in the Contract Sum Analysis or cost plan. This cost ceiling is the first constraining factor placed on the design development.

The contractor will be looking for two qualities in the construction information. The first is the actual production of the information, the relevance of the content at each stage, the selection of the manner of presentation and the coordination of all elements. This could be considered as the quality of the produced information. The second quality is the accuracy, build-ability, practicality and longevity of the detailing.

Management of the construction information is important. There is a construction programme that must be fed and the information must be relevant for the specific package. However, a superb set of information, delivered on programme, will be of little use if the detailing is not up to standard. In a standard design-build contract the defects liability period is only 12 months, but the contractor is not going to want problems. Bad news spreads quickly!

A PFI project is slightly different. The contracting organisation will have a period of maintenance, possibly up to 30 years. By using materials and details that will last, maintenance and capital replacement costs can be reduced.

Good detailing is absolutely essential. It is how the aesthetic qualities of the scheme design are translated into the built form. However, the standard of detailing must be much more than simply a vehicle for transferring the design intention. A detail that fails to consider building tolerance is probably going to cause trouble.

The allowable tolerances for each building element are specified in the relevant British Standard, but even if the tolerance allowance is not known, it is better to consider variations. Trades such as brick/blockwork rely on the ability of the specific brick/blocklayer. It is not difficult to imagine that an element in the masonry such as a window could vary by plus or minus 20 millimetres in both horizontal and vertical directions. This may not be a problem, but it depends on how other elements relate to it. A window is manufactured in controlled conditions, so the tolerance here is likely to be millimetres. How does this relate to fitting in the opening, which could vary by tens of millimetres? This is probably not a problem if the opening is too big, but what if it is too small? Do the jamb/head/sill details give the contractor a chance?

What happens when you have the variations expected from a masonry element mixed with a dimensionally stable product? A terracotta rainscreen is exceptionally dimensionally stable; it will vary from design position by only millimetres over the entire length of a building. If the inner leaf is masonry and the outer leaf is terracotta rainscreen, are the window openings going to line up? Can the detail be such as to allow for the variations in the window position in the blockwork?

Some elements are rarely considered, but if you construct a specific detail, it is possible to test the element in an unusual way with very unusual results. A plastered wall is considered to be flat, there is normally no way of checking and it probably would not matter anyway. In reality, plastering is a manual trade relying on the abilities of the plasterer; the thickness of the plaster must vary. A plastered wall must be a series of convex or concave shapes, although these deviations are so small they should not be noticed. Light is a good test; either a luminaire or sunlight positioned vertically above the wall may cast a shadow on any imperfection. Suppose you detail a change to the vertical plane, say that at door head height the wall is inclined inwards to meet a roof light. At the change in the plane, if all the plaster were exactly the same thickness, a straight horizontal line would be created. Needless to say, the plaster is not the same thickness and a straight horizontal line is not created!

Tolerance needs to be considered in the detailing. Failure to do so is likely to mean that the original design intent will be compromised. The above case of the plaster is interesting to consider further. The line created is not straight or horizontal and unlikely to be visually acceptable to the employer's agent. So whose fault or problem is it? In simple terms it is the contractor's problem; he has constructed something that is not of acceptable quality. He will need, hopefully with the architect's help, to modify the detail to provide a junction that will be acceptable. However, it was not possible to construct the element suitably from the details provided. The detail failed to consider the effect of standard building tolerances.

It needs to be possible to build the details, so there will be a logical sequence to construction. Is it possible to complete the detail in a logical sequence? Does something in the detail involve the contractor in a double movement, or perhaps gaining access again after perhaps the scaffolding has gone? You need to consider the build-ability of what you are proposing. If it involves the contractor in excessive preliminary costs, then it will probably be resisted.

One of the largest constraints, if not the largest, upon the design development will be cost. The Contractors Proposal and subsequently the contract are based upon cost. A building of given quality will be delivered in a given time for a given cost. The cost will be summarised in the Contract Sum Analysis (this is a contract document) or cost plan. Since this is part of, if not the whole of, the brief, you will need a copy.

Design-build contracts attract criticism and it is claimed that it is not a procurement route for the delivery of detailed or complex buildings. This is not true; increasingly complex buildings are now being procured in this manner. However, it is important to remember 'That you only get what you pay for.'

To criticise the contractor for 'cutting corners' or doing everything cheaply is a little naïve. The Contract Sum Analysis was submitted with the Contractor's Proposal and is one of the contract documents. This CSA will define the cost parameters of each element. If the employer or employer's advisers felt that elements of the CSA were costed cheaply, they should check the Employer's Requirements to determine how the element was defined.

Outside of a PFI contract, it will generally be the case that the contractor will not be interested in providing a grade or standard that is above the minimum established by the ER/CP, and again, it should be said, the standard accepted and paid for by the employer. There is nothing stopping the employer from raising the standards by issuing an instruction for the post contract change.

However, that is not the end of the story. The contractor has several other things to consider. The first is the relationship with the client. Every contractor would like to get away from competitive tendering and negotiate the contract. If there has been an omission in the ER, the contractor may take the view that the inclusion of the omitted element may be good PR.

The contract will have a Defects Liability Period, normally 12 months. It is very expensive for the contractor to have to carry out remedial works to defects; it is much more cost effective to ensure that there are no defects in the first place. It may be that the upgrading of the detail reduces the risk of a specific defect, eg a cavity wall is a standard component that works (providing the ties slope to the outside and that the cavity is not full of mortar!), but puncture it with a door or window and risk is introduced. Standard detailing will have a cavity tray above the lintel and a damp-proof course (DPC) as part of the jamb closer. We have already said that the opening increases the risk of the wall failing and that risk is reduced to a minimum by the incorporation of a stop-ended cavity tray below the window, to divert any water to the outside. It is an additional cost, but a fraction of the cost of remedial work. If there are many windows positioned closely together, it may become more economical to have a continuous tray rather than an individual tray above each window.

You must consider the risk posed by the detail. The contractor will not wish to return to the building; so producing decent construction standards is in everyone's interest. The contractor is likely to pay to reduce the risk of failure, whether it is claimed that the money is in the CSA or not. The Employer's Requirements did not ask for a building that leaked, even if they did not specifically state that the building must not leak.

The architect, engaged as lead designer, will need to thoroughly coordinate the work of all the other designing subcontractors. Beware! This is not sufficiently covered in the original RIBA plan of work. The contractor has made you responsible for the coordinated design, which will involve much more time at meetings and considering the work and design information produced by others. As lead designer, your communication skills will be tested along with your technical abilities. A sense of humour will most definitely help!

The Printworks, Manchester

RTKL have designed the largest leisure premises in the UK (completed in 2000). The £110 million redevelopment project involved the transformation of the former regional headquarters of the *Daily Mail* and was the final piece in the regeneration of Manchester city centre following the devastation caused by the IRA bombing in 1996.

The project includes a 20-screen cinema, the North West's first IMAX cinema, a leisure centre with a pool, 36 bars and 15 restaurants. The site was a severely restricted city centre site, with existing facades retained on two sides and the Metro rail link on a third. The contractor elected to use prefabricated brickwork panels on precast concrete backing; the off-site manufacture shortened the programme by three months.

The project for Richardson Developments was constructed by Carillion plc.

Street scene view of the iconic Printworks

The Project Team

(Who's Who)

MANY PEOPLE ARE INVOLVED IN A DESIGN-BUILD PROJECT, EMPLOYED BY EITHER THE EMPLOYER OR THE CONTRACTOR. THIS SECTION IDENTIFIES EACH OF THE ROLES AND EXPLAINS EACH SPECIFIC JOB FUNCTION, INTENDING TO REMOVE A LITTLE MORE OF THE MYSTIQUE SURROUNDING CONSTRUCTION. THE SECTION ACTS AS A GENERAL 'WHO'S WHO' AND OUTLINES THE JOB FUNCTIONS AND RESPONSIBILITIES OF ALL INVOLVED IN THE DESIGN-BUILD CONSTRUCTION PROCESS. THE PROCESS RANGES FROM THE INITIAL TENDER ENQUIRY TO THE COMPLETION OF THE BUILT PROJECT.

The People Involved in the Employer's Team

Project manager

The client will normally nominate someone from his own organisation to act as the project manager, providing answers to any questions the contractor may have about the Employer's Requirements. This person will monitor progress and report back to the client authority. The project manager keeps a fairly high level of involvement. Although he is representing the client or employer, an employer's agent will normally be engaged to administer the actual construction contract and handle the general day-to-day administration.

Employer's agent

Although an architect could adequately undertake this role, a quantity surveyor normally holds it. The contractor is contractually obliged to issue two copies of construction information. The employer's agent receives this information and then distributes it within the client team.

The employer's agent is responsible for administering the contract and will need to carry out periodic inspections to satisfy himself that the construction is proceeding in a manner specified by the Employer's Requirements. The employer's agent will issue any

Palestra
Initial design image

comments in connection with the received construction drawings and will also issue and administer any instructions for change that are required.

Quantity surveyor

A quantity surveyor is required to monitor the financial performance of the project. This will include performing monthly valuations and issuing the relevant certificates for payment, as well as valuing and agreeing the value, of any change instructions, with the contractor. This financial reporting role is essential for the employer and it is probably for this reason that the quantity surveyor and employer's agent have generally been amalgamated.

Since there will also be quantity surveyors within the contracting organisation, the employer's quantity surveyor is often called the project quantity surveyor, or simply the PQS.

Architect

The employer requires an architect to develop the design to a stage where the contractor can provide a relevant tender. Since this is a standard construction project, it would be fair to assume that the architect is the team leader and will remove all administrative hurdles. The project should not be tendered until planning permission (at least outline permission) has been received, unless the successful contractor's costs are underwritten in the event that planning permission is refused. Any other legal agreements, eg section 104, 106 or 278 agreements, should be clearly identified.

If the Employer's Requirements are silent, then there is no question that the Contractor's Proposals will prevail. If it is important to have a specific standard, quality, element or material, then this must be on the drawings or in the specification contained in the Employer's Requirements. Please try to ensure that significant information is not hidden away in some obsolete detail in the corner of the drawing. Clarity will provide its own reward!

Specification is a 'catch 22' situation. If you want something then it must be specified, but if you specify something and then the contractor can procure an alternative at a more attractive rate, what do you do?

If the architect is not being novated to the contractor, then the employer could or even should retain him to advise on the contractor's design. The architect will have a clear understanding of the original design intent.

If the architect is being novated, then the potential for problems exist. It is not uncommon for the employer's pre-novation contract to include some form of retained duty, probably a monthly report on the quality of construction. However, at the time of the report the architect's employer will be the contractor and the architect's appointment will be with the contractor. Is it possible to be contracted to two parties at the same time on the same project?

Structural/civil engineer

Consideration needs to be given to the required speed of the project. If the employer requires completion as soon as possible then it makes a lot of sense to predesign much of the structure; this might also allow a preorder in the case of steel. If the structure is going to be designed, then it is essential that the design be based on a geotechnical survey. If assumptions are made about the design and the contractor commissions a geotechnical report that highlights different CBR readings or depths of load-bearing strata, then any speed advantage from the design will be lost.

If the structural/civil engineer is not being novated to the contractor, then the Employer should retain him to advise on the contractor's design.

Services consultant

A services consultant normally prepares the mechanical and electrical (M&E) specification and sometimes a schematic design, but is rarely novated. It is normal for the individual mechanical and electrical subcontractor to complete and be responsible for the detailed design.

This needs a careful balance. The M&E content of an air-conditioned building could equate to 25–30 % of the capital cost of the building. The consultant's specification and/or performance specification and schematic design may be required to ensure that adequate standards are met, but what if these standards are higher than required and what if the specification is forcing the design down a path that may not be the most cost efficient? The obvious statement is that the employer is not receiving one of the potential benefits of the 'design-build' contract. If the contractor is too tightly constrained and cannot use market forces and buying gains, then the employer will pay an additional cost.

Why do the systems need to be predesigned? It will not help the construction programme but will provide uniformity in tenders, but the fact that the tenders are uniform means that you are not taking advantage of 'bright ideas' or other alternatives. Would a simple environmental performance statement in the ER not suffice? If you define the temperature range and add absolute maximum and minimum temperatures and define the acceptable humidity range, what else do you need to say?

A statement on the visual appearance of mechanical and electrical elements could be included in the architect's outline specification. The drawback to this situation would be that the contractor will probably not include the architect's specification in the enquiry for mechanical and electrical subcontractors, and so the subcontracts will be placed without the architect's outline specification requirements. However, this is the contractor's problem, not the employer's.

Planning supervisor

The CDM 94 regulations require the appointment of a planning supervisor. The appointment is to ensure that health and safety is systematically managed on the project. Contractors are aware that construction activities are dangerous. They will have their own safety procedures, in many cases dwarfing procedures for quality and the environment, which demonstrates how seriously safety is taken within the industry. A competent contractor will manage safety on the construction site, but he can only manage the elements over which he will have control. Health and safety needs to be considered and systematically managed on the whole project, and this very much includes the pre-contract design stage.

The planning supervisor's duty is to ensure that designers cooperate when considering safety. This should ensure that the design is safe to construct. The responsibility carried by designers and the planning supervisor is slightly lessened in the design-build environment, as the contractor will not allow a design to proceed if he considers it unsafe. Contractors have done a tremendous amount of work in establishing and implementing safety procedures; this is producing results in reducing accidents.

The final pre-contract act of the planning supervisor is to prepare the Pre-Contract Health and Safety Plan. This document should include the designer's risk assessments and sufficient information for the contractor to be able to understand all risk to health and safety presented by the project.

The People Involved in the Contractor's Tendering and Project Planning Team

Director
The director's role comes at the end of the tender period. He will determine the amount of risk (money) to be associated with various elements.

The first element is the construction programme. This must be as short as realistically possible, for each additional week is an additional week of preliminary costs, but the programme must not be dangerously shortened. If all contingency and float are removed then a small mishap could push the project beyond the contractual completion date and into liquidated and ascertained damages, which in a very short time will erode the hard earned profit.

The next element is the value of the preliminaries. These include all the fixed costs, manpower, site setup, scaffolding and hired equipment. This is specific to each project.

The director must take responsibility for determining which subcontract prices are to be used in the build-up of the tender figure. The figures available will be a combination of directly placed enquiries, subcontractors identified as tendering for a competitor who are prepared to supply the figure and unsolicited figures from subcontractors tendering for a competitor who have not been approached or subcontractors who have received the information directly from the client or employer's agent. There is a risk in including a low figure from a subcontractor about which very little is known and there will also be some subcontractors who will provide a low figure and then continually fail to perform. A decision must be made on their use.

The director must then determine the 'buy down' figure to be used. This is an assumption on the amount of discount that can be expected from subcontractors and suppliers. Although this figure is to be added to the profit margin, some of it can be used to reduce the tender figure and increase the probability of being successful in the first place.

The profit margin is a variable figure. The actual figure to be applied to this project must be determined.

Quantity surveyor
The quantity surveyor (QS) is engaged to 'take off' the bills of quantities. The bills of quantities are the industry standard way of describing and quantifying elements of work and are produced to comply with the Standard Method of Measurement, currently SMM7. The construction industry is slowly becoming standardised; SMM7 numbering adopts the CI/SFB classification system.

It is common practice for the quantity surveyor to be an external consultant. Take off is very specialised and even harder on design-build projects with limited design information. If the tender period is five weeks, the QS has to receive his copy of the documentation on the first day, as many of the subcontract enquiries cannot be issued until the relevant bill page is available. A major irritation with preparation of the bills in this manner is that the take off QS will only bill what is clearly described; when the element is not clear the bill will simply refer to an item. This simply puts the question back to the contractor; he still cannot describe the element of work and this time has lost a further week off the tender period.

Estimator

The estimator is the person who issues enquires to subcontractors and material suppliers, applies figures to the bills of quantities and develops the tender figure, unlike all the other Players in the tender process. The estimator is only involved in tenders and has no other function during the project.

The estimator will receive the tender documentation, and having had prior warning of the impending arrival of the documentation will have arranged for the services of the take off QS. The estimator arranges the copying of the documents and forwarding to the take off QS. There are many parties who will require a copy of the documents, it is not unusual to make five copies. Documents that cannot easily be disassembled will create a problem. Most contractors can easily copy A4/A3 documentation and drawings up to A0.

The estimator, possibly with the help of the design manager, compiles the subcontract and supplier enquiry list. All subcontractors/suppliers on the enquiry list will receive an enquiry comprising: a relevant preambles section from the ER, relevant bill of quantities pages and drawings and specification clauses. It should be noted that the enquiry cannot be issued until the bills of quantities have been received. The subcontractor may have a design input and could take several weeks to determine his figure. These have to be received by the main contractor before the tender build-up can commence.

The estimator will begin building up the tender figure by pricing the bills of quantities. He will have current rates for trades such as plastering, bricklaying and carpentry, and it might also be possible that the contractor will use some of its own labour. Specialist input will be completed from the returned enquiries.

The preliminaries are determined from the construction programme and construction method. These are priced out and normally refer to a weekly figure.

Supply Chain Management (The Buyer)

It is normal for larger contractors to have somebody or even a small department responsible for the procurement of materials. They will have contacts with all the local suppliers and will have set up various trade discounts.

The procurement or buying function is to procure the materials as economically as possible. Many options for using alternative products will come from the procurement department, since they will have better discounts for some products than others.

The buyer will advise the estimator of the cost of various materials for pricing the bills of quantities, working closely with the estimator to develop the keenest tender.

Planner

Project planners set out rigorous plans for construction projects, establishing milestones in order to meet the requirements of a project, and will then work with the construction team to ensure that everything runs to those plans. Their work requires technical knowledge, business skills and the ability to communicate with all types of people.

Using the bills of quantities, design and Employer's Requirements, the planner will determine the method statement and develop the construction programme, showing the critical path. The programme is important because it is used to calculate the preliminary cost for the project. Since this cost is per week, it follows that the longer the programme the greater the preliminary cost. The programme must also be compared to the time imposed by the Employer's Requirements. If there is a difference then the contractor must consider the risk of Liquidated and Ascertained Damages.

The planner will consider different forms of construction; a steel frame will normally cost more than a concrete frame but will be completed several weeks earlier. The tender team will consider if it is possible to 'crash' or pay to speed up a critical path element. They will then consider the economic balance to achieve the optimum construction cost and programme.

Services design manager

The largest single commodity commonly involved with a construction project is the services content. With the services being the most expensive element, it follows that this area is one that will easily make or break the tender. The services design manager will fully understand mechanical and electrical services.

The first job function will be to analyse the Employers Requirements fully, compiling the basis of the enquiry. It is not uncommon for the Employer's Requirements to contain comprehensive documentation relating to the services even though the building detail is exceedingly limited.

Analysing the ER will provide the opportunity of proposing alternatives that may take more advantage of a specific subcontractor's buying agreement. There may also be a more economic method of achieving the specified environmental conditions.

Having compiled the enquiry list, the services design manager will arrange for the dispatch of the enquiries. When the enquiries are received it is essential that the services coordinator fully analyses them for compliance with the ER.

When the tender is the two stage type and time does not permit enquiries to be made for the mechanical and electrical services, the services design manager will advise a rate per square metre to be included in the tender figure.

Design manager

The design manager's role during the tender period is mainly coordination. He will visit the site and make notes on the available access, constraints, potential CDM (Construction (Design Management) Regulations, 1994) problems and existing services.

The next step is to try to obtain information on statutory services, both existing services and those to serve the subject of the tender. It is becoming more difficult to obtain accurate cost information on statutory services, perhaps not surprising when you consider that they could be asked to price a supply to the project from five or six different tenderers. Statutory services will normally only price for the winning contractor. It is for this reason that the contractor will insert a provisional sum, even if asked not to!

The design will be considered: are there any 'bright' ideas that would save money or make the design more economical and are there any disproportionately expensive elements that are out of place with the general standard of construction? If the ER required a design proposal then the design manager will help with the design development. When the architect is to be novated, it is unlikely that any design development will be undertaken. After all, it might be considered unreasonable to expect the architect to develop five different designs (variations on the design) for the five tendering contractors.

The design manager will write and oversee the production of the Contractor's Proposals. These will include the basis of the tender and any clarifications or qualifications.

The final task for the design manager is on adjudication day. He is responsible for briefing the director on the proposal, as well as ensuring that any modifications required by the adjudication are incorporated into the Contractor's Proposals.

The People Involved in the Contractor's Site Construction Team

Contract (construction) Manager

Control of site operations is normally delegated by the contractor's directors to a contract or construction manager. The title 'contract manager' is a little ambiguous; he will not manage costs or design, but will manage the construction-related activities. The term is probably historic and related to traditional forms of contract. The title 'construction manager' would be much more appropriate.

The construction manager's role involves the management of the project planning, monitoring of the placing and performance of subcontractors, the monitoring, procurement and quality of construction materials, and monitoring and reporting on construction progress. The individual concerned will determine how 'hands on' the management style will be. This could include attending and chairing internal project review meetings and attending design team meetings or workshops.

An important aspect of the role is at the interface between design and construction. Feedback from the construction side is important to help progress and refine the design information required. Working closely with the design and cost managers will provide the basis for better and more efficient production of construction information. Experience is probably better than qualification for this role. The construction manager must be able to pre-empt problems, deal with personnel issues and report internally as well as externally to the client.

The construction manager is responsible for reporting construction related elements to the client; this is basically a progress report. This report is normally given at monthly intervals directly to the employer's agent and any other representatives.

Site manager (project manager)

The construction industry likes to provide titles for its operatives. The senior site agent or site manager is often referred to as the project manager. He manages the day-to-day operations on site, including the monitoring of subcontract performance and material procurement. From the point of view that he manages the construction aspects of the project on site, he is the project manager.

The site manager will ensure that there are sufficient resources available to enable the subcontractors to perform their subcontracts. This could involve simply ensuring that there is adequate scaffolding to allow access to specific points and that this scaffolding is adapted as the building progresses. It could also be helping a specific labour-only subcontractor, eg the bricklayer. The bricklayer will require the information to allow him to build, set out information provided by the site engineer and be supplied with bricks and mortar to comply with the ER/CP.

As the subcontract progresses, the site manager will need to be aware of the quality and progress of the work. Fast or slow progress will influence other trades and preliminary elements; eg it will affect when the scaffold is adapted. Slow progress could impact on the whole project and will need to be reported to the construction manager.

Site agent

The site agent will report to the site manager. Normally only involved on larger projects, he will probably be responsible for a specific package or subcontract. A site agent with bricklaying experience will oversee the bricklaying subcontract. Smaller projects will use a site agent instead of a site manager.

Site engineer

The site engineer is the contractor's engineer. He is only called the site engineer here to try to differentiate his job function from other engineers working either directly for the employer or as part of the design team.

The site engineer's function is to provide the dimensional information to allow other subcontractors to construct the building. His first task is to check all of the dimensional information provided, checking site surveys, location and invert levels of services.

Once he has established his base station, in terms of position and datum, it is not difficult to perform quickly a level survey and plot all boundaries and other obstructions. If the levels and/or obstructions vary from information provided at the tender stage (presumably now a contract document), then the reconciliation is the subject of negotiation and probably best left to the PQS. If the boundaries differ from information previously provided, then this is a different case. It is a contractual requirement that the employer provides a definition of the site boundary. If this definition turns out to be inaccurate, the original definition must be corrected by issuing an instruction for the change. It is often a requirement in the Employer's Requirement that the contractor takes responsibility for all the information contained within the ER, ie check the site prior to entering into a contract!

The site engineer now needs to establish the structural grid on the site, which will allow for accurate positioning of the foundations. Establishing the grid also allows a quick check to be made on the building's position. By taking offsets from the grid lines at each corner of the building it is very easy to spot any divergence from the original intent. It is normally this exercise that first shows a problem with the site size or boundary information.

The site engineer will now set the locations of most elements of the building, manhole locations, roads, walls and windows. He will provide dimensions and datums as requested by various subcontractors for the main construction elements. As the project moves to becoming watertight, the site engineer's function is complete (If the roads and drainage are not already complete, he will return later).

The accuracy of information provided by the site engineer is exceptional. Modern survey stations and lasers are allowing the contractor to set the building out to within millimetres of the intended location. This raises the question of drawing accuracy. A site plan may be to a scale of 1:100 and for clarity the building is drawn with a 0.7 millimetre pen; in reality the line is 70 millimetres thick! As the locations of corners might become critical, the contractor might prefer to receive the set-out information as a series of coordinates.

Quantity surveyor

In some aspects, the quantity surveyor is the most important member of the construction team; it is he who delivers the profit! The tender will have included an incredibly low profit margin, which will probably have assumed a level of 'buying' savings. The QS now not only has to deliver these 'buying' savings but also has to improve on the assumption.

Going back to the market to re-evaluate the available subcontracts predominantly does this. Now that the contract has been placed, there will be a significant number of subcontractors and suppliers who will have priced for the opposition but not the successful contractor. These subcontractors and suppliers may be of interest, so once the successful contractor is known, they will send through their details.

Note that the QS should give the subcontractors who tendered every opportunity to win the work. If a new quote arrives that is cheaper, do not necessarily accept that quote without giving the tendering subcontractors an opportunity to match or better it. As it is the subcontractors who tendered for you that won you the job, they deserve the opportunity. This also provides an incentive for people to give a price at the tender stage, which is essential for the business.

Once successful, the contractor has a 'real' project. This is not simply a pricing exercise but offers the opportunity of work to the subcontractor. This is a further incentive for a more competitive outlook.

The QS is responsible for the placing of subcontracts. The actual placing may provide further opportunities for savings, ie a further discount for prompt payment. It may also be used as a carrot to resolve old accounts.

It is important that the QS and the design manager have discussed the programme and the significance of subcontract input. Many of the subcontractors will have a design input, which will be critical to the development of the overall design. Delaying the placing of the subcontract and subsequent design information could begin to impact on the design progress. However, it is always a judgment call as to whether the longer time spent trawling the market for a cheaper quote will really disrupt the design.

The QS must monitor project expenditure against the cost plan and anticipated cash flow. This will need to be reported to senior managers and directors, normally done on a monthly basis in meetings, typically titled 'cost value reconciliation'. This report will highlight any problems with the project, because the senior managers can affect what is to happen and hence save money or avert a clash with the client or architect. The meeting also needs to predict future expenditure and income, producing an estimate of the eventual final margin, profit!

The QS is responsible for the cash flow, income being generated by the issue and agreement (with the employer's agent/QS) of monthly valuation and actually monitoring the delivery of payment for the valuation. (This may be done in conjunction with the contractor's accounting function.) Outgoing payments for subcontracts and suppliers will be arranged and monitored.

Note that with regard to valuations with the client, the QS tries to get paid for more work than has actually been carried out, by overclaiming on the percentage of work carried out for elements. This provides the contractor with cash that he has not paid out and hence a good cash flow, which is a big plus for a contractor, as he may wish to utilise this to fund other things. However, the QS has to be aware of how much is overvalue and hence make the necessary adjustment in his value/cost reconciliation (VCR), as this money is not profit but simply early payment.

The fundamental relationship that a QS has is with the subcontractors. Therefore it is very important that payments are made:

- When the QS says the money is coming it arrives.
- He informs the subcontractor of how the payment amount is arrived at.

These two conditions can be more important than how much. Everyone argues about how much, and opinions will differ, but if a subcontractor can understand how the amount he has been paid is calculated and it arrives when he was told it would, that forms a basis for a relationship. You can still argue over the amount later.

Estimator

Although the estimator's role is in the tender preparation, there is still the handover of the project to the QS. The estimator will have made all the initial approaches to the various subcontractors and suppliers. He has also costed the preliminaries and compiled the cost plan. Any assumptions and the method of compilation for the cost plan need to be transferred from the estimator to the QS. With the handover complete, the estimator's role in the project is at an end.

Buyer

The buyer's function post-contract is to procure materials. He has an opportunity to go back out to the market to try to better the figure that he provided for the tender. Alternative materials will be offered. These need to be considered by the team before being offered to the client or simply included in the project.

If a material has been specified in the Employer's Requirements, the employer may be willing to accept a substitute if a sufficient financial saving is offered. The contractor will be able to offer a saving, but expect him to start negotiating at something like 30 % of the total saving.

Design manager

This role is relatively new to the world of contracting. It is becoming more normal for contractors who have a high turnover of 'design-build'. The role is simply to translate the ER/CP into construction information through the management of the design team. The mechanics of how this is achieved is discussed in the section on 'Design Management'.

Project planner

The project planner created the programme for incorporation within the Contractor's Proposals. Following any relevant negotiations, this programme will become the contract programme, which includes the time contingency. The planner now has to take out the contingency and produce a target programme. If the contractor met every date on the target programme, the project would finish weeks early!

The project planner must review the project programme at least on a monthly basis, which would tie in with the preparation of the progress report to the employer. If progress is not as it should be, there are several options to be considered:

- If the delay is not the contractor's fault, will the contract be extended?
- Was the delay caused by a 'one off' incident? Is there now little risk of it happening again? Can progress expect to be caught up?
- If the delay is not expected to be absorbed, can other elements be reprogrammed or can a specific element be accelerated or 'crashed'?

The results of this review may need to be incorporated into the programme and the revised programme will need to be passed up the management chain to determine if or how it is going to be issued to the employer.

Contractors would appear to be exceptionally optimistic, assuming that everything 'will come out right in the end'. For this reason it is common practice to continually report that the project is on programme and then suddenly report that the project has now slipped four weeks behind programme in the course of only one month!

The construction and site managers will also need a series of short-term programmes. The target programme will have elements simply identified as a bar lasting a period of time. The site team and management will need this bar to become a programme in its own right. These short-term programmes are often developed by the site manager either with or without the project planner.

Architect

The architect's role, whether novated or specifically appointed to the project, is to develop the design and produce sufficient information to allow the project to be constructed. The first consideration must be to clarify the brief, which will have been defined by the Employer's Requirements and Contractor's Proposals. In fact, the brief is specifically to achieve the minimum standards dictated by these two documents.

The suggestion that the contractor is simply trying to achieve the minimum acceptable standard may seem harsh, or in line with a criticism of design and build that 'quality' buildings cannot be achieved by this form of procurement. This is not true; the employer is getting exactly what he has asked for and in fact paid for. If a higher standard is required, then this should be in the ER, in which case the higher standard would have been included in the tender and contract sum.

It is not the architect's role to 'gild the lily' or 'gold plate' elements of the design. The design criteria have been established and it is these criteria that should be used for design development.

In many cases the architect will know the employer personally, and it may be true that early design intent has actually not been translated into the ER/CP. It is not the architect's role to try to introduce this omitted element now. If the omission is genuine, then the employer's agent needs to be informed, after consultation with other members of the employer's team, whether correction is required and then the change can be instructed. The contractor will recover any additional costs.

If the architect tries to make the change without the employer's instruction, he will need to persuade the design manager that this is justifiable design development. The contractor's team will have two separate contingency sums available to them, the first for design development and the second a genuine contingency to cover omissions and mistakes. Neither of these will be particularly large sums and the contractor will resist expenditure against them, but they are there to cover such eventualities. Any design development against these sums will have to be fully justified.

It is possible that the financial health of the project may not be very good. There may have been poor or wrong assumptions in the tender, there may have been very significant omissions in the tender or perhaps a subcontractor has failed to perform or gone into liquidation. In such circumstances the contractor is likely to look everywhere to minimise the loss or increase the small profit. One area that he will look at is errors in the construction information. The architect comes into the firing line from two directions. Firstly, as the design team leader he would have been expected to check the coordination of the information. Secondly, as a producer of the information, he would not have been expected to make errors and there should be adequate checking available.

If errors have been made, either in coordination or simply errors in the construction information, you will need to consider your liability. The contractor is likely to ask for a contribution and, depending upon the incident, this contribution could amount to the whole loss. Two things to consider when determining your position and counter offer are that the figures quoted by the QS will be well above the actual loss and, other possibly unrelated costs will have been included. Try to justify the figures being quoted. The second consideration is that the contractor's cost plan includes an amount for contingency. You must determine if it is fair that the contractor pays for your mistake, but equally you must consider whether, for a reduced fee, the contractor actually carried the risk.

Structural engineer

The structural engineer may have been novated or specifically appointed for the project, but his role now is to provide the construction information to allow the structural frame to be procured. If the frame is steel, then the detail design will probably be undertaken by the subcontractor, in this case the engineer will check the subcontractor's design. If the frame is reinforced concrete, then the detail design could be by a subcontractor and, but is more likely to be by the engineer. In this case the design information will consist of the general arrangement (GA), details, bar bending schedules and specifications.

The engineer will probably be designing the below ground drainage. This information will be required at a similar time to the frame information since foundations and drainage are both groundwork operations.

Services consultant/M&E design manager

It is relatively unusual to have a services consultant on the contractor's team, as the services consultant has put together the information in the Employer's Requirements and will be retained to advise the client. Contractors are now engaging their own M&E or services design managers. This makes a lot of sense; with the M&E systems accounting for up to 30 % of the construction costs there must be scope for providing more efficient solutions.

With a performance specification, the contractor is free to design very efficient systems. Provided they control the environment in the specified manner, the system will comply with the Employer's Requirements.

Without question, M&E services will be the largest subcontract. To give the contractor the ability to provide this contract efficiently will benefit the project. The contractor may see most of his profit coming from this direction, in which case there is no need to add monies to other elements; the overall tender will be very competitive. However, the contractor can only expect to make money from the M&E services if he fully understands the opportunities and risks involved.

As M&E engineering is a specialist subject the contractor will need specialist advice from qualified people. This advice could come from either an in-house M&E coordinator or an external consultant. With M&E accounting for up to 30 % of the construction costs, this poses a large risk for the contractor. He will need to reduce the risk by understanding the M&E design development process; again he can only do this with access to qualified people and information.

Landscape designer

Most projects will include a landscape element. This could be a requirement of the employer, but is perhaps more likely to be a requirement of the local authority, tied to the planning application.

The resolution of the planning condition will require negotiation with the local authority and could require the contractor to present landscape design intent. This can only be achieved through the use of qualified and experienced people. The actual landscape subcontractor will rarely have the ability to produce a credible design.

With the landscape design accepted by the local authority in principle, it now requires the detailed design and planting schedules. Either the landscape consultant or some of the larger landscape subcontractors can produce these.

The lower risk approach for the contractor is to engage a landscape consultant. This is simply because most employers will require evidence of the discharge of the planning conditions. If this has not been forthcoming, it is much more productive for the landscape consultant to speak directly to the local authority landscape architect. This should provide a route for resolving any problems.

City Lofts, Princess Dock, Liverpool

Atherden Fuller Leng has designed the prestigious residential development, which comprises 162 apartments split between a 20-storey tower, a 10-storey tower and a 7-storey link.

The construction is of reinforced concrete columns with a post-tensioned slab, with glass, zinc and precast concrete cladding. Retail space is at the ground floor and the car parking makes more economical use of space by employing a car stacking facility.

The project for City Loft Developments was constructed by Carillion plc.

Artist's impression of the
finished complex

Choosing the Correct Procurement Route

THE SUITABILITY OF THE DESIGN-BUILD TYPE OF PROCUREMENT ROUTE MAY VARY DEPENDING ON THE TYPE OF PROJECT. THIS SECTION REVIEWS FOUR DIFFERENT EXAMPLES OF A BUILDING TYPE, DESCRIBING THE VARIOUS POSITIVE AND NEGATIVE ASPECTS OF THE PROCUREMENT PROCESS WHEN USED WITH EACH TYPE OF PROJECT.

Each building type is considered for three procurement routes. The first route is when the design team are employed and retained by the employer (client). This route is most typically referred to as a traditional procurement route, normally using a JCT 98 standard form of contract.

The second procurement route to be considered is a true design-build route. A schedule of requirements is included in the building contract and the contractor is responsible for the selection and engagement of the entire design team. It is probable that the employer will retain his own consultants, and equally possible that many of the consultants will be doubled up. On the employer's side, the employer's agent will lead the team.

The final route is a hybrid design-build route. The design team is engaged by the employer to produce and develop the design. This team are then novated to the contractor, post-contract. The idea is that the team understand the design requirement and so can help produce a building more compatible with the employer's actual requirement. There are inherent risks with this approach, not using the contractor's buying power being just one.

The four types of building to be considered are a steel-framed warehouse with integral office, a speculative office of a given size, a pharmaceutical laboratory and finally a major refurbishment.

Steel-framed Warehouse with Integral Office
It is quite conceivable that an architect and structural engineer could be engaged for this project. The engineer could design the foundations and slab, and could size the steel columns, portals and rafters. The architect could design the layouts, elevations and stairs etc, including specifying the brickwork and cladding. Finally, a specification could be put together to support all the detailing and material specification. This traditional approach will give exactly what is required, but also with full consultant fees and no discounts for materials.

The same argument could be used for the novated design team. It will produce what is wanted, but at a large cost penalty.

If left to the contractor, with simply a required area of warehouse and office, and perhaps an outline design from the planning permission, it is possible to achieve significant cost savings.

The contractor could engage a structural engineer to design the foundations and slab, but it is equally possible that he will simply engage a groundworking subcontractor who is capable of designing the groundworks. The steel frame will be designed by a subcontractor, and since this will be chosen in competition, the design will be the most efficient use of steel (ie the cheapest cost will be the most efficient design, the one that uses the least steel – this element will be checked by the building control officer, and so the calculations will need to prove acceptable).

The cladding will be tendered, so again the most economical market solution available at that specific time will be used. The same applies to all the windows and doors.

The contractor will most certainly have assembled the most cost-effective kit of parts, but not all these savings are passed back to the employer. The contractor is responsible for the design and so will have added a cost to balance the risk.

In conclusion, the design is not complex and the requirements in terms of area and outline shape are easily defined. The traditional or novated team will produce the required building, but will not have introduced all of the cost savings possible. The contractor's own team will produce a building that meets the requirements, carries the necessary warranty and is easily the lowest global cost (global cost is the sum of all consultant and construction costs.) The design-build route, requiring the contractor to appoint his own design team and produce his own design will probably produce the most cost-effective result for this type of project.

It is possible to argue that by the employer engaging the most efficient designers available this would be cost effective. In practice, there are unlikely to be significant gains on the subcontract designs, and any small advantage gained by this process will not attract the savings generated by the contractor's supply chain management. It is unlikely that even the most efficient designers could produce a project that is financially more efficient than that of the contractor alone.

Possibly more significant than cost are the potential time savings that can be made in the overall project. The shortest possible time for the project, from design to completion, comes when the contractor is totally responsible for the design. He knows what is coming and so can pre-order and plan ahead.

The savings in project time are reduced when the novated team develops the design and are totally eroded when the design is fully developed pre-tender. It is possible that this particular example justifies the criticism of design-build. This is a cost-effective building but is not going to win any design awards!

Speculative Office Building

As in the previous example, there are two ways of starting this project. It could be determined that the actual layout and style were so important that they needed to be predesigned and contained in the contract. The other option is to determine that the design could be allowed to vary slightly provided a net lettable figure of reasonable quality office was achieved. Either way, an outline planning permission is required and this will need to be in place before tender enquiries are made.

With the outline planning permission in place, the employer either engages a design team to work up the design to a detailed level before it goes to tender or the employer simply puts the design out to tender as part of the global construction. The latter will provide several different designs, final selection probably being done on cost. However, with different design options being available, it is possible that if costs are close then design quality might win through.

If the employer has engaged a design team to develop the design, it is not uncommon for the design team to be novated, completing the design under the contractor's employ and thus relieving the employer of any responsibility for the design. As previously mentioned, a very 'tight' specification will probably act against any cost savings that the contractor could offer through his various supply chain arrangements.

It is interesting to consider how the contractor can bring economies and 'bright ideas' to the project. When the contractor provides a design as part of the tender, every economy possible will be part of the design. The employer is getting the most cost-effective solution, but will have little control on the final form or arrangement.

If the design team has developed the design to a detailed level and then gone through the tender process, the contractor will be reluctant to offer 'bright ideas' and cost economies during the tender process simply because all too often those 'bright ideas' are simply passed to the other tenderers for consideration or inclusion.

The contractor then faces a dilemma, if he has a 'bright idea' that will save money, he can lower the tender figure on the assumption that the employer's team will accept the change. If the change is not accepted then the contractor has a loss that he must try to recover from. If the contractor determines that such 'bright ideas' can only be offered if he is the winning tenderer, then the employer is likely to be deprived of such ideas. In reality it is a simple choice, a given amount of net lettable space of the required quality within fixed design parameters or the most economic solution for the same net lettable space but with a design that was unknown before the tender.

It is of course possible that different design solutions would have many good ideas, perhaps several in each scheme. To amend the winning design by incorporating or cherry picking from the other designs is at best immoral and at worst a breach of design copyright.

Although slightly more complex than the warehouse project, there are fundamentally two types of procurement. Either a traditional approach or a design-build approach will produce the required building. Design-build is likely to be cheaper, or at least contain the risk, as well as being quicker for the overall project.

Once design-build has been selected, it is simply left to determine how much control the employer requires over the finished layout and appearance of the building. If little control is required, then a simple design-build contract requiring the conceptual design to be submitted with the tender will produce the most economic solution for this building. If more control is needed, then a developed design in the Employer's Requirements is the more suitable route. This will still allow some incorporation of the contractor's savings via supply chain management and so will produce economies. It also caps risk and liability, so gains over a traditional form of contract.

It is very important to consider how significant the design control is. By going with the contractor's design the project will probably be available for let (income!) several weeks before the more developed novated team approach.

Pharmaceutical Laboratory

In this example a specific design is required for the correct function of the laboratory. Such design expertise will be relatively rare.

It is probable that if the design responsibility, certainly initially, was left with the contractor, then the design is unlikely to fulfil its purpose. The statement may be a little harsh, but it is unlikely that an architectural practice with good pharmaceutical experience will already be teamed with one of the contractors selected to tender. It is of course possible that the tender list could be compiled containing only contractors with the relevant experience, but I would not expect many contractors to have this specialist experience and so for this example it is assumed that the contractor will not have the necessary experience.

Following planning permission, the design could be developed to an advanced stage. This could form the basis of a tender enquiry and later form the contract documentation. Such design development would suit either the traditional or a design-build type procurement route.

After the letting of the construction contract, it is probable that the design will be developed, so consideration needs to be given as to how that design development is going to be controlled. If design responsibility is left with the contractor and the direction of the design development does not appear to suit the employer (but the design development is still in accordance with the ER/CP), then the employer has no option but to issue an instruction requiring a change, which will almost inevitably carry additional cost. If the contractor did not have responsibility for the design, then any change or design development could simply be valued at existing rates.

The building shell may provide an opportunity for value engineering or using a contractor's specific buying power to procure a favourable material, but the fitting out will be very specific and come from a limited number of suppliers. The contractor's supply chain management is unlikely to be able to provide any relevant cost saving deals.

In summary, design-build could be used, provided the Employer's Requirements were developed to such an extent that the project was fully specified. There is a heavy involvement from design consultants and so little scope for saving fees. With everything so specifically designed, the only advantage with a design-build contract is that the risk for design development would pass to the contractor, but we have already shown that the risk is minimised by the exceedingly detailed Employer's Requirements.

There appear to be few advantages from the 'single point responsibility' that design-build offers. It is possible that the most suitable procurement route for this type of design will be some form of traditional contract, with the employer maintaining control over the design. It is quite possible to use JCT 98 but utilise the contractor's design for a portion of the project, perhaps the external envelope.

Clearly, simply stating the area required and building type will not produce a building that will suit its function. It is highly unlikely that a design-build solution will cut the project time when a fully developed design is required.

Major Refurbishment

This example is going to consider a major refurbishment project, probably dramatically changing the use of the building from its original intent. The example being considered was constructed long before CDM 94 made it obligatory for a Health and Safety file to be assembled. The project has very limited 'as built' information available.

The design was developed by a concept architect. There is still little information about the existing building and some of the changes proposed to the building are fairly drastic, perhaps moving entire cores or punching an arcade through the existing fabric and structure. The employer could now either retain the concept architect for the detailed design or engage another architect. Structural and civil engineers could be engaged, as well as mechanical and electrical engineers.

The building is an unknown. It could be surveyed to give a much better understanding, but refurbishment tends to keep its secrets until they are released as the building is opened up, and at that stage they can be an unwelcome surprise. A contractor could be engaged to help. The contract would be a remeasurement type and so the contractor would not lose by one of the many unknowns involved before the building is opened up.

Unfortunately, the employer is carrying all of the risk. He is required to fund the contractor and the design team for unforeseen work. The length of the contract is also not known; additional work requires additional time and the contract would allow for this.

Using a traditional form of remeasurement contract could produce a successful project, but much will depend upon the original contingency decisions made by the Employer. What value was placed on the unknowns, and if this value was realised is the business plan still viable? Could the risk be moved over to the contractor by undertaking the project on a design-build basis? In theory the answer is 'yes'.

The contractor will take the concept design and either engage his own design team or receive the employer's novated team to develop the design such that it can be measured and priced. Since the building has not been opened up at this stage, the price must include many assumptions.

The contractor now has to consider the risk associated with the assumptions. If he gets this risk correct, then the employer will fund this risk in the tender figure. If the risk is incorrect the contractor will fund the risk, very quickly moving the project into a loss-making situation. Not only will the contractor need to fund additional labour and materials, but he may also have to compensate the Employer for the additional time.

In a tender situation, the contractor who prices all the risk is unlikely to produce the lowest tender figure, and so is unlikely to win the contract. It follows that the winning contractor is the one who has allocated least money for dealing with unknowns, so it also follows that this contractor is the one who carries the highest risk of something going wrong.

Personally, I think that the risks are too high; I do not feel that using a design-build contract in this situation is fair. Furthermore, I do not understand why a contractor would undertake this type of project with all the associated risks. But they do! Perhaps I am too conservative in my thinking.

Perhaps the answer is a sort of hybrid project. The building could be opened up and most of the demolition or major change carried out under an enabling contract. This has all the risk of the unknowns and so should be a remeasurement type of arrangement. The lower risk required to complete the project could then be subjected to a fixed cost/time design-build arrangement.

This does not need to be as complex as it sounds. It could be undertaken by a single contractor, with the project being in two distinctly separate stages. This would also allow the contractor and design team to learn a lot more about the building as the work proceeds, but of course change would need to be carefully managed. The contractor could not be selected on price, and so the selection process would be based on interview, previous experience and preliminary costs.

The Three Gorges Project, Sandouping of Yichang City, China

This big project, began in 1994 and is scheduled to be completed in 2009. It is difficult to say if it should be in a book about design-build, but it does involve many international partners, bespoke funding arrangements and many aspects that must fall into the design-build remit.

The Three Gorges Project (TGP) is the construction of a $24 billion hydroelectric dam and is a vital project in the development and harnessing of the Yangtze River. The dam site is situated in Sandouping of Yichang City, Hubei Province, approximately 40 kilometres upstream from the Gezhouba Project.

The TGP is the largest conservancy project ever proposed in China or the world. With normal pool level (NPL) at 175 metres, the total storage capacity of the reservoir is 39.3 billion cubic metres, with a further 22.15 billion cubic metres of flood control storage capacity.

This multipurpose hydro-development project will produce comprehensive benefits in flood control, power generation and navigation improvement. It functions as a backbone in flood control to protect the areas in the middle and lower reach of the Yangtze River. Its ideal geographical location will make it possible to effectively control the huge floodwater from upstream.

The dam is being provided with a total installation of generating capacity of 18 200 megawatts and with an average output of 84.7 billion Kilowatt-hours a year, one-ninth of the national total generated power. A large proportion of the electricity supply will go to Eastern and Central China and a small proportion to the east of Sichuan Province, this replaces 40–50 million tonnes of raw coal burnt each year. This reliable, cheap and regenerateable energy will play an important role in economic development and the prevention of environmental pollution.

The 660 kilometre long waterway from Yichang to Chongqing City will be improved after the completion of the project. At least 10 000 tonnes of barge fleet will pass directly to the city harbour of Chongqing. This will increase annual one-way navigable capacity to 50 million tonnes from the current 10 million tonnes and decrease navigation costs by 35–37 %. By regulation of the reservoir, the minimum flow downstream of Yichang in the dry season will be increased from 3000 to over 5000 cubic metres per second.

Is the dam a sustainable development? Hydroelectric production definitely means a cleaner environment, but at what cost? Chinese officials estimate that the reservoir will partially or completely inundate 2 cities, 11 counties, 140 towns, 326 townships and 1351 villages. Spreading over about 23 800 hectares, more than 1.1 million people will have to be resettled, accounting for about one-third of the project's cost.

The project will have a devastating ecological impact. By altering the natural environment an almost infinite number of species will be affected. These include the giant Panda, Chinese tiger, Chinese alligator, the Yangtze dolphin, the Chinese sturgeon and the Siberian crane. In addition, the project requires extensive logging in the area.

Right
Artist's impression of the
aerial view of the dam

Below
The dam in construction

三峡水利枢纽鸟瞰图

PFI

THERE ARE VARIOUS TYPES OF PRIVATE FINANCE INITIATIVE/PUBLIC PRIVATE PARTNERSHIP (PFI/PPP) BUT THE MOST COMMON IN BRITAIN REQUIRES THE PRIVATE SECTOR TO DESIGN, BUILD, FINANCE AND OPERATE (DBFO) FACILITIES, USUALLY FOR 25–30 YEARS. PFI/PPP IS A VEHICLE THAT ALLOWS THE GOVERNMENT TO PROCURE A FACILITY WITHOUT HAVING TO PROVIDE A LARGE CAPITAL OUTLAY AT THE BEGINNING. THE PROJECT WILL INCLUDE THE MAINTENANCE FOR THE CONCESSION PERIOD. THE MAINTENANCE COULD BE MUCH MORE THAN SIMPLY LOOKING AFTER THE BUILDING AND COULD INVOLVE A FULL FACILITIES MANAGEMENT (FM) PROVISION.

THE COST OF THE PROJECT AND FM IS SPLIT OVER THE FULL CONCESSION PERIOD. THERE ARE FOUR INTERRELATED PRINCIPLES AT THE HEART OF THE PFI:[21]

- GENUINE RISK TRANSFER.
- OUTPUT SPECIFICATION.
- WHOLE LIFE ASSET PERFORMANCE.
- PERFORMANCE-RELATED REWARD.

THERE HAS BEEN MUCH CRITICISM OF THIS TYPE OF PROCUREMENT, MAINLY SUGGESTING THAT THE DESIGN IS NOT SUITABLE FOR THE REQUIRED FUNCTION.

The Private Finance Initiative was announced by the Conservative Government in its 1992 Autumn Statement. Its aim was to achieve closer partnerships between the public and private sectors. Although this is fact, some infrastructure schemes, such as the second Severn Crossing, had been funded in this way in the late 1980s. In the 1992 Autumn Statement the government stated:

> The British government is committed to partnerships with the private sector to deliver modern and effective public services. Partnerships enable the public sector to benefit from commercial dynamism, innovation and efficiencies, by harnessing private sector capital, skills and experience with the high standards and commitment found within the public services.
>
> Public Private Partnerships place risks with the party best placed to manage them. The private sector partner puts its own capital at risk, encouraging innovation and the effective management of risks, which helps to deliver projects on time and on budget through the lifetime of the project. Public Private Partnerships can offer better services, delivered more efficiently and thus providing better value for money for the taxpayer.

Public Private Partnerships are not a single model applied to every circumstance but rather offer a tailored approach to the particular circumstances of public services. The Private Finance Initiative (PFI) has been the main vehicle for delivering successful PPP's, a message strongly endorsed by the National Audit Office's report 'Managing the relationship to secure a successful partnership in PFI projects' (November 2001). PFI projects can only go ahead where they demonstrate clear value for money against a 'traditional' procurement. This involves a comparison between the PFI proposal and a Public Sector Comparator that estimates the costs of a 'traditional' procurement in which separate arrangements will exist for the construction, maintenance and operation of a service.

The following is an extract from the Budget Speech 2005:[22]

> Under the Private Finance Initiative (PFI) the public sector contracts to purchase services on a long-term basis so as to take advantage of private sector management skills incentivised by having private finance at risk. The private sector has always

been involved in the building and maintenance of public infrastructure, but PFI ensures that contractors are bound into long-term maintenance contracts and shoulder responsibility for the quality of the work they do. With PFI, the public sector defines what is required to meet public needs and ensures delivery of the outputs through the contract. Consequently, the private sector can be harnessed to deliver investment in better quality public services whilst frontline services are retained within the public sector.

The Government only uses PFI where it is appropriate and where it expects it to deliver value for money. This is based on an assessment of the lifetime costs of both providing and maintaining the underlying asset, and of the running costs of delivering the required level of service. In assessing where PFI is appropriate, the Government's approach is based on its commitment to efficiency, equity and accountability, and on the Prime Minister's principles of public service reform. PFI is only used where it can meet these requirements, and where the value for money it offers is not at the expense of the terms and conditions of staff. The Government is committed to securing the best value for its investment programme by ensuring that there is no inherent bias in favour of one procurement option over another.

Since PFI began in 1992, the following are some interesting facts:

- Over 400 projects, each with a capital value of over £15 million and a combined capital value over £42 billion, have been authorised.[23]
- 78 % of projects have been delivered to the price agreed at contract.[24]
- 88 % of projects have been delivered on time or early.[24]
- Almost 60 % of PFI projects by value are on the government's balance sheet.[25]

The National Audit Office (NAO) recently published a report that demonstrated that PFI is delivering on time and to budget better than projects traditionally procured. In summary:

	Traditional (%)	PFI (%)
Projects over budget	73	20
Projects late	70	24

The PFI report found that where there were cost overruns, these were generally the result of changes to the project instigated by the client and not the contractor.

PFI projects appear to be able to deliver on time. This is probably because payments do not commence until the asset has been built and the consortium is delivering the required service. The payment mechanism incentivises the consortium to complete the construction as soon as possible.

PFI allows the government to take advantage of private sector expertise to manage complex investment programmes. A Treasury commissioned report by Mott MacDonald concluded that publicly procured projects tended to underestimate project costs and duration and overestimate benefits. The report showed that PFI projects, however, benefited from higher levels of diligence and were able to reduce these risks. By introducing private sector investors who put their own skills and own capital into the project, the public sector gets the benefits of commercial efficiencies and innovations as well as timely delivery. This results in not only better public services, but also better value for money.

There has been wide coverage on the use of PFI in health and education, but PFI is also being used in a diverse range of projects like helicopter simulators for the Ministry of Defence and the redevelopment of the main Treasury building.

PFI has an inbuilt mechanism to ensure delivery. Payments to the private sector contractor will be linked to a level of service based on specified performance standards. The contractor is incentivised to perform up to an agreed standard, as deductions are made from the payment to the contractor for substandard performance. Many contracts have provisions that allow the termination of a subcontractor for a particular service, eg cleaning, if that is the only area of weakness. If there are overall serious shortfalls, the whole contract can be terminated and may be re-let to another contractor.

The government can borrow more cheaply than the private sector, but determining value for money is not simply about comparing interest rates. Any additional costs of borrowing are more than offset by the private sector taking on the risk of construction cost, time overruns and project performance, using their ability to innovate, and making more efficient use of resources. HM Treasury is currently consulting on new proposals for a value for money assessment, to include the reform of the Public Sector Comparator in order to reflect these advantages.

Does PFI compromise on design standards? When bidding for a PFI, both the construction and design teams are working together to decide the best way to deliver the required service over the contract life. This encourages the contractor to take a longer-term view of the design of the asset and a reduction in problems of implementation of design during the construction. In over half the projects looked at in the recent NAO report, the department and project managers rated design and build quality as good or very good.

PFI is much more than the construction project and will normally involve the transfer of staff to the operating vehicle. Government ministers will not approve a PPP scheme unless the terms and conditions of service of transferred staff are protected by the Transfer of Undertakings (Protection of Employment) Regulations 1981 (TUPE).

These regulations do not cover occupational pensions, but ministers will not approve a PPP scheme unless staff are offered broadly comparable pension terms by the new employer at primary and subsequent contracting rounds, and the new pension scheme allows staff to move their accrued credits to that scheme on a fully protected basis.

Legal costs were high in the early days as the PPP market was developing. However, as the market matures, we should see the length of time spent in the bid stage decrease and therefore the cost of advisors go down. Also, PPPs require greater due diligence than for traditional procurement to enable risks to be identified and effectively managed. The costs represent only a small proportion of the value of investment that will be delivered over the life of the contracts.

Britain has led the field in PPPs, but almost every government in the world has been looking at the PPP model and reviewing how the private sector can help develop their public services. These include Holland, South Africa, Portugal and Finland.

Sir Stuart Lipton, chairman of the Commission for Architecture and the Built Environment, gave a speech to a union conference in September 2002. He was asking if PFI was failing our future, and although he quotes that at the moment the majority of PFI buildings are poorly designed and will fail to meet the changing demands of this and future generations, he concluded that there was no inherent reason why PFI could not deliver exemplary buildings.

However, he was quite clear that the onus was on the end user. All too often the public client fails to demand the necessary design quality. He felt that if the client takes the time to define the brief and set the quality standards and benchmarks, then we will get the functional, sustainable and beautiful public buildings that we all deserve.

Another major criticism of the PFI process is that the contractor will not understand the design or operational requirements of the end user, e.g. the hospital or school. This is quite correct, the contractor will probably not have much experience of the operation, but the design team certainly will! If the experienced design team work with the client representatives, an efficient functional design should be developed. There is nothing inherent in a PFI contract that prevents good design.

The main conditions of contract are not JCT 98 WCD; the contract is for the PFI vehicle and the construction contract will be based upon this. It will almost certainly be bespoke for the project. Consultant appointments are not an RIBA format but will be the contractor's standard form and will include various sections taken directly from the main contract. The contractor will try to offset any obligations on him by making them specific obligations on the consultant.

Various architectural media report that the RIBA is very much against this form of procurement, the stated reason being that PFI cannot achieve design quality. However, there is no reason why this should be so; the consortium can engage top architectural practices to produce leading designs, but care is needed in ensuring that the design is deliverable.

The Employer's Requirement part of the contract is likely to be a very small high level document, containing non-specific requirements. This then allows the Contractor's Proposals to contain all the detail of the design. This situation arises because the consortium is the client for the construction contract, but the consortium will not be the user of the completed facility. The end user will be the hospital or other beneficiary of the PFI proposal. As discussed previously, client involvement is required in developing the design before it becomes part of the contract.

The Contractor's Proposals will be very detailed, and will be the vehicle by which to measure or assess the construction. It is often the situation that the PFI beneficiary's requirements may change several times during the course of the project. This could be because inadequate effort was used at the beginning of the project to define the brief. It could also be that because the projects tend to have a relatively long time span, often years, the PFI beneficiary's requirements may have altered for many reasons. The Contractor's Proposals is the document that defines the detail of the construction. These will need to be amended each time the requirements are changed.

The design of the project obviously needs to satisfy the end user's requirements, and it is normal for the end user to form a 'committee' to investigate and help develop the design. The contractor will normally introduce some form of 'sign off' procedure, allowing compliance with the project requirements to be checked as the design develops. Again, this should help to avoid the earlier criticism of bad design.

In principle, a PFI project has two budgets: a capital budget dealing with the delivery of the building and infrastructure, and a maintenance budget for the operation of the facility. These are often referred to as Capex and Opex budgets.

Life cycle costing has had an influence on the Opex costs. Over the project life each material will have been considered in terms of the number of times it will need to be replaced, or maintained. This cost is included in the budget.

If the designer can show that by increasing the standard of material, the replacement cycle is altered or maintenance costs reduced, it may be possible to demonstrate that money is actually saved by using higher quality or more expensive materials.

The construction and material standards are defined by the Contractor's Proposals, so these are known at the outset of the project. The consortium will have chosen material and construction techniques that comply with the required life cycle proposals in the Opex budget. There is some concern that the contractor is unregulated and will 'cut corners', but this would seem illogical since if the material does not last the defined time, additional expense will be incurred over the life of the building. The suggestion that PFI projects lack quality would not seem to be supported by the requirement to maintain the building over the project life.

Clearly the project must be efficient. PFI will not have unnecessary design elements or superfluous design detailing. It could be argued that this setup will not provide 'cutting edge' design, but if such design cannot be financially justified, I am not sure that this is a valid criticism. Why should the end user (or client) pay for unnecessary design?

I would argue that PFI should provide quality buildings that stand the test of time. The initial design was selected by competitive process, albeit that the driving factor will almost inevitably have been cost. The materials and construction methods cannot be inadequate as this project has been subjected to vigorous life cycle costing and set up to perform over the term of the project. A traditional contract, or even a JCT 98 WCD type design and build contract, is not subjected to life cycle costing.

The main problem with a PFI contract is the bid cost. If these could be reduced, then as a procurement route it is providing competent, if not exciting, architecture. I do not have an answer to the bid costs; numerous consortia will develop designs before these are reduced to two to further develop their schemes. At the end of this development, a preferred bidder is selected and with only one consortium involved, the design and PFI contract are developed. Allowing a smaller number of consortia to develop schemes and moving to developing with single consortia at an earlier stage could reduce costs, but this would reduce the competition and so may not produce the best result.

HM Treasury produced a step-by-step guide[26] to the PFI procurement process. The following is a summary of the steps:

Stage 1 – Establish business need. No significant capital or service procurement, whether by PFI or otherwise, should proceed until after a rigorous examination by the client of business objectives and constraints, including the constraint of affordability.

Stage 2 – appraise the options. If it has been determined that investment is necessary, an option appraisal should be carried out. This strategic examination involves identifying and assessing options – realistic alternative ways of achieving the change that appears necessary.

Stage 3 – Business case and reference project. If the outcome of the option appraisal is that there is a strong case for investment, which is expected to be cost effective, then the possibility of a PFI solution should be explored. The outline business case should be an assessment of what is possible and should incorporate a reference project (a particular possible solution to the output requirement). This should be a combination of capital investment, operations, maintenance and ancillary services.

Stage 4 – Developing the team. The procurement team, often led by a full-time project manager, and a project steering board to which it reports and which can take decisions are developed.

Stage 5 – deciding tactics. The client's professional advisers should be able to advise on the procedure best suited for the particular business, including how much information to request from the bidders and when to seek fully costed proposals. Where the project is relatively straightforward it may be possible to select the 'final' tenderers directly from the prequalified respondents. When the project is novel or complex, a two-stage process, passing via a long list of at most six to a final tender list of two or three, might be preferred.

Stage 6 – Invite expression of interest, publish OJEC notice. The formal procurement begins with the publication of a contract notice in the *Official Journal of the European Community* (*OJEC*). The advertisement should include sufficient explanation of the project to attract a provider. In general, the negotiated procedure with a call for competition is appropriate.

Stage 7 – Pre-qualification of bidders. The list of respondents to the *OJEC* notice should be evaluated and reduced to a long or short list, whichever is relevant.

Stage 8 – Selection of the shortlist. Elevation to the shortlist must be on the grounds of ability and commitment. This could include a technical submission.

Stage 9 – Refine the appraisal. The business case should be further refined in the light of new information available, and the affordability and funding arrangements for a period with the specified scope should be reaffirmed.

Stage 10 – The initiation to negotiate. The invitation to negotiate is issued to the shortlist and should include:

- The services required, in output terms.
- The boundaries or constraints on service.

Design-Build

- The proposed contractual terms.
- The timetable and process for negotiating.
- The criteria for evaluation of bids.
- The extent to which bidders are encouraged to submit variant bids.

Stage 11 – Receipt and evaluation of bids. It is essential to establish that the bids meet the value for money and affordability criteria. The client may request a best and final offer (BAFO).

Stage 12 – Selection of preferred bidder and the final selection. As the preferred bidder is selected, the PFI proposition should be retested against the key value for money and affordability criteria.

Stage 13 – Contract award and financial close. Provided best practice has been used in the evaluation of the preferred bidder, the process to contract award and financial close should be relatively straightforward.

Stage 14 – Contract management. The structure of the contract will have defined the basis for the new long-term operational and managerial relationship between the client and supplier.

The Edge, Booth Street, Manchester

Broadway Malyan has designed the prestigious residential development near to the River Irwell and the Lowry Hotel. The project consists of a four-tower block and a three-storey podium. The construction is a reinforced concrete frame, with glazed façade.

The project for Countryside Properties was constructed by Carillion plc.

Artist's impression of the
finished block

Case Studies

THIS SECTION OF THE BOOK INCLUDES VARIOUS CASE STUDIES. EACH CASE STUDY CONTAINS DETAILS AND IMAGES OF A SPECIFIC PROJECT THAT HAS BEEN PROCURED USING A DESIGN-BUILD APPROACH.

The case studies have been selected not only to span different building types but also to cover different countries. Personally, I have been involved in the construction of a number of the following studies. All studies were selected because I felt that there was some aspect to the project that shows that design-build can be used to provide good architecture. Two of the studies contradict the main text. Design-build is not a good procurement route for a refurbishment project normally the risks are far too high, but if they can be successfully managed, then, as the studies show, a successful project can be achieved.

Case studies include:

Australian Bureau of Statistics, Canberra

A government landmark building leading the rejuvenation of the existing town centre.

Brindleyplace, Birmingham

This is not a single building but the development of a whole business district, taking over a decade to complete. It comprised more than 10 buildings, each with its own distinctive style, but achieving the developer's required quality objectives.

Café in the Square, Birmingham

A small landmark 'gem' in the centre of the new business district.

Capitol Area East End, Block 225, Sacramento

A government building designed to set sustainability standards.

Dean Close School, Cheltenham

An interesting piece of architecture located on the edge of the Regency conservation area in Cheltenham's town centre. The school selected design-build to try to control costs and the project achieved their aims.

Government Communications Headquarters, Cheltenham

A major award winning PFI project, using standards of design and materials that are rare on any project.

Great Western Hospital, Swindon

A leading project in terms of sustainability. Although a PFI project, the consortium selected stringent sustainability targets for the project.

Mile End Stadium, London

The completion of the park by a prestigious refurbishment and addition to the existing stadium.

Museum in the Park, Stroud

The relocation of the existing museum collection, including the refurbishment of the existing listed manor house. The project should not have been design-build, but it was and it worked!

National Trust New Central Office, Swindon

Award winning 'green' architect, linking with the National Trust to set sustainability standards while paying homage to Swindon's railway heritage.

Oklahoma State Capitol Dome, Oklahoma City

The completion of a landmark building constructed early in the 20th century. The existing building should have been too risky for design-build, but the risks were controlled and the project a success.

Princess Royal University Hospital, Orpington

PFI project amalgamating several sites into one efficient unit.

Southern Cross, Melbourne

Commercial high-rise development, with civic space.

The Custom House, Redcliffe Backs – Bristol

Prestigious accommodation in a harbour-side location.

The Stevenage Centre, Stevenage

One of the largest further education projects in the UK.

Wellington E Webb Municipal Office Building, Denver

Amalgamation of government functions into one new building, integrating several existing features.

Australian Bureau of Statistics, Canberra, Australia

Project: Office development
Employer: Bovis Lend Lease
Architect: Woods Bagot
Engineer: Taylor Thomson Whitting
M&E engineer: John Raineri & Associates
Contractor: Bovis Lend Lease
Contract value: A$61.8 million
+ 25.6 million fit out
Contract type: Design and Construct
Contract period: 28 months

Introduction

The headquarters for the Australian Bureau of Statistics (ABS House) is the first component of a substantial urban rejuvenation of the Belconnen Town Centre. The building creates a local landmark with a strong public presence within the commercial hub of Belconnen. This is achieved by creating a contemporary yet civic development that responds to the mission of the Bureau, the surrounding urban design a palette of existing Cameron offices and the environmental context. The design has already proven to uplift the morale of ABS staff. As such the building has been an effective tool to assist cultural integration and organisational change.

General

The site was part of the Commonwealth Government's asset disposal programme and the sale of the land included the precommitment of some 35 000 square metres of new office space. To meet the government's brief, the Bovis Lend Lease team developed a unique financial structuring arrangement and a comprehensive master plan, which has set a new industry benchmark in Australia, and returned A$41 million to the government.

A central atrium creates a vertical 'village common', which fosters permeability and visual interaction between the larger community and building users. The atrium forms an 'internal street', providing a continuous public realm within and through the building. The sky bridges that cross the atrium at upper levels provide informal breakout spaces for casual interactive exchanges within the workplace to assist in supporting the new culture of the ABS.

Architect's Input[27]

Integrating environmentally sustainable design principles were fundamental to the design approach. The design team were committed to creating an energy efficient building. The building utilises passive and active environmental systems that provide opportunities to maximise natural light and fresh air for workplace and breakout areas.

Central to the design concept has been the need to integrate the ABS organisation in a building that fosters a sense of community within the various divisions that make up the Australian Bureau of Statistics. A key contributor to this is the use of a central atrium space, which unites two wings of office space under one roof. The atrium and scheme design acts on a number of levels to facilitate an integrated ABS building.

Primarily, the new building responds to workplace problems encountered in the existing Cameron offices on the adjacent site. The large separation of divisions experienced in the Cameron offices resulted in both physical and psychological fragmentation of the ABS for many years. This has been overcome in the new building by the creation of an environment that fosters visual and psychological integration. ABS House promotes the productive operation of the organisations as a whole, ensuring the wellbeing of staff and projecting a unified and professional ABS public image. The transparency of the atrium space allows the whole organisation to be perceived from any one point within the space, promoting a sense of belonging and connectivity between divisions and staff. The more dynamic and social spaces, such as group meeting areas, breakout spaces and public liaison spaces, are located around the atrium. More private and secure spaces are located within the office zone or on the external perimeter of the building in order to create a logical hierarchy from public to private space.

The organisation of the external spaces similarly address organisational issues as well as being responsive to environmental and urban design factors. A private courtyard is located to the north of the building to optimise solar penetration. It is accessible from the public level within the building yet secure access is maintained. This space is also cut into the existing site contours to isolate it from acoustic and visual interference of the adjacent bus station.

A public cafe is located at the front of the building to activate the primary address and streetscape. This facility provides a meeting place for the public and staff as well as assisting in humanising the public face of ABS.

The core concept of ABS House is to integrate the ABS organisation physically, visually and psychologically. Located centrally in the building, the atrium forms the heart of this complex and creates a spatial device that effectively addresses the primary challenges of the brief. It is a shared or common space where functions such as public liaising, informal meetings, public presentations and workplace 'breakout' activities take place in an uplifting and exciting environment. The space is flooded with light from a glazed skylight and protected from unwanted climatic elements such as harsh sunlight, the cold, wind and dust. Primary circulation paths and open stairs are combined with informal breakout spaces to encourage casual and unplanned social and intellectual exchanges between staff.

The brief called for a building that represented the ABS mission and core values. ABS is a prominent federal government organisation that has been central to the growth and wellbeing of the Belconnen Town Centre for many years. As a founding member of the Town Centre and as a major source of employment, it was important to create a building that had a strong and visible presence in the heart of Belconnen. As such, the physical stature of ABS House reflects the social importance of this organisation on a local and national level, and the building is timeless and enduring in its expression.

In addition to ABS House being responsive to its social and functional roles, it was also important to deliver a 'Canberra' building that employed secondary design 'moves' appropriate to contemporary stylistics and construction technologies. The large building mass is eroded at its edges and along its length to assist in rescaling this development to its context. This massing strategy has enabled ABS House to be perceived as a series of 'additive' horizontal shifted planes in counterpoint to 'subtractive', or recessed, vertical zones.

The material palette is strictly composed of two systems to emphasise the formal qualities of the building. Large-format precast concrete units cantilever beyond the edges of the building, revealing their thickness and the inherent construction technique of the building. These panels visually connect with the adjacent Cameron offices and provide a sense of solidity compatible with the stature of the organisation. The panels are highly textured and contain titanium dioxide to ensure a brilliant fresh white appearance that will increase over time.

Conversely, the recessed vertical zones contrast in colour and texture to the pre-cast concrete to emphasis the formal narrative. These zones are smooth textured aluminium panel assemblies, dark in colour with similarly coloured glazing units. Expressed panel fixings reveal the nature of the aluminium material and provide at key points a finer texture to the building skin.

A floating 'halo' roof unifies the external articulation and the two accommodation pods. This halo folds and becomes a wall element to address the corner of Benjamin Way and Cameron Avenue. This element grounds the building at its most prominent address and reinforces the building's gateway quality to the commercial hub of Belconnen Town Centre.

Integrated with the massing strategy and façade articulation is an internal storyline that also reflects the services and intentions of the organisation. The central atrium is recentred by a blade wall that recalls the shifted planes of the building skin. This blade structures the atrium space by accommodating reception facilities, breakout areas and vertical circulation. It also extends externally to support way-finding graphics and disabled access ramps.

In contrast to this smooth aluminium blade wall, the skin of the perimeter walls to the atrium are stripped away to reveal the structural concrete frame. This unfinished concrete frame expresses the construction logic of the building and creates a scale suitable for this 'outdoor' space. Perforated timber spandrel panels are inserted between the expressed frames to provide acoustical conditioning of the space and textural warmth.

The atrium floor is folded and articulated as a blade adjacent to the grand stair. The texture of the Panna limestone warms the space and plays a similar visual role to the elevated timber panels. At ground level, inserts of darker stone comfortably articulate the expansive floor. Upon viewing the atrium floor from the elevated sky-bridges, the pattern making is revealed to express an abstract representation of the binary code or punched 'Chad' cards of technologies used by ABS to perform their mission.

The interior has been designed to make the most efficient use of space, with a layout designed to take advantage of emerging technologies and to accommodate future changes. It does this by providing a high degree of commonality between general workplaces in open plan areas close to windows and enclosed rooms located around the core of the building. The workspace has been designed to offer varying environments for ensuring effective working arrangements for staff.

M&E Input[28]

The project contains the Australian Bureau of Statistics data centre, which houses their mainframe computer system, a major component of the building. A majority of services to the data centre are standalone, with the power supply backed up by an uninterruptible power supply (UPS) and a diesel generator, meaning that the data centre can operate independently from the rest of the building in the event of an emergency.

Summary

The project not only created a landmark building but provided the accommodation ahead of schedule. Early 2002 saw a major milestone in the history of the ABS with Central Office staff moving into purpose-built accommodation. ABS House provides a modern, professional and well-equipped office environment in keeping with its standing as a leading national statistical agency. The design is compact and concentrates access through two main entries. In addition to ensuring appropriate security of the building and workplace, these arrangements have provided greater opportunity for informal staff interaction.

As an indication of how this has been received by the ABS, on opening day their choir performed a version of 'Amazing Grace' (aptly titled 'Amazing Place'), to literally sing the praises of their new home. The opening of ABS House on 21 February 2002 by the Treasurer, the Hon Peter Costello MP, was a particular highlight for the ABS.[29] The Treasurer emphasised the importance of the work done by the ABS for Australia. In opening the building he observed that the move to ABS House was achieved within budget and ahead of schedule and would do much to strengthen the Bureau's ability to undertake its work.

ABS House has already won two significant awards – the first was the 2002 ACT Master Builders Association Project of the Year Award (builders – Bovis Lend Lease Pty Ltd) and the second was the 2002 Royal Australian Institute of Architects, ACT Chapter, Canberra Medallion (architects – Woods Bagot Pty Ltd). ABS House is now eligible for the national judging of both awards.

In awarding the prestigious Canberra medallion, the Royal Australian Institute of Architects said:

The Australian Bureau of Statistics headquarters building is a positive expression of the mission and organizational needs of the Bureau. Located within the strong existing architectural environment and planning framework of the Belconnen town centre, the building has been designed to project an image of transparency and public accessibility while providing the high levels of security required by the client. The open, central atrium of the headquarters provides an abundance of natural light and ventilation that fulfils a key element in the environmental performance of the building.

Andrew Metcalf, Professor of Architecture at the University of Canberra, cited four new buildings as ground breaking,[30] but said that enhancements to Canberra's many government buildings might not translate into rental dollars from commercial tenants elsewhere: 'ABS house in Belconnen got the Canberra Medallion. It was principally because of the clever way the social agenda of the ABS was built into the design.'

The building has a giant central atrium traversed by wide bridges (complete with lounges and coffee points) from which staff could see and be seen by the occupants of the various sections in the complex. Metcalf says that this provides a sense of social cohesion.

Brindleyplace, Birmingham

Project: Brindleyplace development
Employer: Argent Group plc
Concept architects: Anthony Peake Associates,
Allies & Morrison, Demetri Porphyrios, Stanton
Williams, Sidell Gibson Partnership, Lyons Sleeman
Hoare, Sir Norman Foster
Contractor's architect: Weedon Partnership
Contractor: Carillion, HBG and Tilbury Douglas
Contract type: JCT 98 WCD (plus partnering
agreements)
Contract period: 1993–2004

Introduction[31]

Up until the 1760s the area now occupied by
Brindleyplace was open countryside on the west
side of Birmingham town, with a sandstone ridge
forming the route into Birmingham; even then it
was known as Broad Street. In 1768 an Act of
Parliament was passed to enable a canal to be built
from Wolverhampton, in the Black Country area, to
Birmingham. The engineer in charge was called
James Brindley, which is where Brindleyplace got
its name. The canal opened on 6 November 1769.

By 1810 the canal which forms the north and
east edges of Brindleyplace was well established.
The canal terminated at the old wharf, now the site
of Central Television, which forms the western
boundary of what is now Brindleyplace. In July
1847 landowners in the area agreed to sell the
substrata beneath their premises for a railway tunnel,
to carry the main Birmingham to Wolverhampton
Railway. The route runs under both the National
Indoor Arena and International Convention Centre.

The Birmingham Brasshouse was established in
1781 and brass was made at the rear of the
Brasshouse until about 1850. The array of furnaces
and chimneys were demolished by 1866 when the
Birmingham Water Company took over the building.
This building was converted to a restaurant in 1988.

Broad Street became known as the Gateway to
Edgbaston, as wealthy businessmen travelled along
it to their residences in healthy Edgbaston and
Worcestershire. The Town Council looked after the
street and in 1876 it became one of the first tree-
lined streets with the planting of 100 trees.

By 1907 all the roads had been constructed and
the railway and engine sheds were in place in the
area now occupied by the National Indoor Arena.
The Sheepcote Street Stables were located at a
point between the canal and the railway. In 1937
work started on a development for Odeon cinemas,
but with the onset of the Second World War, the
project remained a 'steel skeleton' for 14 years. The
City of Birmingham's Housing Department
completed the project by turning the skeleton into
offices. 'Bush House' was opened in March 1958,
which was said to be the largest Housing
Department Headquarters in Europe. The building
closed in 1989.

The land along Broad Street between Five Ways
and the City was partially occupied by the remains
of the declining manufacturing industries, typical of
the inner city, with much low-grade, semi-derelict
industrial properties. It was this area of land that
the City chose for the site of the International
Convention Centre; the Convention Centre was built

Right
Two Brindleyplace

Below
Three Brindleyplace

152

Four Brindleyplace

on Bingley Hall, which itself had been built on Bingley House.

The promotion of Birmingham as an International City was part of the strategy to change the image of the City and to create a business and leisure sector in this part of Birmingham. The area on which the International Convention Centre stands was cleared in 1987 and building work led to the opening of the International Convention Centre in 1991, topped with an official opening by Her Majesty the Queen on 12 June 1991.

The Convention Centre contains 11 large halls, which are used for conventions or conferences, held by business organisations from all over the world. Hall 2 at the International Convention Centre is know as Symphony Hall and is the most up-to-date concert hall in the world.

By 1990 the largest remaining area of derelict land became known as Brindleyplace. The site had been cleared and was ready for redevelopment.

General

In July 1987 developers were invited by the City Council to draw up a blueprint for the vacant 26 acres of land adjacent to the International Convention Centre site. The overall scheme, which would be a 'magnet to attract thousands of people', was scheduled to be completed and operational by spring 1991. The site was leased to a consortium of three companies: Merlin, Shearwater and Laing (MSL). MSL planned to create a 'huge leisure and entertainment area'. Their experience in developing a major city attraction in Baltimore, USA, which

attracts up to 26 million visitors, was said to have been a major factor in their tender being accepted.

The consortium paid £23 million for the development rights and much of the money was used to build the National Indoor Arena (NIA). Their masterplan for a £200 million development included the NIA and a tourist visitor led Festival Market and National Aquarium.

A monorail system linking the complex with other parts of the city centre was discussed, based on a system used in Merlin's Darling Harbour scheme in Sydney, Australia. The National Aquarium, 'A Whale of a Tourist Attraction', was expected to attract 2 million visitors a year and would be similar to those already existing in Baltimore and Boston, USA.

The 'Go for Big Broad Street Plan' was the headline of September 1989 when the development was given planning permission. The agreement, however, did not include the multimillion pound monorail, but included 600 000 square feet of office space. This was to be the 'final piece of the jigsaw' to transform the Broad Street area into a commercial and leisure development. It was said to be one of the most exciting regeneration schemes ever seen in this country.

The exchange of contracts between the developers and the City Council took place at the topping out ceremony over the NIA railway tunnel in October 1989.

In July 1990 Merlin pulled out of the scheme due to fears about the property slump and the project was taken over by Shearwater's parent company,

Rosehaugh. The Festival Marketplace was said to be 'unfundable'. Rosehaugh relooked at the masterplan for the development and together with Birmingham City Council drew up a new scheme, which contained many of the components of the Festival Marketplace proposals, but in a form whereby each phase could be separately financed and built. The planning committee was concerned that the area could be a 'dead zone' after dark, but were in the end convinced that this was not the case.

By March 1991 the press were informed of 'exciting proposals for a high quality, mixed-use redevelopment'. In December 1991 another plan was submitted for approval based on the revised masterplan. The development was now to include Birmingham's fifth public square, constructed and paid for by the developers, but for the benefit of all the residents and visitors to the city who wished to enjoy it. The development included 19 restaurants, shops and bars in Birmingham's first ever purpose designed leisure venue overlooking the canals. The development proposals also contained 120 homes to encourage more people to live in the city, rather than outside it. There were 1 100 000 square feet of offices, which would create 6000 jobs. The leisure element was not absolutely certain but possible options at the time were Science of Sport, an Imax Cinema, bowling alley and rebuilding the existing Crescent Theatre.

The developer's intention was that Brindleyplace would be a thriving place from early morning through to the early hours of the following day. A property research company (hired by Brindleyplace)

found that the site was 'outstanding in a local, regional and national sense' in terms of the amount of new office space available.

Outline planning permission was gained in July 1992. This meant that the scheme would be implemented in phases and led by 'market demand'. The area would employ 6000 people on completion.

The obstacles had not only been financial, but also ecological! In the recession, progress had been slow and ecologists 'discovered' that the site was home to the very rare black redstart, a bird that is a protected species. Work could not begin until the birds migrated.

In November 1992 the development once again almost came to a halt. Rosehaugh's shares were suspended at 7.5p where they once traded at 925p. The company's debts were reported to be at £350 million. After an anxious wait Brindleyplace was declared to be safe. Brindleyplace plc as a subsidiary of the Rosehaugh parent company continued its work.

In June 1993 the Argent Group plc, a privately owned UK property company, purchased Brindleyplace for an undisclosed sum. By September 1993 development was under way. Workmen moved on site on 6 September 1993 and the building project was officially launched on 29 September 1993. The first part of the development to be completed was the Water's Edge – a canal side scheme of shops, restaurants and bars – which was officially opened in November 1994.

Architect's Input

The developer, Argent, wished to revitalise the area of the city. They chose to do this through careful master planning and creative design. The mix of styles and ideas, all contributing to one of Europe's largest inner city mixed-use developments, was achieved by using different architects to design many of the buildings. Mixed-use projects on brownfield sites are being widely promoted as the best way to revitalise our cities, but at Birmingham's Brindleyplace – with its shops, offices, housing, leisure and cultural facilities – theory has been turned into practice.

The developer chose a concept architect to establish the parameters of the project, developing the Employer's Requirements for each building. The contractor's design team then undertook the detailed design. Details of the specific buildings are as follows.

One Brindleyplace

One Brindleyplace is a five-storey office building fronting on to Broad Street. It is situated between the former Church, now a popular nightclub, and the Brasshouse. It provides 68 553 square feet of office space and was completed in October 1995 after a 15-month construction programme.

The façade has been designed to blend in with the adjacent buildings. The air-conditioned building has a glazed central atrium and 134 car parking spaces and was the only brand new office building to be completed in Birmingham in 1995. The occupiers of the building are the well-known mobile communications company Vodafone.

Designed by Anthony Peake Associates, constructed by Carillion with Weedon Partnership as the production architect.

Two Brindleyplace

Construction started in November 1995. The six-storey office is located in the Brindleyplace Central Square, which has become one of Birmingham's most prestigious business addresses. Over 600 Lloyds TSB employees operate from this 75 000 square feet building, completed in June 1997.

Designed by Allies & Morrison, constructed by Carillion with Weedon as the production architect.

Three Brindleyplace

This classically designed seven-storey building was completed in April 1998. The striking red brick building, with front colonnades and a clock tower, is now a recognised city centre landmark. The building houses International Property Consultants GVA Grimley and the international serviced office provider, Regus.

Designed by Demetri Porphyrios and constructed by HBG.

This building was voted Office of the Year 1999 by the British Council of Offices.

Four Brindleyplace

Four Brindleyplace was completed in 1999. This 114 000 square feet speculative office building is home to the award winning Bank Restaurant & Bar on the ground floor. Tenants include Accord Sales

and Lettings, Deloitte & Touche, Michael Page, Mercer Human Resource Consulting and Perceptive Informatics.

Designed by Stanton Williams, constructed by Carillion with Weedon Partnership as the production architect.

This building was voted Office of the Year 2000 by the British Council of Offices.

Five Brindleyplace

Five Brindleyplace was pre-let to BT in 1994 and is used as their regional headquarters. This 120 000 square feet office building is designed to be people friendly and enable individuals to reach their full potential within a comfortable and adjustable working environment. The BT building is now a well-recognised landmark within the Brindleyplace development.

Designed by Sidell Gibson Partnership and constructed by HBG.

Six Brindleyplace

This 92 000 square feet headquarters style office building is situated at the heart of the development and was completed in 2000. Two retail units overlook Oozells Square and are occupied by restaurant units. The Thai Edge opened in 2000.

The building was designed by architects Allies and Morrison, constructed by Carillion with Weedon Partnership as the production architect.

Seven Brindleyplace

This 85 000-sqare feet office building at the

gateway to Brindleyplace was completed in 2002.

Designed by Demetri Porphyrios and constructed by HBG.

Eight Brindleyplace

Eight Brindleyplace provides 92 000 square feet of offices, situated below 35 fully serviced apartments, in addition to ground floor retail/restaurants units. It was completed early in 2002.

Designed by Sidell Gibson Partnership and constructed by HBG.

Nine Brindleyplace

Nine Brindleyplace is conceived as a mixed-use building bridging the space between Broad Street and Oozells Square and announcing Brindleyplace to Broad Street. It is adjacent to the grade 2 listed Presbyterian Church, dating from 1849, which is prominent in long views in and out of the city.

Nine Brindleyplace combines 26 800 square feet (2500 square metres) of restaurant space with 43 000 square feet (4000 square metres) of offices and 60 parking spaces.

Designed by Sidell Gibson Partnership and constructed by HBG.

Ten Brindleyplace

Ten Brindleyplace is a 62 000 square feet office building and is the last building to front Broad Street. A 5000 square feet retail unit is incorporated on the ground floor Broad Street elevation.

Designed by architects Sidell Gibson Partnership.

Symphony Court

This consists of 145 houses and apartments constructed by Crosby Homes and designed by Lyons Sleeman Hoare. Designed to be a 'city living' concept occupying a triangular site across the Brindley Loop Canal, the development fitted into Argent's masterplan. The Dutch gable theme created an instantly recognisable and marketable image. The project was completed in 1996.

Crescent Theatre

A new £14 million theatre for the Crescent Theatre has a superb 340 seat auditorium together with a studio theatre, rehearsal room, meeting rooms and a fully equipped workshop.

National Sea Life Centre

The £15 million National Sea Life Centre opened in June 1996. It features more than 30 displays of native British marine life and some freshwater fish. The building was designed by Sir Norman Foster and continues to be one of the city's leading visitor attractions.

Water's Edge

Work began in September 1993 on the Water's Edge – 60 000 square feet of retail (shopping) and catering facilities located on the canal side, directly opposite the International Convention Centre (ICC). It was completed in September 1994, forming one of the first parts of Brindleyplace. The Water's Edge is busy all day, but especially in the evenings after a concert or when a sporting event is held locally.

Experts say that up to 2 million people could visit the Water's Edge each year, spending up to £13.9 million.

Contractor's Input

The whole of the Brindleyplace development was constructed by three contractors, who worked within a design-build and partnering arrangement, taking the concept architect designed Employer's Requirements and turning them into the delivered environment. Much of the development land was heavily contaminated and needed to be remediated before the phased development could begin.

Summary

This particular case study is quite personal, not because I was involved in any way with any part of the development, but because I was a student in Birmingham at the beginning of the 1980s and remember Broad Street as a run-down area. Comparing those memories with the vibrant lively sector of the city now is very emotive.

Many of the buildings have received individual awards, including the Icon Gallery (not specifically detailed above), which is an imaginative conversion of a grade 2 listed Victorian school building. This was awarded the Institute of Civil Engineers project award in 1998 and the RIBA Award for Architecture in 1999. In 2004 Birmingham received a European Award for Excellence from the Urban Land Institute and Brindleyplace played its part in securing this award.

The development works because it is a balanced

approach to land use; the developer did not try to economise on the public spaces. Roger Madelin said:[32] 'Birmingham's Brindleyplace, an Argent scheme, was profitable because the developer had taken care to create a set of genuinely public spaces rather than a sterile office park.'

At the Better Buildings Summit in London, October 2003, John Prescott,[33] Deputy Prime Minister, said that the Brindleyplace development was a 'fantastic' example of a housing development where 'people were proud to live'. Highlighting the city's modern architectural achievements, he went on to say that town planners need to be more ambitious in their designs. Good architecture should have the 'wow factor' and everyone involved with developments had to look at design as an investment and not a cost. Brindleyplace, along with other developments in the southeast, were 'fantastic' examples of urban design.

In response, Gary Taylor, director of Argent Group, developers of Brindleyplace, said:[33]

We are obviously delighted that Brindleyplace has been highlighted. The quality of design and attention to detail at Brindleyplace has been paramount from day one and its importance in the future success of the scheme was never doubted.

It is not enough to deliver just well-designed buildings. To bring a scheme to life you have to have a sustainable vision and the ability to deliver it – something we were determined to do at Brindleyplace.

Our vision included a combination of high quality buildings and an eclectic mix of bars, restaurants and shops in a safe and clean environment.

The reality is the vision and it is these major ingredients that underpin the success of Brindleyplace.

We are committed to ensuring that the scheme will stand alongside the Bullring as a landmark development that Birmingham can be proud of and will continue to be proud of many years into the future.

The Commission for Architecture and the Built Environment[34] championed the government's move towards better design and the introduction of the Better Public Buildings Initiative. The document contains a picture of Brindleyplace with the following note: 'Birmingham City Council is working closely with private sector developer, Argent, and the council also extended the centre with the development of Brindleyplace, where high standards of design have demonstrable economic benefits.'

The developer had chosen to use design-build to create a striking piece of urban development. This development is outstanding because of the quality of design, the sheer size and value of the whole development and finally the fact that the architectural vision has been maintained for more than ten years.

Café in the Square, Brindleyplace, Birmingham

Project: Stand-alone café
Employer: Argent Development Consortium Ltd
Architect: CZWG Architects
Landscape architect: Townsend Landscape Architects
Engineer: Adams Kara Taylor
M&E engineer: F Bailey/N&G Bailey
Quantity surveyor: Silk & Frasier
Contractor: Kyle Stewart (now HBG construction)
Contract value: £350 000
Contract period: 3 months – completion 1997

Introduction

When the square within the Brindleyplace development was conceived, the client and landscape architect intended to create a building of sculptural form to act as a main feature and focus within the square. When the square was completed in 1995, an eye-shaped area was left uncompleted. This formed the footprint of the focal point, the café.

The Pevsner architectural guides[35] describe the building as 'small, angular, sculptural: a pointed oval of grey-painted steel and glass, its roof slopes extended across each other and up, like the wings of a bird about to fly.'

General

Although the requirement was for a piece of architecture that would form an iconic structure, the developer decided against an open architectural competition and approached the architect CZWG and its figurehead Piers Gough directly. The architect responded with a purple glazed brick structure, which was rejected by the developer,

arguing that they would prefer a more transparent, lighter structure to be the centrepiece of the square. The second submission was more successful with both the design team and developer and developed into the built form.

The brief was to provide a self-sufficient café that could seat 40 people inside and have provision for over 100 people outside. All had to be contained in an area of 50 square metres.

The developer, Argent, had already completed two of the Brindleyplace office buildings using a partnering basis. For the café, Kyle Stewart was appointed as the design-build contractor. The design development and detailed design were completed concurrently with the costing exercise for the scheme.

Architect's Input

The intent was that the café would act as a focal point for the whole of the Brindleyplace development. The square is surrounded by buildings, which are generally six storeys tall, with some rising as high as 48 metres. The available footprint is only 14 metres by 7.6 metres at its widest point.

To create the airy feel to the café, the walls and roof comprise double-glazed units. The front walls are clear glass whilst the roof has a white dotted pattern fritted on to the outer pane for glare and solar protection. The canopies are made from single glazed 12 millimetre toughened glass, with a similar white frit. Nonoperational and more private areas, WCs etc are hidden from view by their

External view of café showing
elegant roof 'wings'

View of café through square

location behind the rear partition to the bar area. They are protected from external view by fritting with a solid white enamel screen print to their perimeter wall. To maximise the building's transparency, secure storage is provided in a basement that is accessed from an external trapdoor. This is located next to the pumping plant for Brindleyplace's external fountain.

The building control approval procedure was helped by the developer's ongoing relationship with the Local Authority. Meeting the regulations for certain areas provided a significant challenge during design development, eg the provision of WCs, which used valuable floor space within the small footprint of the building.

The quality of detailing was very important to the realisation of the design concept. This was helped by early contact with the subcontractors, who provided designs for steel and glazing. Ironmongery was specially designed for the project and was fabricated from stainless steel.

Engineer's Input

The structure of the café consists of a number of 114.3 millimetre diameter tubular steel portal frames. The structure is braced by two horizontal tapering ovoid frames. The vertical structural columns are continuous with the roof members. They cross over at the ridge of the roof pitch to form canopies resembling butterfly wings. These give the building added height, while their profile reinforces the building's footprint.

The building is fully glazed. The design team had to ensure that movement of the steel frame was compatible with the glazing design.

M&E Engineer's Input

The building is effectively a 'greenhouse'. Comfort cooling/heating is provided to deal with summer/winter conditions. Heated air for winter warming is pumped in from external vents, which appear as stone 'toadstools' in the grassed areas of the square. This is supplemented by underfloor heating. Opening the 12 millimetre toughened single-glazed fold-back glass doors, which are hinged to open 180° against the adjacent wall, provides summer cooling. This is supplemented by blowing external air overhead.

A separate supply and extract system to the kitchen uses the sculptured stone vents in the adjacent grassed area, with ducting routed out through a louvred funnel.

Contractor's Input

The early involvement of the design-build contractor enabled the client and design team to involve specialist contractors early in the programme. The three-month construction was achieved by prefabrication and preforming the steel structure and the glazing panels, and by preordering and manufacturing the servery counter and all the M&E equipment prior to construction commencement.

Summary

The building performs as intended – a focal point within the Brindleyplace development, a visual magnet even in dull weather. Part of the café's asset is its setting; the buildings bordering the central open space of Brindleyplace provide a defined edge and the enclosed square has good-quality materials.

The building is clearly well designed, achieving the desired visual focus. The sculptural quality heightens the impact, which is reinforced by the standard of detailing together with the consistent size of structural members. However, the initial desire to serve meals has proved too optimistic, being reduced to drinks, pastries and sandwiches. A review[36] concluded that 'At £700 per square metre, the Café in the Square was a very expensive building to deliver. However, its positive complement to the surrounding buildings and its popularity in use has satisfied the client, who perceives it as much a work of art as a functional building.'

Because of the design lead-in required for the various components, the three-month construction period could not have been achieved without the involvement of the contractor. Design-build was found to be a suitable route to control cost and the construction programme. It should be noted that a very high quality of design has also been achieved.

Capitol Area East End, Block 225, Sacramento, California, USA

Project: 460 000 square feet office accommodation
Employer: State of California (City of West Sacramento)
Architect: Johnson Fain Partners (conceptual design/master planning)/Fentress Bradburn Architects
'Green' consultant: SMWM
Engineer: Paul-Koehler Consulting Structural Engineers
M&E engineer: Critchfield Mechanical
Contractor: Hensel Phelps Construction
Project consultant: 3D/International
Contract value: $56.7 million
Contract type: Lump Sum Design-Build
Contract period: 16 months – completion July 2002

Introduction

The East End complex is a group of five office buildings constructed for the State of California to house the Department of Health Service and the Department of Education. The project includes 1.5 million square feet of office space and 750 000 square feet of parking structure space. The State of California is using this project to showcase a variety of sustainable features and evaluate the results.

This study considers only one block, block 225. This block used the raised floor for both cable management and for ventilation.

Before the project commenced, the State had to amend the existing legislation, initially to raise capital to fund the project and then to allow a design-build procurement route to be used on a government project. The procurement method is known as 'bridging', in which design criteria and related documents define the requirements before proposals are solicited from teams of contractors and architects, called design-builders.

Prior to design completion, the state sponsored a competition in which the design-build teams submitted proposals on how to make the building design more energy efficient and sustainable. The design-build team were selected on the basis of 'best value (technical and price)'. This was judged from the contractor's response to the Employer's Requirements, in this case a conceptual design and performance criteria.

The winning proposal included approximately 125 green building enhancements, intended to reduce energy consumption, improve indoor environmental and air quality in the final occupied building, utilise resource efficient materials and systems, and ultimately improve the building performance within the allocated construction budget. Although it had been mentioned that the 'greening' of the building was to be done within the original construction cost, it was accepted that there would be a 'green' premium. Estimates of the green premium for this project are approximately $1.6 million or 2.9 % of the $56.7 million construction cost. An interesting note is that 30 % of the premium was attributed to additional design and documentation fees.

General[37]

There is quite a long history to this project, starting

Right and below right
External views of corners of
the building

Below left
Motifs in external wall

Reception desk and art in the entrance lobby

in the 1960s when the State of California purchased 42 blocks for a downtown state office campus. In 1977, the Capitol Area Development Plan was amended to achieve the planning objectives of including a mix of office, housing and retail uses on quarter-block modules. In 1993 assessment of the Capitol Area Plan found that the intended quarter-block development modules were impractical and after a series of public workshops, new land use synthesis was completed to improve development opportunities for consolidated state office space and housing. In 1995 the Urban Land Institute Panel identified the Capitol Area as high risk for blight and endorsed a mixed use of housing, office and retail, recommending development of state offices at the east end to improve the neighbourhood and protect the Capitol Building and Park.

Senate Bill 1270 authorised the construction of the facilities for use by the departments of Education and Health Services. The office project is located on existing state-owned land within the Capitol Area. The bill authorised financing of the facilities by the sale of Public Works Board revenue bonds not to exceed $392 million. Senate Bill 776 authorised the Director of the Department of General Services to use the design-build route for the procurement of the project. In 1998 master architect Johnson Fain was selected to design the East End Office complex project. The Governor's Sustainable Building Task Force, a unique partnership of more than 40 government agencies, helped ensure that this project would be the 'greenest' in the state.

It is the goal of the Department of General Services that state-owned buildings be models of energy efficiency and utilise cost-effective sustainable building design measures and technologies. This meant that the building was to achieve a gold standard in the Leadership in Energy and Environmental Design (LEED) programme and exceed the 1998 mandatory energy efficiency standards by 30 %.

From the beginning, the East End team looked beyond the initial cost of construction and recognised the value of a healthy, energy-efficient environment that would help increase-productivity and reduce utility bills. This meant choosing durable materials that do not use harsh chemicals during manufacturing, installation or maintenance. Specifically, the East End team developed a new specification that required each building material to be examined for need, source, durability, maintenance and eventual re-use. This performance-based specification required manufacturers to pay for the testing – about $3000 per test – prior to acceptance and use on the project, and at no cost to the project itself.

Before construction could begin on site, project managers had to remove a 1930s eight-storey apartment building. Rather than demolishing the structure, the building was moved to a new location.

Architect's Input

Johnson Fain Partners initiated the design of the project with a historical and urban analysis. The

Diagramatic 'green' poster for
the building

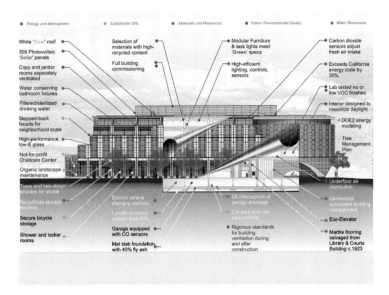

Capitol Area East End Complex extends the visual boundaries east of Capitol Park and provides an eastern gateway and a neighbourhood amenity, which is highly accessible and responsive to the surrounding context. The project was always intended to be 'green', so a specialist consultant was engaged to advise the project, the consultant was SMWM.

The contract required that the design-build consortium submit an energy model to support their design. This model (DOE-2) required the input from all members of the design team, and influenced the detailed development. The adoption of underfloor heating meant the inclusion of a 400 millimetre floor void.

The building envelope includes a combination of windows and curtain walling. These are highly efficient and reduce solar heat gain and the cooling load. The windows contain spectrally selective, low emissitivity (Low e) glass. This glass allows most of the visible light to pass but blocks the infrared frequencies. Open workstations are placed around the perimeter to make maximum use of the natural light and allow maximum light penetration into the building. This light penetration is further enhanced by the use of high ceilings and light coloured decoration to increase daylight reflectivity. Two storey arcades provide shading at the lower level to reduce heat loads.

The materials specified had to meet the aggressive State requirements for recycled content. This included recycled content in access flooring, acoustic ceiling tiles and fly ash as an aggregate in

the concrete. The overall East End project will use 300 000 square feet of rubberised asphalt, which equates to recycling approximately 1100 car tyres, while 30 000 square feet of grey marble recovered from the historic Library and Courts Building is to be used in the ground floor lobbies. Storage and Collection of Recyclable Materials Used by Building Occupants was to form part of a waste management strategy, which included providing space plans that include recycling rooms at each floor with compaction facilities in each loading dock area.

Engineer's Input

The six-storey steel framed building sits over below-ground level parking and is an eccentric braced frame lateral system. The design of the foundation system was such that the use of noise generating pumps to relieve hydrostatic ground water pressure was kept to a minimum.

M&E Engineer's Input[38]

The team also chose to utilise an underfloor air distribution (UFAD) system as opposed to a conventional overhead HVAC system. UFAD introduces conditioned air from an underfloor plenum at a higher temperature and lower velocity than traditional systems. As the cool air warms, it rises out of the space through natural convection. The warm air is then exhausted from return vents at the ceiling.

From an energy standpoint, UFAD delivers conditioned air at 63°F versus 54°F from a conventional overhead system. This higher

Ground floor lift lobby

temperature means significant savings in energy bills as well as reduced equipment costs because of the lower velocity delivery of air. As required in the contract documents, the East End Complex was to be 30 % more energy efficient than California's Energy Code. After third-party verification (energy modelling was about 0.09 % of the project budget), it was determined that the entire complex met the requirement, thus saving the state over $500 000 per year in energy bills.

To reduce energy costs further, the East End Complex utilised occupancy sensors in conjunction with an energy-efficient direct–indirect lighting system. This reduced lighting power density to 0.9 watts per square foot, well below the California Energy Code. Daylighting sensors were also used to dim the lights when natural light increases, typically when energy use is at its peak. The combination of dimming and occupancy sensing provides a high degree of energy savings, as well as enhanced user control over the lighting at 0.01 % of the construction budget.

Contractor's Input

A majority of the contractor's input on this project was limited to the disposition, recycling or limitation of construction and demolition waste to meet State and government targets. The goal for recovery from demolition materials, and the recovery from new construction waste is 75 %

Recycling is very important to the American waste management strategy, and includes targets for recycled content of materials. For this project, the recycled content goals were as follows:

Structural steel	60 %
Reinforced concrete	25 %
Precast concrete	25 %
Glass	10 %
Asphalt concrete pavement	50 %
Drywall	30 %
Acoustic tile	85 %
Toilet partitions	10 %
Telecommunications cabling	20 %
Irrigation materials	20 %
Metal signs	40 %
Work station components	40 %

Summary

The building is a success, providing abundant natural light and allowing employees to control their own environment by adjusting a unique underfloor air distribution system. The building has achieved the required gold LEED rating. The M&E subcontractors considered the construction of the building a great success, mainly because none of their work involved an overhead installation.

The project exceeded the energy standards in the Title 24 Energy Code by over 30 %. Compared to the previous buildings, this project saves the taxpayers $400 000 annually in energy savings alone.

The building has a very high indoor air quality, mainly due to the emphasis on reducing volatile organic compounds and dust. The structure contains low or formaldehyde-free building and plumbing insulation; formaldehyde-free ceiling tiles were also used.

The use of design-build clearly helped this project. The main contractor was able to persuade the suppliers to provide the required material-testing regime at no cost to the project. At the time of construction, the testing was specific to this project. The same testing regime and information is now required on all state projects in California.

Right
Interior view of conference room

Below
External landscaping

Dean Close School, Cheltenham

Project: Boarding house, Cheltenham
Employer: Dean Close School
Architect: Associated Architects
Engineer: Shire Associates
M&E engineer: Couch Perry Wilkes
Contractor: Moss Construction
Contract value: £1.7 million
Contract type: JCT 98 WCD
Contract period: 49 weeks – completion December 2001

Introduction

Dean Close School is a private school located in the centre of Cheltenham. The school grounds lie on the A40 arterial feed into Cheltenham, just outside the major conservation area of Montpellier. Several of the schools buildings are large grade 2* regency buildings. The school has acted as an architectural patron, providing Cheltenham with some interesting architecture, particularly the theatre complex.

Jonathan Lancashire,[39] Bursar of Dean Close School, stated:

> The School had completed a number of major building projects in the 1980s and 1990s using Associated Architects in Birmingham and following the traditional architect-led procurement route.
>
> The experience had been that buildings of a high quality were delivered but at some cost in terms of exceeded budgets and difficulties in negotiations with the architects throughout the projects.

Two projects were completed in 1999 using contractor's design and build. In both cases, although the budget costs were achieved there were significant quality failures and the buildings were felt to be of a lower standard than the rest of the recent projects.

The school employs Faithful and Gould as Employer's Agent and QS on all its projects. F&G recommended the procurement route of design and build with novated consultants, with the specific advice that a detailed specification should be developed first to reduce scope for variability of quality.

This proposal was unanimously supported by the Governors and, indeed, everyone but the architects.

John Christophers,[40] Associated Architects, stated:

> The form of contract was agreed between the QS, client and architect. We expressed some reservations over design control, and it was therefore agreed to delay tender until RIBA stage E was complete in order for key elements of the design to be more closely defined.

Kevin Merris,[41] Faithful & Gould, Employer's Agent, stated:

> The previous project at the school had been done on a D&B basis. Given that that had been completed on time and in budget it seemed appropriate to extend the philosophy to this

External view of the building

Right
View along intermediate
corridor

Far right
View down top corridor,
showing glazed rooflight and
floor

project. As lead consultants with the bulk of our work being done on a D&B basis we were also comfortable with the process and considered it the best way of keeping the project within budget. Carrying the works out with Novated consultants with the bulk of the design being done up front also ensured that quality would be retained. Employing a reputable contractor also helped considerably.

The Employer's Requirement consisted of a fully designed building, the conditions of contract were the JCT 98 WCD and the contractor was responsible for the detailed design. Jonathan Lancashire stated:[39] 'Despite the detailed specifications at tender stage a number of omissions were later discovered and these were remedied via Employer's Change Orders, at cost!'

General

The accommodation is to provide a boarding house for the use of pupils during term time and to generate income during holidays. In addition to the student rooms, family accommodation was provided for the 'house parent' and also facilities for the 'house mistress'. The accommodation is spread over four storeys, the ground floor being a reinforced concrete frame and upper floors constructed from load-bearing masonry. The roof structure is timber.

Architect's Input

The architect had completed several previous projects for the school. Using this developing relationship with the Local Authority gave all parties the confidence to promote this rather striking addition to Cheltenham's Regency stock.

John Christophers had very strong views on the aesthetics of the building, including the requirement for the exterior to appear to flow into the building and the internal central corridors to be lit by natural top light. The intermediate floors were to receive top light through glazed floors.

The external appearance was to be strongly modular, with elements being enhanced by a neutral render. The school had suffered an expensive window failure on a previous project. As a consequence, the architect carefully specified exacting standards or specific products for most of the materials.

John Christophers[40] responded to the question 'did the finished project match your expectations?' as follows:

Very close. The internal glass block flooring and terracotta external cladding panels were important design features that were fully specified and designed in principle before tender. They remained intact. One or two changes of material were made to meet the project budget, but these were not related to the design-build route. The M&E coordination and roofscape did change.

Kevin Merris stated:[41]

On the subject of Quality: I believe that quality

Staircase detail

achieved would have been no different had we gone down say a traditional route. Again choice of contractor and subcontractors is important and possibly the contractors input in design made some aspects more buildable.

Structural Engineer's Input

Although the building is relatively simple in structural terms, with a reinforced concrete ground floor and first floor slab with load bearing masonry above, the engineer had to ensure that none of the external finishes were affected by movement. The exterior of the building is modular; this needed to be considered when positioning the movement joints, ensuring that the resulting detail would look exactly the same as other details.

The architect had equally strong views on the simplicity of the interior. The structure was to be clean and simple, beams were not to be seen, only flat slabs. This was made more complex by the ground floor being mainly open spaces, with very few limited places for the service drops from above, particularly the multitude of soil and vent pipes. These were set in trenches in the Reinforced concrete structure, being collected before dropping in discrete locations.

M&E Engineer's Input

Although the electrical, heating and ventilating systems cannot be described as complex, they were not to interfere with the clean aesthetics of the building. The glazed floors restricted circulation, meaning that above the first floor level, the two halves of the building had to be separately serviced.

With very limited space in the roof, equipment needed to be selected for its size and service routing carefully coordinated.

Contractor's Input

The contractor had won the project through a competitive tender, and although there was a very detailed specification and exacting set of scheme design drawings, the contractor was to take responsibility for the design development and detailed design required to complete the project. Jonathan Lancashire stated:[39] 'The contractor provided a number of significant "buildability" savings at tender stage, which helped greatly in achieving a tender figure, which met the School's objectives.'

There were several buildability issues that the contractor was required to solve. The glazed floors were to be imported from Germany. The procurement, manufacture and delivery time meant that the floor panels would not be on site before the blockwork was nearly up to eaves level. The architect did not want to see any structure, just simple joints between materials; the glazed floors had been detailed as being built into the blockwork. This was not a suitable solution for two reasons: firstly, the long delivery time would not allow this construction method without long delays and, secondly, the manufacturer would not warrant the product if used in this manner. The contractor changed the method of support and increased the gap at the side of the panels, this would still provide the architect with the required aesthetic and allow the contractor to crane the floors through the building. Jonathan Lancashire commented:[39] 'A large number of design development issues also arose although the contractor resolved most of these with no noticeable lack of quality. The contractor successfully managed one or two serious supply difficulties such as the delay in delivery of the glass block floors.'

The architect wanted to create the appearance of the outside flowing into the building; the external paving was used as flooring on the internal ground floor. This seamless effect was to be created using frameless glazing. The contractor could not be persuaded that water would not be blown under the door, eventually declining to warrant this detail. The client followed the contractor's advice and framed glazing was introduced.

The contractor was very concerned about tolerance issues on the external wall. The window openings would be formed in blockwork, with a tolerance of ± 20 millimetres horizontally and vertically on a good day. The terracotta cladding had a tolerance of virtually zero. This meant that there was no guarantee that the window opening in the terracotta would line up with the window opening in the blockwork. The architect solved the problem by oversizing the blockwork window openings, reducing them later on with a dry lining detail. John Christophers stated:[40] 'The contractor brought a useful and active constructional project management skill to the team, and contributed to buildability issues.'

Summary
This is a very complex building; without the contractor's input on buildability and material procurement, the project would not have been as successful. Making the contractor responsible for the design was the correct solution and 'design and build' was the correct procurement method.

Without the design being completed pre-tender, it is doubtful that the aesthetics could have been achieved. If the Employer's Requirements had consisted of a performance specification, a building of this quality would almost certainly not have been delivered.

The contractor contributed to buildability and helped resolve several problems, but even so was let down by a few construction issues. The ground floor paving had to be totally relaid; it had originally been put down with too dry a screed base and as a result the mortar in the joints turned to dust and the stones eventually began to rock. After consultation with the manufacturer the floor was relaid with the same specification but this time with greater attention to moisture content.

The bathrooms had been designed with a sloping floor to take the shower water to a drain, but the design of the slope was probably inadequate to deal with building tolerance, and as constructed simply did not work. The shower was intended to have a simple fabric curtain, which water would run down, and the falls in the floors would take the water to the outlet. The powerful shower would make the curtain bow out, with water dropping in the wrong place. Several bedrooms became

waterlogged. The contractor had to retrofit wall-mounted glass screens.

The school and their project team had chosen to use a design and build form of procurement to try to control cost, but the project was not delivered for the tender sum because there were in excess of 20 contract variations. However, the project was delivered within the school's budget for the project.

The building not being delivered for the tender sum, and indeed with over 20 variations, is rather disappointing. If the variations were as a result of the Employer's Requirements changing, then that cannot really be blamed on the design team. If, however, these changes were the result of a technical inadequacy in the original design, then this is the fault of the design team. Technical problems could be resolved by the introduction of the contractor much earlier in the procurement process, but then this raises the competition issues. It is the employer's choice.

The finished building is very close to the original design intent contained within the Employer's Requirements. The main difference is that the original design required frameless glazing for all the doors on the ground floor. The contractor questioned the ability of such a system to prevent air leakage and keep out water; the architect reluctantly accepted the change.

Jonathan Lancashire commented:[39]

The building has not been universally welcomed, either by the users or commentators, although the points of difference are relatively minor, and

are to do with its visual impact.

The occupants find most aspects of the accommodation very satisfactory although there are some problems with privacy, which might have been foreseen given the use to which it was intended that it should be put.

From a practical point of view, I would describe the building as a success.

In general, the Governors' view is that this procurement route is likely to be appropriate for most major projects where quality of finish is important. Moss Construction was on the tender list of the next project to be let and it is likely that this will continue in the future.

Kevin Merris stated:[41] 'Did it work? The school's criteria were for a good end product, on time and within budget. All three criteria were met. I can think of a number of issues where had the designers and contractors not been one team, claims and delays could have occurred.'

Government Communications Headquarters (GCHQ), Cheltenham

Project: A new headquarters facility for GCHQ
Employer: Integrated Accommodation Services (BT, Group 4, Carillion)
Architect: Gensler
Engineer: TPS Consult
M&E engineer: Crown House Engineering
Contractor: Carillion
Contract value: £360 million
Contract type: PFI
Contract period: 42 months – completion June 2003

Introduction

GCHQ previously occupied 50 inefficient buildings spread over two sites several miles apart in Cheltenham. Their objective was to use the PFI process to develop a flexible, modern building into which they could decant their 4500 staff. This huge new accommodation building will enable a flexible response to rapidly changing security situations and the threat of global terrorism.

The project comprises the design, construction and management of the new Government Communications Headquarters (GCHQ) building, including the provision of a comprehensive range of support services over a 30-year period. The PFI consortium was called Integrated Accommodation Services and comprised Carillion Building, British Telecom and Global Solutions Limited (Group 4). Financial close on the project was achieved in 2000.

General

The aim of the project was to integrate the GCHQ operation on to one site from their current two sites. The sites were located on opposing sides of Cheltenham. Farmland was acquired adjacent to the current Benhall site.

The plan was to construct the new accommodation without demolishing the existing building. GCHQ could then move their operation into the new building, allowing the demolition of existing accommodation. The existing land was then to be used for car parking, with any remaining land being sold off for housing.

The £350 million four-storey building encompasses 100 000 square metres of floor space, equivalent to 17 football fields. The huge computer hall is the size of the Royal Albert Hall and is housed beneath the central courtyard. The main facility comprises doughnut-shaped offices surrounded by four separate support buildings, which comprise a visitor reception centre with training and conference facilities, a logistics centre and power supplies.

Security is a major consideration. This led to the innovative doughnut shape, which minimises the area of the external envelope for the plan area, giving the optimum level of security.

The doughnut shape provides an inner court, which could fit the Royal Albert Hall. The original design intent was that this would provide a landscaped sanctuary for staff. The trees were later removed from the design because of fears over lightning strikes. The court sits over the computer room.

As part of the planning process, the agreement

Bellow left
Entrance to internal court

Below right
Stainless-steel staircase,
sculptured wall and glass lift
within lower level entrance
foyer

Main entrance showing stone, glass and cladding material

with Cheltenham Borough Council required the upgrading of the main A40 road adjacent to the site. This involved modifying two roundabouts as well as upgrading the carriageway and building a new bus priority lane. On the site itself, new roads were built which would serve the new housing areas identified in the Cheltenham local plan.

Architect's Input

The building is circular on plan, with an open central court. The circular accommodation is divided by a circular atrium. The circle itself is divided into three radial sections, the area between these three radial divisions acting as hubs for entering the building. Each radial section has two vertical cores containing lifts and stairs. The central atrium is bridged at each level, three bridges per radial section.

The existing land slopes. The design has taken advantage of this with the entrance at one side being a storey height above the entrance at the opposite side.

Chris Johnson MD of Gensler[42] and principle design architect commented:

On GCHQ, the output spec provided by the client allowed the design teams (with the contracting partner) to develop more innovative solutions other than the traditional workplace and architectural designs. This allowed the project to mould itself so it became more representative of the client's ambition both physically and emotionally. The result is a series of buildings, which the organisation sees as its natural home as opposed to a building it simply occupies. The behavioural changes, which have been witnessed by GCHQ and engineered by design solutions, are now reaping the rewards for the organisation.

Gensler were involved with the subcontract procurement process. Knowing that the detailed design/construction information would be developed by the subcontractor allowed them to produce their design as a detailed concept. They were then involved in the development process.

The internal aesthetics of the building are emphasised by the natural finishes, the circular *in situ* concrete columns are simply sealed and the concrete is exposed. The atrium floor (which forms the main horizontal circulation route, called the street) is finished with granite. The balustrading is a combination of stainless steel, glass and oak. The doors and frames are oak.

The exterior of the building is simple. Where a solid material was to be used, this was a local Cotswold stone (2500 square metres), albeit prefabricated offsite on to a precast concrete backing. The glazing consisted of double-glazed units separated from a single-glazed toughened glass outer protective layer by the maintenance walkway. The intent of the design is to provide some protection from a bomb blast.

Structural Engineer's Input

The frame had to be designed so that it could be

built in repetitive sequence. TPS selected an *in situ* concrete column and main beams, with precast 'double T' beams making up the floor. The building is so big that from the casting of the columns on the first gridline it would be several months before the circle was completed.

Darius Aibara, TPS Consult principle engineer, stated:[43]

One of the successes was the integration of the structural design with the requirements of the frame contractor. Early agreement of the construction methodology and the means of exchanging design information contributed to the relatively smooth construction of a complex facility. Maximum utilisation of precast concrete elements facilitated rapid construction.

The roof top plant rooms with their curved cladding have a steel structure. Each floor plate required two groups of secure data rooms. To provide the security these rooms were constructed from *in situ* concrete. The engineer used this feature opportunity to provide rigidity to the building. This removed the requirement for braced bays leaving the building to have uninterrupted galls walls around 360° on both the inside and outside.

M&E Engineer's Input

Crown House Engineering was the mechanical and electrical subcontractor. Their design department acted as the consultant engineer.

On-time completion was critical to the project's success, so the construction period was significantly shortened by designing the building frame around modular M&E components such as risers, heat exchangers and pump circuits. These components were fabricated off-site while the frame was being constructed, and then brought to site and craned into place through predesigned openings. This brought massive programme savings and greater certainty of completion.

GCHQ had very stringent rules on the locality of services, both horizontally and vertically, to their data network. To allow the necessary crossovers, an access floor was provided to the entire building; the void beneath this access floor is 900 millimetres deep.

The void below the access floor is used to supply and extract air. The original design concept had been to install exposed chilled beams between the exposed precast 'double T' beams, but this concept was later changed and a ceiling installed.

The building needs to be extremely flexible to enable the client to change team structures on a rapid basis when necessary. The chosen solution was to house all the power and IT beneath flexible floors and by having a generic furniture layout this allowed new team areas to be set up overnight with the minimum of effort. The introduction of a common 'desktop' computer system and 'hunt me' phone system means that staff can operate from any desk in the building.

The layout of the building meant that there were three separate roof level plant rooms. Services were distributed vertically within each of the three radial segments.

Security and secure services meant that there had to be a certain amount of duplication. Power had to be supplied to the building from two different directions, ensuring that a single incident could not isolate the building. Power is critical to the GCHQ operation. For this reason two of the four external ancillary buildings are diesel-powered generators.

Many substantial features were designed to save energy, including passive solar and heat recovery systems. BT was responsible for all the data cabling. The length of cabling used is a record in itself, with 5500 miles of cable and 1850 miles of fibre optics.

Contractor's Input

The contractor had a major input in bringing all of the designing subcontractors together and managing their output. At peak Carillion had 15 design managers on site, all managing different packages and associated with different cost plan teams. Darius Aibara stated:[43]

> One of the keys to a successful contractor–consultant relationship is the presence of a co-ordinated design programme and the early involvement of key trade contractors. This contributes greatly to efficient design and construction and hence to delivery on programme and budget.

The roof had to be left off until the modular prefabricated plant had been craned in to place. To ease mechanical service construction, all firewalls were also left down, to be completed after the mechanical installation.

The programming of design, procurement and construction activities was essential. Each radial sector was considered as an individual project with its own construction project manager. Internal competition enabled progress to get ahead of the construction programme. Safety and communication were paramount; the contractor insisted that there would be a briefing every morning, so every team was aware of what would be happening.

The contractor ran a safety reward system. Good safe behaviour meant individuals being entered into the monthly draw to win a car; poor safety behaviour left the individual being awarded 'points', the culmination of too many points meaning exclusion from the site. This proactive safety attitude resulted in the project being awarded the prestigious British Safety Council Sword of Honour 2002 for exemplary health and safety performance.

The PFI contract required the provision of a complete building, which included furniture and all supporting facilities. Supporting facilities included restaurants, shops, coffee and sandwich bars etc. The furniture installation was a major project in its own right, made even more complex by the need to allow BT time and space to install the data infrastructure and then connect up all of the workplace computers once the furniture was installed.

Summary

The building is breathtaking, both in terms of scale

Approach to visitor centre

and quality of design and finish. PFI has helped the building. Many materials were upgraded to achieve longevity and reduce maintenance costs over the 30-year concession period.

Since completion this project has achieved several awards. The building won the best-designed PFI project and best PFI project of the year, 2002. Commenting on the project,[44] the judges said:

> Inside GCHQ we met a tremendously enthusiastic construction team who are ecstatic about what they have created. The result is a building with real presence of calm quality.
>
> The reason GCHQ is special is the superb quality – far superior to the norm of PFI projects. It is very, very high quality design and build.

The building was one of 17 included in the Prime Minister's Better Public Building Awards shortlist and, although it narrowly missed out on the top prize at a ceremony in London on 28 October 2004, the project was awarded a special judges award, presented by the British Construction Industry in recognition of the intelligence centre's inspirational architecture. According to the judges,[45] the new headquarters – affectionately known as the Doughnut – was 'a superbly designed and finished building with real presence of calm quality perfectly fitting GCHQ's post Cold War aspiration to be flexible and able to respond to change rapidly, 24 hours a day'. Additionally, the internal street within the Doughnut was described as: 'refreshingly different … encouraging accidental interaction between staff'.

Stephen Gale, GCHQ's director for business support, who accepted the award in London, commented:[45] 'We're chuffed to bits. The judges' comments are very gratifying. The new building really does make a difference to our ability to tackle our national security mission effectively. This award really is the icing on the doughnut.'

The new GCHQ building has won the corporate category for the South of England and South Wales region at the British Council for Offices (BCO) Awards 2004. Judges praised the building, commenting on the part it has played in 'a massive change in culture' at GCHQ and describing it as 'an investment that could last many decades and is expected to improve productivity in more than 20 business areas'. Accepting the award on behalf of GCHQ at a special ceremony in London on 5 October 2004, Alan Green, the new accommodation programme director, said:[46] 'The building is already proving to be a great asset, with its open plan design and unified IT systems enabling new teams to be formed quickly and effectively to deal with a variety of new threats to the UK.'

Her Majesty the Queen, accompanied by the Duke of Edinburgh, officially opened the building on Thursday 25 March 2004. After a short tour of the building, during which the royal visitors met a wide range of staff and others responsible for the design and construction, Her Majesty unveiled a plaque commemorating the event. A spokeswoman for Buckingham Palace said:[47]

View of building across car park

Her Majesty and the Duke of Edinburgh were very impressed by this state-of-the-art intelligence centre. They were particularly interested to see how the building contributes to GCHQ's effectiveness in delivering intelligence and information assurance for the nation.

A GCHQ spokesman added:[47]

This has been a memorable day not only for GCHQ, but also the IAS consortium, which is responsible for the building, and Chris Johnson, the architect. The royal couple previously visited GCHQ's Oakley site in 1995 so they were able to appreciate fully the improvements in our working environment and the business and cultural benefits that we are deriving from the move to a purpose-built single site headquarters.

Foreign Secretary, Jack Straw, stated:[48]

This is my second visit to GCHQ's new headquarters, but the last time I was here – 2 years ago – it was a very large building site. I have been extremely impressed today with what I have seen. Even at this early stage it is obvious that this state-of-the-art building will enhance GCHQ's ability to provide vital intelligence, which will help counter global terrorism and other serious threats to the UK and its allies.

The contribution made by GCHQ to safeguarding national security and the UK's interests across the whole range of foreign policy, defence and economic priorities cannot be overemphasised.

The project was completed 10 weeks early, meeting all of the client's criteria for high levels of security, flexibility and state-of-the-art resilient IT systems. It has achieved a 'very good' rating on the BREEAM sustainability index.

Was the project a success? One of the main driving criteria behind the project was to amalgamate the GCHQ function on to one site. The logistical exercise of building a new building, decanting the staff from the existing buildings, demolishing the existing buildings and completing the car parks all worked reasonably well. However, the original PFI staffing model was based on GCHQ reducing its staff numbers to 3500.

Politics has interfered; 11 September 2001, unrest in the Middle East and the emergence of Al Qaeda as global urban terrorist forces have all served to increase staff numbers. This has resulted in the temporary retention of two buildings on the Oakley site while GCHQ considers how best to accommodate the unforeseen surplus.

It could be argued that the project has not satisfied its prime objective, but this cannot be a criticism of the IAS consortium or PFI in general. The provided building is clearly a huge success.

Below left
Detail of circular glazing

Below right
Bridge across atrium at upper
level

Great Western Hospital, Swindon

Project: A 551 bed acute hospital
Employer: Swindon and Marlborough NHS Trust
Architect: Whicheloe Macfarlane (later to amalgamate with BDP) in collaboration with USA healthcare designer HDR
Engineer: TPS Consult
M&E engineer: Crown House Engineering
Contractor: Carillion Building
Contract value: £135 million
Contract type: PFI
Contract period: 46 months – completion March 2004

Introduction

The Swindon and Marlborough NHS Trust was operating on three sites, some miles apart. Faced with the need to expand capacity to meet rising demand, it made sense to rationalise health facilities on to one large greenfield site.

The new 551 bed acute general hospital will have around 55 900 square metres of floor space in an 'L' shape, with a dramatic curved quadrant forming the main entrance. A wide range of services will be offered including Accident and Emergency, Radiology, Orthopaedics, Rehabilitation Therapy, Breast Screening and Cardiology Departments.

This new development gave the Trust an exciting opportunity to ensure that health care provision in the 21st-century would place patients first. In line with current best practice, the aspiration was to provide a high-quality integrated service, organised around individual needs.

The scale of the project on its 32-acre site presented a number of challenges. Not least was the need to manage the health, safety and environmental aspects of a project on this scale being driven at high speed, while minimising its impact on local communities.

The ability to predict, control and reduce running costs, particularly energy costs, over the whole lifetime of the hospital gave the Trust the chance to plough resources back into the hospital. Carillion were able to draw on the knowledge gained at Darent Valley Hospital, particularly in the areas of environmental performance and fast track construction using off-site manufacturing. Working in close partnership with the Trust, Carillion managed the transfer of staff, services and patients to the new hospital with minimal disruption.

Thanks to excellent collaboration between users, managers and the public, the hospital has been fully operational since November 2002. The Hospital Company (the PFI vehicle) is now operating the facility under concession for the next 27 years, on behalf of the Trust, striving to provide excellent service in every respect. The Hospital Company have now commissioned a significant addition, a new diagnostic and treatment centre. This addition is not part of this case study.

General (The Environment)

Sustainability is creating major change in construction. Carillion used this project to advance their sustainability knowledge, ideas and techniques. From Gandhi's quote[49] 'be the change that you want to see in the world', Carillion named this major leap

Main hospital entrance

forward for construction 'Be the Change'.

Business is intended to make profit. From the outset it was important that sustainable construction did not cost more or carry an additional premium. Les Meaton,[50] Technical project manager of Swindon and Marlborough NHS Trust, commented: 'A sustainable hospital is one which is better for patients, better for the medical staff who work there, better for the local community and better for the team who build it, and better for the planet earth.'

Carillion engaged Dr Mark Everard, director of science from the Natural Step to facilitate a two-day workshop for the entire project team, providing a thorough insight into sustainability and the four system conditions. From this workshop came the sustainability action plan together with its hard targets to control carbon emissions, eliminate chlorofluorocarbons (CFCs), use materials from managed sources and provide the building as an asset for the community. Paul Dempster,[51] Carillion's project manager, commented: 'The Natural Step were introduced to the project to help us understand sustainability and to help us achieve real sustainable benefits.' From the workshop, the empowered team produced a design which:

- Achieved maximum flexibility for future use.
- Achieved maximum repetition throughout design.
- Made maximum re-use of excavated materials and minimised waste.
- Made maximum use of off-site prefabrication opportunities.

For the action plan to work, suppliers and trade contractors had to be fully involved. As the plan advanced over 50 initiatives were put in place to increase sustainability, including:

- The plasterboard manufacturer Lafage and the trade contractor BR Hodgeson helped to develop an enhanced product that saved labour costs and reduced the amount of waste.
- Because the project is PFI and the consortium has a 27-year concession, it was possible to increase capital spending on the roof insulation with the knowledge that this would pay for itself within the concession period by reducing energy costs, reducing atmospheric carbon emissions as a consequence.

Architect's Input
The Great Western Hospital features 7600 square metres of rich cream-coloured precast concrete cladding, replicating the appearance of the natural stone commonly used in Wiltshire. The high-quality finish and careful detailing of the cladding contributes to the clean and attractive lines of the building. Precast cladding was used in order to dispense with the need for scaffolding. To speed up construction and minimise the numbers of joints and fittings the strategy was to make the precast units as large as possible. The panels weighed 14 tonnes and spanned 7 metres x 4 metres. The other major part of the façade is aluminium-faced insulated Spanwall panels.

For further increased efficiency and ease of

installation, window frames, glazing and installation were installed in the precast concrete factory. With the units at ground level such installation is both safer and simpler due to accessibility.

The contract was signed against a very basic design, which included 1:200 drawings, outline specification and room data sheets, a design development procedure. The 1:50 drawings were developed with the Trust clinicians, but this relied on the clinicians understanding the drawings and the full engagement of the Trust clinician teams.

Structural Engineer's Input

For a shorter construction programme, simplified construction, fire protection benefits, inherent energy saving through thermal mass and the maximisation of service zones, TPS Consult designed a straightforward concrete frame for the construction of the new hospital.

Flat slab concrete floors are supported by a nominal 7.2 metre x 7.2 metre grid of concrete columns. The floors are 300 millimetres deep (the optimum depth for the bay size to control deflections within code limits) and finite element design enabled maximum service zones and a provision for large cast-in and drilled service openings, to be accommodated within the slab depth without having to use downstand beams.

Each section of the building was designed separately to achieve horizontal stability. Concrete shear walls were introduced at stair and lift cores, extending from foundation to roof level as well as around the external perimeter of the building, so that horizontal loads are shared and torsion is not introduced into the building. The shear walls then act together with the diaphragm action of the floor slab construction to brace the building and transfer horizontal loads to the foundations.

The concrete panels were designed to span off the edge of the slab from corbels cast to tight tolerances on to the back of the concrete, and located adjacent to the columns. The concrete panels thus utilised their height to span between corbels and did not require the slab to act in bending.

M&E Engineer's Input

The servicing strategy involved an 'energy centre' located some 250 metres from the main building. This energy centre provides the basic servicing needs, which are further enhanced in the rooftop plantrooms.

Because of the programme requirements, it was necessary for Crown House Engineering to design and prefabricate as many items as possible. Services in riser shafts were prefabricated so that they could simply be craned into position. Horizontal service runs were designed so that they would be repetitive and then modular. This allowed individual modules to be fixed to the structure and then connected together. This provided the service runs and was significantly quicker than installing single pipes.

Contractor's Input

The contractor's requirements for sustainability

filtered down through the designers, suppliers and trade contractors. Through the waste management philosophies, the standard of the site and welfare facilities was exemplary, demonstrating to all involved that sustainability was the future.

Working to strict timescales, windows were supplied direct to Trent Concrete – producers of huge precast concrete panels – for fitting off-site. Trent Concrete then stored the complete concrete panel and window assembly ready to be supplied to the hospital as and when required. This subsequently reduced labour and programme timescales that would have otherwise been required for an on-site installation.

Undertaking these operations while panels are readily accessible and at ground level makes much more sense from an efficiency and safety viewpoint, and it also makes the early enclosure of a dry envelope possible. This in turn allows following, weather-sensitive, trades to start work earlier, which is especially important in hospital construction due to the significant amount of M&E services to install.

One of the primary reasons for specifying precast concrete was a desire to dispense with external scaffolding. On a multistorey project of this size, scaffolding represents a considerable cost and also hinders other work from starting at the earliest opportunity.

On-site, finished components are lifted directly from the delivery vehicle to their final position on the building on a carefully scheduled just-in-time basis. This reduces the number of traffic movements and therefore lowers CO_2 emissions, as well as lessening dust and noise.

Summary

This summary is taken directly from Carillion's promotional material[52] for this project:

The Great Western Hospital has been a journey

for all those involved, from an initial desire to do something different and better, it now represents one of the most remarkable and important developments in Britain. Not because it is a major health care centre or because it was procured through Public Finance Initiative, but because it was the first development in Britain to take that great leap to becoming more sustainable, sustainable for Swindon and North Wiltshire.

The Building Research Establishment said[53]:

The adoption of Sustainability Action Plans by Carillion demonstrates a joined up approach to sustainability rare in construction generally and possibly unique in the construction of NHS buildings.

Trevor Payne, director of estates and facilities at Great Western Hospital, said:[54]

The Great Western Hospital is a landmark NHS Building – providing an excellent and well planned patient environment. The challenge for us and our private sector partners – The Hospital Company (THC) – is to ensure that a sustainable approach is taken to service provision and operational activities now that the new hospital is open.

A presentation to the RIBA Healthcare Forum[55] concluded that a quality building had been achieved but criticised the width of doors and provision of showers. The services installation was also highlighted, questioning the quality of some of the installations and the performance of the theatre ventilation.

Elevation showing stone and
metallic cladding

Mile End Stadium, London Borough of Tower Hamlets

Project: New sports facilities
Employer: London Borough of Tower Hamlets
Employer's agent: CM Parker Browne
Architect: Limbrick Limited
Contractor: Jackson Construction Ltd
Contract value: £15 million
Contract type: JCT 98 WCD
Contract period: Commenced 7 June 2004 –
completion due early 2006

Introduction

Mile End Park is a park located in London. It was
created on land originally devastated by Second
World War bombing. Extensive development of the
park was completed in 2002, including linking the
park over the main road with a 'green' bridge, by
architects CZWG. The final phase of the park
development is the creation of the sports facility.

The new masterplan and park buildings were
designed by Tibbalds TM2. In April 1995, Tower
Hamlets Council, the East London Partnership and
the Environment Trust formed the Mile End Park
Partnership (MEPP) to complete the vision set out
in the post-war Abercrombie Plan.

The submission to the Millennium Commission
for funding stated:[56]

> Our vision for the Mile End Park of the 21st
> Century is to transform this segmented and
> under used open space into an active and
> vibrant regional park – the best in East London.
> We seek to create a park which will offer
> facilities for the widest possible range of open-air

pursuits, from sport and play, to appreciating the
arts and enjoying the environment; which will
demonstrate excellence and innovation in all
aspects of its creation: design, engineering,
landscaping, nature conservation; and which will
be enjoyed and cherished by the people of Tower
Hamlets and the whole of East London.

Mile End Stadium is at the south end of the
park and is being redeveloped to form sports
facilities fit for the twenty-first century. In
addition to the stadium, the project involves the
creation of mini-soccer facilities.

The park has already had a high profile opening.
His Royal Highness the Duke of Edinburgh,
President of the National Playing Fields Association,
made a return visit in May 2001 to one of London's
most important public parks. He last visited in
October 1952 when he opened the park. 'The park
has been remodeled by local people in a way which
should be an example for communities all over
London,' says the director of the NPFA, Mrs Elsa
Davies.[57] 'The Duke of Edinburgh has been involved
with the work of the NPFA for over 50 years, and
he was anxious to see this development for himself.'

Mile End Park is one of 475 playing fields
dedicated as a memorial to King George V. The
proposed sports development, minifootball facilities
and stadium, completes the final part of this project.

General

Funding for this project was quite diverse, and
included:

Right
Site plan

Below
Visual of main approach

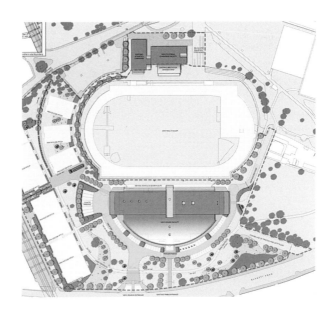

Right
Visual impression of the
building seen from the
running track

Opposite right
Visual of the entrance area

Opposite far right
Visual impression of the pool

Sport England	£5.483 million
Millennium Commission	£1.8 million
The Football Foundation	£800 000
Tower Hamlets Council	£5.7 million
Ocean New Deal for Communities	£1.15 million

The Stadium is designed to be attractive and welcoming to all sectors of the community, particularly hard-to-reach groups or those who traditionally have shown low interest in sports, such as Bengali women, with a women-only fitness suite, direct access from the women's changing rooms to the secondary pool with flexible water depth and health suite, and a crèche that caters for newborn babies to five year olds.

Ray Gerlach,[58] acting corporate director of environment and culture at Tower Hamlets Council said:

Local athletes have used Mile End for a long time, and the new facilities will offer unprecedented opportunities in the borough for training and fulfils the council's commitment to excellent public services that will benefit the entire local community.

Roger Draper,[59] chief executive of Sport England, said:

We are delighted to be contributing to the development of these facilities. They will give many more people in the area the opportunity to start, stay and succeed in sport – key Sport England objectives – and will also make a contribution to a generation in Tower Hamlets. We are particularly pleased that every effort has been made to make the facilities as inclusive as possible.

Councillor Rahman said:[60]

Once completed, Mile End Stadium will be the biggest amenity of its kind in the borough and will plug a real gap in facilities for the community in and around the area.

The stadium was procured as a two-stage project. The architect and client completed detailed design prior to involvement of the contractor.

Architect's Input

The design comprised an eight-lane 25 metre pool, 17 metre training pool with movable floor, four-court sports hall, aerobics studio, general fitness suite, women's only fitness suite, spa facilities, meeting room, changing rooms and crèche.

Summary

At the time of writing, the project is not complete and so it is not possible to comment on the success of the stadium.

What is interesting is that a design-build route has been selected, although the contractor is only involved post-design. The architect is a gifted sports and leisure designer, the project is very high profile, with the funding body including Sport England, yet a procurement route that is often criticised for not providing the desired quality was selected.

The truth is of course that the funding body required the removal of risk of a cost overrun, while the two-stage process ensured quality of design.

Museum in the Park, Stroud

Project: New Museum, Stratford Park, Stroud
Employer: Stroud District Council
Employer's Agent: Ridge Chartered Surveyors
Architect: David Hutchison
Engineer: Buro Happold
M&E engineer: Buro Happold
Contractor: Moss Construction
Contract value: £1.45 million
Contract type: JCT 98 WCD
Contract period: 41 weeks – completion January 2001

Introduction

Stratford Park lies on the outskirts of Stroud and was created from the original manor house. Stratford House has been in the ownership of Stroud District Council since Stratford Park became a public leisure park in the 1930s. Stroud District Council needed to rehouse the existing museum and the existing 17th and 18th century house was also in need of major renovation. The two requirements were combined and the 'Museum in the Park' was created.

The project consisted of refurbishing the existing manor house with the addition of a single-storey extension to create the museum, shop, resource centre and art gallery. The extension was to be built over an existing listed wall, so Stroud District Council employed their own archaeologists (The Gloucestershire Building Recording Group) to painstakingly record every brick and stone before the new works could commence.

The existing building contained a plunge pool. It was important that this was maintained, including the spring that filled it, so this was to become a constraint on the design.

The Heritage Lottery Fund helped fund the project.

General

This was a high profile project for Stroud District Council and they were determined to try to make it a successful project. The Local Authority took a very proactive approach to Building Control. The existing house required a 'change of use', which could cause major structural dilemmas such as an increase in floor loadings etc. Building Control provided alternative solutions to any of the possible problems created by the change of use classification.

The potential conflict between the conservation requirements and the current Building Regulations could also have been a problem. For example, the existing sash windows were single glazed; the conservation requirement to keep the original glazing bars meant that there was no opportunity for double glazing. An internal acrylic screen was provided to increase security, but this added little to the thermal properties of the window. There was also little opportunity to increase the thermal properties of the wall without disturbing the listed plaster cornices. The Building Control department ensured that this was not a problem.

The following is taken from the report that accompanied the Listed Building Consent application.

Material

The original house was built in coursed, rough tooled, oolitic limestone with large quoins, some of

which have survived on the northeast and northwest corners of the projecting wing. It is most likely that the stone was quarried on or near the site, although no evidence of the existence of a quarry has been found to date. The new work by Anthony Keck in the latter part of the eighteenth century is also oolitic limestone, but both the material and the craftsmanship are of a finer quality than the remains of the early house. Guiting Cotswold Hill stone probably provides the closest match in colour, texture and geological characteristics to the original material.

The North Elevation

The stonework on this part of the Mansion has been severely damaged by damp and frost action, which has caused cracking and spalling. The problem has been exacerbated by local subsidence thought to have resulted from the presence of a spring close to the house and a defective drainage system, leading to leaching out of the subsoil next to the house.

Defective stone adjacent to (blocked) windows W12 and W13 is to be carefully cut out and replaced with matching stone laid in the bed, in lime mortar and pointed to match adjoining work.

Roof

The roof of Stratford Park Mansion is remarkable for the roof covering of large sandstone flags, which are generally larger and thicker than limestone slates, and require a heavier and stronger roof structure. At the Mansion the pitch is 30°. The coarse textured sandstone, dark grey buff in colour, has a similar grain to Forest of Dean sandstone.

Windows

The late seventeenth century stone mullioned windows in the west and north walls, windows W6, W7, W8, W12, W13, W23, W24, W25, W26, W32, W33, show a range of detail and scale in the mouldings of architraves, cills and mullions which include both ovolo and cavetto forms. The sequence of repair and alteration is not yet clearly established; however, it appears that windows W12 W13 and W33 were blocked as part of Anthony Keck's scheme to extend the earlier house.

A significant number of plain glazed lights have survived: however, many of these will require repair as in some lights the lead cames have deteriorated and weakened, while in others the plain glazing is at risk from distortion and buckling of the frames.

Extensive repair will be required to repair damage and insensitive alterations, which have been carried out in recent years. Where alterations have been made to windows W6, W7, W8 and W26, they are to be taken out and plain glazed lights to match adjacent reinstated.

Much early iron window furniture has also survived. It is proposed that this should be repaired where necessary, and new furniture to match made to replace missing items.

The scope of this report allowed the contractor to cost the refurbishment with more accuracy than could normally be anticipated.

Architect's Input

David Hutchison commented:[61] "I first became

aware of the enquiry through Tony Frost of J Nisbet and Partners, who thought I would be interested. I first approached Buro Happold, who were renowned designers, and then Paul Cullen of Moss Construction. Paul saw the opportunity as a positive challenge; we had our team !'

The extensive refurbishment of the Mansion has seen floor strengthening, reroofing and elimination of infestation and rot. Many original external and internal features, including original windows and glazing, doors, roof tiles, plasterwork, timber panelling and decorations are retained. The conversion includes installation of fire and security systems to meet the national standards of the Museums and Galleries Commission.

The new single-storey extension is designed to carefully fit along the kitchen garden boundary wall and incorporates the existing plunge pool from an old outbuilding. This arrangement enables a semi-enclosed south-facing courtyard to offer an attractive entrance to the complex.

The materials chosen are of local natural origin including stone walls, timber and skate roofing and lead panelling. The design follows the Council's sustainable energy efficient policy. The landscaping respects the large mature parkland trees and uses the change of level to provide a meeting space for visiting educational parties to gather within the enclosed courtyard for group activities.

Structural Engineer's Input

The existing building would have changing use categories, the uplift from domestic classification meant that the floors would require strengthening. It would not be possible to simply place new steel beams below the existing floors (as per the Employer's Requirement) because of the existing listed plaster cornices. Buro Happold's engineer worked very closely with the Moss in-house structural engineer to develop a scheme that would upgrade the floor construction but keep the strengthening within the depth of the existing floor.

Although this sounds a very simple exercise, the solution to this problem without disturbing the existing plasterwork significantly contributed to the success of the project.

M&E Engineer's Input

The completed building was to function as a museum. This has demanding constraints on the internal environment for the preservation of artefacts etc.

The environmental constraints were further heightened by the refurbishment of the existing building. As the old and new buildings reached equilibrium in terms of humidity, the existing building. would dry out, giving rise to concerns about timber cracking etc.

The M&E was further complicated by the accessibility requirements. The requirements to have doors held open meant that different zones simply flowed into each other. The M&E consultant working directly with the contractor's selected specialist M&E subcontractors produced a solution correctly conditioned to the internal environment for the museum.

Detailed view of extension
elevation

Contractor's Input

The contractor had won the project through a competitive tender, and although there was a detailed specification and a set of scheme design drawings, the contractor was responsible for the design development and detailed design required to complete the project. By engaging a team of specialist subcontractors, the contractor was able to make use of essential technical advice for the completion of the design. Such specialist subcontractors included specialists for glazing for the refurbishment of the existing Georgian Lamb's tongue glazing bars, dampproofing, roofing and green oak for the new build.

Summary

The project is clearly very successful. The museum is now functioning well in the green surroundings of Stratford Park. David Hutchison stated:[61]

> The rest is history insofar as the outline design was developed to the finished product which is evident to all who now regularly commend the building and the facilities, and the Moss crew very clearly took on board the notion of adding to the design with a well constructed and very good looking building.

The following is an excerpt from a letter to the Heritage Lottery Fund (HLF):[62]

> The award has enabled the creation of a high quality accessible new home for the Museum's

display and education services. Stratford Park Mansion has been refurbished and the centre of its historic parkland setting has been regenerated and restored for public use. We are delighted to report that all the project objectives have been met and the scheme was completed on time and on budget.

On the strength of the success of the project and the public response to the new facilities, the Council has increased the Museum's revenue budget by £46 000 to fund free admission and extended opening hours. At the same time, the Council and the Trust are now planning a second phase of capital development for the Museum Service. The aim will be to release all of the Museum's off-site premises by creating a new purpose-built centralised collections centre within Stratford Park. The proposal is also to include the restoration of the historic walled kitchen garden adjacent to the Museum and provision of public access. It is envisaged that a further application will be made to HLF for this project.

The following is part of the Heritage Lottery Fund completion report:[62]

Principal Project Objectives

[1] Create an accessible home for the public services of the Museum in Stratford Park.

[2] Refurbish the buildings and surroundings to a high standard and in a manner that serves to

Interior view of refurbished
building

interpret their history and development.

Summary Report on Achievement

[1] The Museum in the Park opened on 20 January
2001 and comprises core displays of the
Museum's collections and a range of exhibition,
education and visitor facilities. Accessibility was
one of the key design criteria for the project. The
Museum and its services have been (and
continue to be) designed in close consultation
with target audience groups, including the local
Access Group for people with disabilities.

[2] Prior to the building works, the footprint of the
new extension building was excavated and
recorded by Gloucestershire County Archaeology
Service.

Gloucestershire Buildings Recording Group
have researched and recorded the history and
development of Stratford Park Mansion. They
have produced a detailed paper on the
development and documentary history of the
building. They also examined the building fabric
during the opening up of the building by the
main contractors.

All of this work has informed:
(a) the programme of work to refurbish Stratford
Park Mansion, the adjacent plunge bath and
courtyard;
(b) the use, interpretation and display of the site.

One of the conclusions of this text is that design-

build is not an appropriate procurement method for
refurbishment as the risks to the contractor are too
high. However, this project was certainly a success.
Stroud received a Museum of some acclaim, while
Moss and the design team completed the project,
returning the required profit. It is clear from the
success of the project that the contractor allowed
sufficient risk within the pricing, and since not
many problems materialised, this risk money could
be added to the profit.

Opening up the existing building provided few
surprises that had not been anticipated by the very
comprehensive Listed Building Consent application
prepared by Stroud District Council or could not be
integrated into the design. This potential uncertainty
is the area that makes design-build unsuitable for
the procurement of refurbishment projects.

There were also a significant number of
employer-instigated changes. As discussed
previously, change inevitably carries a higher profit
margin and so will help to compensate for any
minor losses on other elements.

National Trust New Central Office, Swindon

Project: New central office building for the National Trust, Swindon
Employer: Kier Ventures (funding by Kier Property)
Tenant Project Manager: Buro Four
Employer's agent: Wakemans
Architect: Feilden Clegg Bradley
Engineer: Adams Kara Taylor
M&E engineer: Max Fordham and Partners
Contractor: Moss Construction (Kier Regional)
Contract value: £14 million including fit-out
Contract type: JCT 98 WCD
Contract period: 18 months – completion July 2005

Introduction

The National Trust is a well-renowned organisation, founded in 1895 to protect the natural environment and buildings of the UK. Having made the decision to amalgamate its offices in a new central building, it was important that the Trust was seen to be 'green', architecturally aware and sensitive to the needs of its staff while avoiding accusations of extravagance or empire building.

Financial risk has been minimised by the decision not to develop the site itself but to find an institutional partner to build the office and then lease it back to the National Trust for 35 years. Kier Property undertook this PFI type role.

Kier Property director Tom Gilman commented:[63]

We are delighted to be working for the National Trust on this prestigious project and have every confidence in the Moss Construction team who have a wealth of experience in constructing award-winning central HQ buildings. This is an excellent opportunity for Kier Property to continue with plans to expand the commercial portfolio.

National Trust project director Sue Holden said:[64] 'We hope the project will demonstrate how commercially viable buildings can be built in a more sustainable way.'

Swindon was selected because of its good transport links to London and its proximity to three of the four offices that will move to the new headquarters (and thus minimise staff disruption). Within Swindon, the National Trust has chosen an existing heritage site: the centre of Brunel's Great Western Railway works with its close neighbours English Heritage and the Steam Museum. The site has a fascinating historic significance with many listed buildings – built by Brunel, Gooch and Armstrong between the 1840s and 1880s. At its peak it was the largest integrated railway works in Europe, employing 14 000 people.

By choosing an old industrial site, the National Trust is making the point that in the 21st century it has to start engaging more seriously with Britain's urban and industrial past and not remain overwhelmingly focused on the countryside.

General

For the new Central Office, the National Trust chose an intriguing site that once formed part of Brunel's Great Western Railway Works. It was the adjacent 19th century engineering sheds that provided the

View of external corner
showing shading and
photovoltaic panels

View of recreational space in
the atrium

concept for the new offices. Lofty, two-storey buildings with high-quality daylighting and ventilation through a regular rhythm of pitched roofs, these buildings were designed before the days of artificial lighting.

One of the key requirements of the Trust was that the disparate parts of the organisation that were coming together into the new building all needed to feel part of one organisation. The regular rhythm of an all-embracing roof supported on slender columns, visible from all workstations on the ground or mezzanine floors, seemed to fulfil this objective. The deep plan that this building form suggested initially seemed to be counterintuitive, though redefining the building with the roof as the major connection to the environment means that in effect each workstation is no more than 7 metres from daylight and ventilation. Two internal courtyards were added to provide an indoor garden space and a greater connection to the outside.

Buro Four project director, Iain Roberts,[65] said:

The choice of the design-build procurement route I believe was integral to the Trust achieving their objective of securing a new headquarters building that met their operational and sustainability objectives without exposing the Trust to the risks of development.

The following text is taken from the National Trust Trustee's Statement:[66]

As part of the Organisational Review we agreed that locating the vast majority of staff from our four offices under one roof would bring significant benefits to the Trust, including long term cost savings.

Swindon was identified as the best location in terms of staff retention, site availability and good transport links. We identified a site on the footprint of the historic Great Western Railway works. Following a series of interviews, the architects Feilden Clegg Bradley were appointed to design the new building that will be home to 430 staff and will also contain a reception, shop, exhibition area and meeting rooms.

The Trust set a challenging brief to ensure that whilst being frugal the building is sympathetic to its historic surroundings, is as environmentally sustainable as possible and provides an effective 21st century office space.

Through orienting the building at a north–south angle on the site, and drawing on roof features, which reflect our great industrial heritage, the building will be one of the most daylight-lit buildings ever constructed. Natural ventilation will also remove the need for air-conditioning.

The initial National Trust requirements were:

- Create an excellent working environment, facilitating internal communications and helping to develop a sense of community.
- Achieve high standards of sustainability.
- Be appropriate for a charity and demonstrate quality without ostentation.
- Be a warm and welcoming building and create a

Interior view showing the double height recreational atrium space and first floor workspaces

new public face for the Trust.
- Creating an enjoyable pedestrian environment between our office, the Steam Museum and the outlet centre.
- Be a building that is institutionally fundable.

In addition the building was to contribute to the surrounding area by:

- Making an appropriate new architectural contribution to the area.
- Creating an enjoyable pedestrian environment between the railway station and the Steam Museum.

Architect's Input

The design that emerged uses a very similar form to the existing railway sheds, with the orientation of the ridge turned so as to provide south-facing roof slopes for solar collection and north-facing rooflights for daylighting. The orientation of the building provides a powerful diagonal line, which picks up the route to the town centre. The remaining three sides have gable walls revealed and are clad in blue engineering bricks, again picking up on the decorative detail of many of the remaining buildings. Jo Wright, from architects Feilden Clegg Bradley, said:[67] 'We have tried to show that it is possible to meet institutional funding requirements and deliver a sustainable building which will provide a long term home for the Trust.'

The design concept aimed to ensure that each workspace should be able to see the sky. The most difficult zones in which to achieve this were

obviously under the mezzanine floor areas, which were designed to be 9 metres wide to provide reasonable flexibility and workstation layout. A floor to ceiling height of 3.75 metres was used under the mezzanine and 6 metre voids were introduced between mezzanines. Analysis showed that daylight factors ranging from 3 % at the centre of the underside of the mezzanine floors to an average of 9 % on the mezzanines themselves could be achieved.

The rooflights are shaded by extending the leading edge of the south facing roof slope over the ridge to shade from high-level summer sun, and by incorporating ventilators that consist of a raised enclosure around the section of the rooflight. The ventilators at roof level are designed to operate independently of the wind direction and also provide rain protection to the opening sections of rooflight. This system is automated to provide night cooling in summer and daytime ventilation from spring to autumn, with vents being controlled by the building management system (BMS) with local manual override.

One of the problems with naturally ventilated buildings is the provision of the very low rates of ventilation that are required to maintain oxygen levels during the winter. Casement windows or even trickle vents tend to admit too much air and cause draughts. A very low level mechanical ventilation system has therefore been installed with an integral heat recovery system, which introduces air to raised floor plenums and provides a single point of extraction adjacent to the fan unit itself in order to provide heat recovery.

Naturally ventilated buildings often incorporate 'safety net' measures to deal with excessive summertime conditions. Here, an extract ventilation system is incorporated in eight of the roof ventilation 'snouts' to enhance cooling potential and air movement through the building if absolutely necessary.

Power consumption by office equipment, however, is more difficult for the design team to control, and will remain the largest source of CO_2 emissions in the low energy office building. The only way to meet this electrical load without importing electricity is to incorporate on-site photovoltaic generation. The roof form of the National Trust Office maximises this potential with a total potential area of 1400 square metres of ideally oriented collection area facing due south at 30° to the horizontal. Around a third of the collection area consists of the extensions to the south-facing roof slope that form shades for the north lights. The remainder is located on the south-facing roof itself in a position where it is exposed to direct sunlight above an altitude of 20° due south. A low-cost thin-film amorphous silicon panel was selected for the project.

The National Trust sustainability agenda extends way beyond energy use. Studies of water usage showed that by installing 4 litre flush WCs and waterless urinals, spray taps and class A kitchen appliances, it will be possible to reduce water consumption by 60 %.

The materials selected for use in the buildings were checked against the rating in the Green Guide Specification. Blue engineering bricks chosen for the outer walls of the building have been laid in lime mortar to ensure recycling. Brunel had used the same bricks in the original building design and for the adjacent canal. Both the roof and the windows are made of aluminium, which now has a very high percentage of recycled stock.

The National Trust is very keen to utilise materials from its own estates, and one of the more significant undervalued products is the sheep's wool from the Herdwick flock on the Lake District fells. Elsewhere it is hoped that the internal fittings of the building will utilise timber from nearby local National Trust estates.

The Trust's sustainability policy also extends to the transportation strategy for the building as well as its management. The site was selected because of its proximity to the main line station, and the number of car spaces provided has been reduced to below what commercial developers might expect and the planning authority might accept. One car space for every three workers will mean that a green transport plan will be forced to reduce car dependence.

Social facilities both for staff and for public form the heart of the building. There will be no cellular office spaces, giving greater credence to the democratic working principles of the organisation.

Structural Engineer's Input

Various options were examined in relation to the superstructure frame with timber/concrete composite solutions evaluated against steel. Studies showed surprisingly that the embodied energy of highly processed timber as against steel sections with a high percentage of recycled steel made very

Interior view of entrance area

little difference to the overall embodied energy. The refinement of the steel frame and the reduction in thickness of the slab were of greater consequence.

M&E Engineer's Input
M&E worked with the architect to set out the best orientation and massing of the building to achieve good natural daylight and ventilation, and to accommodate the photovoltaic (PV) array, which also acts as solar shading for north-facing rooflights.

The resulting design is a two-storey, deep plan, building with a mezzanine first floor plate and rooflights; naturally ventilated via automated windows and rooflights; and daylit on both floors using the rooflights and mezzanines so that artificial light is required for only 15 % of working hours.

The PV array received the largest grant awarded in the UK by the DTI scheme for photovoltaics and it is anticipated that overall energy use will be among the lowest in the country for an office. Energy Minister, Stephen Timms, said of the government's £25 million Major Photovoltaics (PV) Demonstration Programme:[68] 'Including today's announcement, we have awarded £13 million worth of grants to 110 different projects throughout the UK, further proof of our commitment to reach our renewable energy target of 10 % by 2010.'

Contractor's Input
Moss Construction became involved in the project with the design at RIBA Stage D. From then they were involved in making a complex design buildable.

The building has a very complex roof, with ridges and valleys at complex angles. The architect had specified a standing seam roof for aesthetic reasons. The roof shape was going to mean that the complex junctions in the standing seam would be prone to water and air leakage. This was significant as the contract required air leakage standards to be better than Part L of the Building Regulations. Through the standing seam roof were a multitude of penetrations for bolts holding the protection to the opening lights and the photovoltaic panels.

Below the standing seam finish, the roof was given mass by the use of concrete planks. These planks also acted as the structure for fixing all of the bolts. Moss took the decision to apply a waterproof membrane to this structure, which would guarantee that the standing seam roof could now not only achieve the required aesthetics, but the roof construction as a whole would achieve the required performance. The application of the membrane made the structure waterproof earlier than had been envisaged by the construction programme. This allowed some trades, like painting, to be advanced.

The project uses a brickwork construction, with modular 'Staffordshire blue' blocks stack-bonded. Moss were proactive in developing the detailing, with the very wide cavity and large amount of insulation.

The project achieved an 'excellent' rating (72 %) under BREEAM.

Summary
The new 7200 square metre Headquarters in Swindon sets the standard of demonstrating good environmental practice while providing open,

well-designed flexible space to suit modern ways of working. Facilities for its 430 staff include a library, offices and a public information area.

The building has been designed to be the lowest energy consumption office building in the country. Such an approach should provide rewards in terms of running costs as well as the internal environment. The 'excellent' BREEAM rating is reward for the sustainable practice adopted by client, designers and contractor alike.

Iain Roberts, Buro Four project director, commented:[65]

> We were able to achieve the objectives by:
> (a) Splitting the scheme into base build and fit-out. This enabled the Trust's detailed requirements to be developed to a different timescale to the main building.
> (b) By novating the design team to the contractor facilitated continuity of design.
> (c) By including the scheme design report as the Employer's Requirements and by including a joint environmental statement of intent.
> (d) By selecting a developer and contractor who were genuinely aligned to the Trust's objectives.
> (e) By administering the contract in a non-adversarial manner.

Design-build delivered this project. Without a proactive contractor it would have been almost impossible to achieve the 'excellent' BREEAM rating.

Oklahoma State Capitol Dome, Oklahoma City, USA

Project: New dome and structural refurbishment for existing capital building
Employer: State of Oklahoma
Architect: Frankfurt-Short-Bruza Associates, PC
Engineer: Frankfurt-Short-Bruza Associates, PC
Contractor: Capitol Dome Builders (joint venture between Manhattan Construction and Flintco Inc)
Contract value: $21 million
Contract type: Lump sum design-build contract
Contract period: 18 months – completion November 2002

Introduction

Between 1914 and 1917, Oklahoma City built its State Capital, a Greek revival style statehouse by Soloman Andrew Leyton and S Wemyss Smith. Although a central dome and cupola were part of the original design, the First World War drained funds so it was constructed without one. In 1934 the existing shallow domed ceiling of the rotunda was remodelled; the architect for this is unknown.

This project is really about the completion of the original design – the addition of the dome. The completed dome is 50 metres high, 27 metres in diameter and has a 6 metre high bronze statue of a Native American on top.

Frank Keating, Governor, stated:[69]

This week, I announced that we have completed raising the funds to build a dome on our State Capitol building.

It's important to keep three things in mind about the dome:

First, the Oklahoma State Capitol was originally designed to have a dome, like our nation's Capitol does and like most other states do. In fact, ours is the only state capitol in America designed to have a dome, which lacks one, for an interesting historical reason.

Construction of the Capitol began in 1914. When America entered World War 1 in 1917, structural steel needed for the war effort was diverted from domestic projects. For that reason the dome was not completed then.

Second, the state will contribute only $5 million of the estimated $20 million it will cost to finally place a dome on our Capitol. The rest of the funds have been contributed by private donors – individuals, corporations and charitable foundations.

The $5 million state contribution will come from bond money, not from general appropriations used to finance day-to-day business of government.

Third, the dome is expected to be completed by November 16th 2002 – statehood day. We are approaching our statehood centennial in 2007. Along with other improvements in the State Capitol complex, like the new historical museum and revitalisation of the Lincoln Boulevard, the dome will help symbolise our first 100 years as a state.

Our public buildings are symbols of our government, and our government belongs to the people. I think that it is appropriate that the people, through their voluntary contributions,

Internal view looking up into
new dome

have decided to finish the Capitol as it was originally planned 86 years ago.

Oklahoma has lots of other symbols of our past, from the Oklahoma City National Memorial to the Greenwood district in Tulsa to statues and courthouses across our state.

The dome says we're determined to grow, I think that's a good symbol for our future.

General

The two construction companies, Flintco, Inc, based in Tulsa and established in 1908, together with Manhattan Construction Company, were chosen through competitive selection. The Oklahoma Department of Central Services oversaw the selection process. Blake Wade, executive director of the Oklahoma Centennial Commission, stated:[70] 'On behalf of the Oklahoma Centennial Commission I am pleased that two such respected Oklahoma companies will join as one to complete our state Capitol. I'm looking forward to seeing the cranes go up.' Later he commented:[71] 'we are extremely delighted that an Oklahoma firm with the outstanding credentials of Frankfurt-Short-Bruza will be part of the design-build team for the Capitol dome and will direct the architectural planning and engineering for this project.'

The idea of fitting the dome was first muted in the 1960s, when Frankfurt–Short–Bruza (FBS) assisted an earlier governor.

Architect's Input

Frankfurt-Short-Bruza Associates (FSB) completed

the State Capitol Dome feasibility study in 1998 for the Oklahoma Department of Central Services. The analysis was based upon the original construction documents and specifications from 1914.

This project had to have a high profile, to ensure that adequate funding was raised. The Governor wanted the project to be a topic of discussion in schools. Together with FSB he created a goal of designing and completing a flier that helped to educate children about the dome, its various features and its history. The flier was an immediate success and scooped a journalism award.

The architectural detailing of the dome includes both the external dome and an internal dome visible from the rotunda. Much of the existing structure was saved, including the stained glass skylight, which was intended to be used in the inner dome but later replaced with new stained glass, plaster crown and cut limestone.

The base of the dome has a ring of 16 pairs of columns, each being 10 metres tall and 1 metre in diameter (the columns are actually circular steel with a stone outer casing). These surround an inner ring which is 22 metres in diameter and contains 16 windows, each being 1metre wide by 5 metres high.

The portion of the Capitol that was built in 1915 was constructed of limestone with a granite base. Architectural precast concrete and stone were selected as modern replacements. The manmade materials can span structurally and are a colour that will match the original weathered stone.

The interior of the dome is themed from the colours of the state wildflower, the Gaillardia. The

'Indian blanket', its common name, provides a deep red-brown centre, sunset red tones for the encircling coffers and yellow tips on the recessed panels. The flower is on a green base. A lower drum of blue symbolising the vibrant Oklahoma sky is accented with bands of gold punctuated by darker reds, blues and greens, depicting Indian beadery.

The new canopy over the opening in the upper dome is stained glass artwork, which replicates the original stained glass. The new window is 7 metres in diameter and has an image of the state seal at the centre. Triffo's Glassarts, the same glass company who produced the original stained glass at the Capitol, produced the new stained glass window.

Engineer's Input

The engineer started by collating all available original photographs, and linking these with current observations and testing to confirm that the structural framing to support the large dome was actually installed during the original construction. Special testing for the large dome included coring of the basement floor and footings, compressive strength tests of concrete cores, bearing capacity of the soil and rock materials on which the Capitol is built and tensile strength testing of the original steel. Part of the governing codes and standards require the building to resist certain seismic forces; this had to be included in the design.

The original 1914 structural design for the large dome incorporated a cast-in-place ribbed concrete superstructure with a compression ring at the crown and a tension ring at the base. For the current project a steel superstructure was selected as the best solution. The steel structure will be hidden behind the cladding.

A complex computer analysis was undertaken to determine the impact of the new dome on the existing rotunda structure. A 1:175 scale model was constructed to use in a wind tunnel. The model included all buildings within a 500-metre radius and was coated in plaster to simulate the actual texture of the dome material. Nearly 100 pressure sensors were used to collect that data, mimicking wind speeds of up to 90 miles per hour and from 16 different directions.

M&E Engineer's Input

The only real input from M&E was for the lighting design. The dome is brightly lit at night and is visible from most of Oklahoma City. The lighting is a mix of internal lighting, which provides a glow, and external direct lighting highlighting elements. The lantern at the very top is designed to change colour.

The stained glass is backlit with accent lighting to enhance the variety of colours used.

Contractor's Input

For the project to be a success, it was essential that the design and construction sequence and management were coordinated.

The first major input from the contractor was the site management. The location of the tower crane had to be determined such that it could span the existing building but its base and associated loads would not be detrimental to the existing building.

The location had to be determined with consideration for deliveries, the parking and unloading of delivery vehicles etc. Four piers were drilled into the bedrock; a 1.5 metre deep cross-shaped beam sits on the piers and supports the crane.

The basement and lower three floors were not affected by the dome construction and so had to be protected, including building protective covers over openings in the floors and a false ceiling to further protect the third floor. Existing artwork had to be protected against water, dust and sunlight damage even though the existing building was going to be protected when the rotunda and stained glass were removed. A 30 metre x 30 metre x 12 metre tall temporary warehouse was installed on top of the Capitol. The warehouse has 200 tonnes of steel and protects the interior of the existing Capitol from rain and snow. A 14 metre high temporary partition with steel studs, insulation and board finish was set up in an existing arched opening. This acted as a 'dust' wall offering protection to the existing building and artefacts.

The scaffolding was very complex with construction/protection platforms needing to be built at several different levels. The lower platform sat on a temporary steel work deck installed over the existing saucer dome and clear glass skylight.

Many of the existing features were then removed, including the existing flagpole. The Oklahoma State Seal was removed from the existing skylight. Although it was intended to reuse this later it was replaced with new stained glass.

Many existing components were going to be replicated. These had to be surveyed and scanned to allow them to be manufactured. This specifically included the stone columns, stone column capitals, stone cornice, plaster coffer and plaster panels. (The coffers and plaster panels were replicated using glass fibre reinforced plaster and modern technology.) Most of the precast concrete and stone was manufactured in Arkansas.

The remaining parts of the building were then opened up, including exposing the huge concrete arches of the saucer dome, which were exposed for the first time in 84 years. The existing cornice to the saucer dome, which was not going to be reused, was taken down and given to the Oklahoma Historical Society for display in the new History Museum.

With all of the structural protection in place, the existing building was considered safe enough to allow artisans to work. Mural painters from local colleges were engaged to complete a mural. Senator Haney was engaged as the artist to create the statue for the top of the dome. This Native American is called 'the Guardian'. Allied Steel manufactured the statue in their Oklahoma plant. Brass rails to the cupola were designed and manufactured.

Before the stained glass could be installed, the lighting system had to be completely checked for errors. This took over 100 hours of testing.

Summary

The dome has clearly been a success, finishing on time and to budget. The dedication ceremony was held on 16th November 2002. The ceremony included a memorial firework display and laser show.

The project involved works to an existing building, which always includes unknowns and risks. Although not clear in the information provided, I suggest that most of the research, analysis and testing had been completed prior to the Joint Venture construction company accepting the lump sum contract, thus greatly reducing the risks of the unknown.

The project has received a long list of awards, including:

- Associated General Contractors of America – Award of Merit.
- Design-Build Institute of America – National Design-Build Award 2003.
- National Council of Structural Engineers Association – Merit Award of Excellence.
- Institute of Classical Architecture and Classical America – Arthur Ross Award.
- Illumination Engineering Society of North America – Illumination Design Award.
- Superior Craftsman Award.
- Quality Craftsman Award.
- Best Precast Award.
- Oklahoma Society of Professional Journalists – Educational Graphic Material Award.

Princess Royal University Hospital, Orpington

Project: Hospital
Employer: Bromley Hospitals NHS Trust
Employer's agent: United Healthcare (Innisfree, Barclays Infrastructure and Taylor Woodrow)
Architect: CODA Architects
Engineer: Waterman Partnership Ltd
M&E engineer: Zisman Bowyer & Partners LLP
Contractor: Taylor Woodrow
Contract value: £100 million
Contract type: PFI
Contract period: 18 months – completion December 2002

Introduction

The Princess Royal University Hospital is the main component of the Bromley Hospitals PFI project. The overall development amalgamates previously dispersed hospital services to create an effective, fluid, efficient hospital.

Bromley Hospitals NHS Trust, in conjunction with PFI Contractor Taylor Woodrow Construction and architect CODA Architects, were fully committed to provide a service that met the expectations of the users, both patients and staff. From an early design stage the Trust service provision was viewed holistically, rationalising acute services across the whole Trust.

Bringing together facilities from Bromley, Orpington and Beckenham sites, development at Farnborough includes the new Princess Royal University Hospital, an existing Day Surgery Unit, Post Graduate Education Centre and the Green Parks Mental Health Unit, completed in 2000 as part of the PFI development. The existing hospital building stock had accrued over many years and was unsuitable for delivering healthcare in the 21st century. The new hospital was required to give the Trust a new start – a new public face.

General

The construction sequencing was carefully considered across the sites, resulting in a single-phase development saving years on the overall programme and minimising disruption through one move rather than decanting over several phases.

The site layout was developed to be legible, robust and welcoming. A hierarchy of avenues and spaces defines the site, which has been given a pedestrian focus despite the requirement for a high number of parking spaces. The hospital is itself a landmark building generating its own urban context. The landscape design and site planning respond to this by creating a sense of place in which the new and existing buildings can comfortably sit.

The site gradient was used to create two ground floor levels, separating access points and simplifying circulation. Staff and patients can easily find their way from site access points to an appropriate entrance of the building and, internally, most users either stay on the entry level or go up or down one floor.

Architect's Input

Craig Bennetti[72] of CODA stated:

The strategic planning of the new hospital

Below left
Glazed canopy at main
entrance

Below right
Detail of elevation

utilizes angled and curved elements to create the appropriate functional adjacencies as well as creating a visually stimulating and legible composition. Curved forms are used both in plan and in section to contrast with and soften the linear elements of the building. The orientation of the principle building elements in an east/west direction enhances internal comfort conditions without the need for heavily air-conditioned spaces.

The height of the building ranges from three storeys for the west building, which fronts the adjoining residential development, to a maximum of four storeys on the central block (one floor being below perceived ground level). The contemporary elevational treatment combines both modern and traditional forms and materials to create a design that is both visually stimulating and human in scale.

The principle elevation is layered vertically using the classical divisions of base, piano nobile and clerestory and also horizontally, with a sunscreen and support structure forming the outer layer and a mixture of terracotta panels and timber/aluminium composite windows forming the inner layer.

Elsewhere a contrasting horizontal layering is achieved by using projecting eaves, highly articulated staircases at block ends and projecting bay elements. Other elevations are faced with a mixture of brick, render and glass block and/or terracotta panels set within an aluminium frame to be cohesive with the timber/aluminium windows and brise soleil.

The facing materials have been carefully selected to enhance the design and to ensure that the building retains its quality with the minimum of maintenance. The roof oversails the external walls to provide summer shading and to provide weather protection for the external walls. The north, east and courtyard elevations are finished primarily in facing brickwork with white render to the ground floor and window/terracotta bands on the upper floors.

Hospitals are in use 24 hours a day and, as a consequence, attention has been given to designing the elevations to reflect both day and night interest. Night-time views of the building with the large areas of window and glass blocks sparkling and with external lighting will provide a night-time panorama.

Externally, a family of hardscape details and street furniture have been carefully chosen to unite the site aesthetically, although use of vertical elements externally has been minimised to reduce visual clutter around the site. The softscape has been designed to proactively benefit the site users, with the planting of over 600 trees, which will increase the biomass and ecological footprint of the site while acting as filters to the emissions caused by vehicles using the site. Colour and texture are used extensively to promote seasonal awareness among site users.

Good hospitals have a feeling of harmony. The appropriateness of materials, colour schemes, interior decoration and artwork, water and landscaping all contribute to a sense of calm.

Internally, the hospital is organized in a simple, legible way with the Outpatients, Parent and Child

Glazed canopy at outpatient
entrance

Departments and entrances in the south block, Treatment and Diagnostic Departments in the central block and wards in the north block. The hospital is naturally ventilated except in areas that require mechanical ventilation for functional reasons.

As with the external fabric, the internal materials have been chosen to enhance the design and minimise maintenance. The internal environment is designed to identify a clear and orderly sequence of spaces and events from the main entrance of the hospital to individual rooms.

The main entrance is designed to create a link between the outside spaces of the hospital and the interior. It will identify the range of materials and detail to be found elsewhere in the hospital. The location of the lift cores and hospital street are clearly defined. Hospital streets are clear and uncluttered with views into the courtyards to assist in orientation.

Within the hospital the 17 courtyards have been designed to provide a year-round foil of attractive calm within the building, adding rhythm and continuity to the diagnostic areas and a sense of discovery and place to the wards. Art has been incorporated as a result of additional funding from the King's Fund, heightening the attractiveness of the three largest courts.

All departmental entrances are designed with a clear focus and refer to reception desks and nurse bases found within the departments to avoid confusion and assist in patient/visitor orientation. Colours are used as part of a way-finding system through the hospital, with matching flooring, back panels and accent colours set against the base palette of pale and natural colours for walls, doors and ceilings.

The interior design reflects the character of the architecture with a unifying base palette highlighted by accent colours.

Structural Engineer's Input

The brief from the Trust was to provide a structure to last for a minimum period of 60 years and to require minimal maintenance throughout the period. The structure selected is part *in situ* and part precast reinforced concrete frame.

The floor construction consists of a precast void former slab with continuous areas of polystyrene void formers to provide flexibility for penetrations through the floors for services. This provision allows for the future changes of use to be accommodated without having to break out areas of concrete. The floor construction also provided the necessary sound reduction between floors for a hospital.

The structure to the plant areas is of solid construction for acoustic reasons to prevent noise breakout. Foundations are mass and reinforced concrete pad bases designed to suit the ground conditions. Geoff Shutt,[73] Waterman Partnership Ltd, stated: 'The structure has been designed to provide the hospital with a robust building which can accommodate the ever changing requirements of a modern healthcare facility.'

M&E Engineer's Input

Steve Pardy,[74] Zisman Bowyer & Partners LLP,

South elevation

commented: 'The brief from the Trust was to provide a modern well-serviced environment, whilst achieving a low energy target.' This has led to a largely naturally ventilated building, utilising mechanical ventilation and cooling where required for clinical reasons. Ventilation systems incorporate high efficiency heat recovery, transferring thermal energy from the waste exhaust air into the incoming fresh air.

Further energy savings are made by the installation of a combined heat and power (CHP) plant within the hospital's energy centre. Electricity is generated for use in the building by a gas-fired engine. The heat from the engine's exhaust and cooling jacket is then fed into the hospital's heating system to heat the building and provide fresh air and hot water. This gives efficiencies in excess of 75 % compared to conventional power stations of only 35 %. Electricity consumption is minimised by the use of high-efficiency luminaires and variable speed pumps to optimise load matching, which can further reduce electricity demand.

The use of these energy saving techniques have contributed to the new hospital achieving an NHS NEAT Assessment Rating of 'very good'.

A number of modern techniques were used to speed installation. These include mechanical crimped joints or small-bore pipework, and integrated bedhead trunking systems containing lighting, power and medical gases.

A 'patient services' system is provided to all beds to give patients access to entertainment and communication. These facilities include individual television screens, radio services and telephone,

funded by a 'pay-as-you-go' system. The services will be extended in the future to give broadband Internet access.

The engineering services installations have been designed to provide the Hospital with a high-quality environment for many years to come.

Contractor's Input

Taylor Woodrow was one of the first companies to embrace PFI and act as sponsor, equity provider, design-build and maintenance provider, and it is using this extensive experience continually to develop its products and maintain its position as a leading provider of healthcare facilities. Taylor Woodrow was instrumental in facilitating the deal and provided a full design and construction service and additionally the ongoing maintenance and management of the asset.

Building integrated project teams that are focused on delivering an improved healing and working environment for patients and staff is now yielding award-winning results for Taylor Woodrow.

Summary

The new hospital provides a 21st century facility for Bromley Hospitals NHS Trust, enhancing operational procedures, providing natural lighting in departments previously with none, ensuring natural ventilation wherever possible and creating an environment for delivering exemplar healthcare. Since opening in April 2003 the hospital has been highly acclaimed by staff and visitors alike. From the first impression of the main elevation, as the

hospital is approached, to the well-ordered departmental areas via the day lit hospital streets overlooking sunny courtyards, each visit is one of harmony and calm.

The hospital has now received several awards, including:

- Contract Journal's PFI Project of the Year.
- HD/NHS Estates' Building Better Healthcare Awards Special Recognition for the Implementation of NEAT.
- HD/NHS Estates' Building Better Healthcare Awards Highly Commended in the Best Designed Hospital Category.

Southern Cross, Melbourne, Australia

Project: Commercial high-rise development
Employer: Multiplex Group
Architect: Woods Bagot
Structural engineer: Bonacci Group Pty Ltd
M&E engineer: Lincolne Scott Australia Pty Ltd
Quantity surveyor: Rider Hunt Melbourne Pty Ltd
Contractor: SX Developments Pty Ltd/Multiplex Constructions
Contract value: A$275 million
Contract type: Design and Construct
Contract period: 39 months – completion due for July 2006

Introduction

The Southern Cross was originally a hotel, opened in 1962 and trading until it closed in 1996. The hotel had a history, being Melbourne's first international hotel, and there had been plans to refurbish it. When the developer went into receivership, the government gave permission for the demolition of the hotel.

The landmark Southern Cross development is situated on the iconic Southern Cross Hotel site, on the western side of Exhibition Street and adjoining the corner of Bourke Street and Little Collins Street. Southern Cross is well located on the eastern precinct of the Melbourne Central Business District. The site also enjoys excellent amenities with shops, restaurants, hotels, major office buildings and public transport nearby.

Woods Bagot's design for the Southern Cross project aims to 'break the mould' of commercial high-rise development. Unlike some high-rise buildings where scale-less bulk contributes little to the built environment, Southern Cross challenges basic assumptions to develop a new built form that is responsive to its context.

General

The Southern Cross commercial development will consist of two towers separated by a central tapering civic space, in the heart of the City of Melbourne. This study is about the first tower; currently the developer does not have permission to construct the second tower.

Stage 1 of the development comprises the construction of the five-level basement car park with parking for 951 cars, the 38-storey East Tower and the substructure for the West Tower pad site. The Stage 1 office tower will have a regular floor plate and a central service core, allowing for efficient and flexible use of accommodation.

The building has been planned by utilising the application of environmentally sustainable design principles of construction, design and operation of major buildings, with a double-glazed façade. This will facilitate reduction in the long-term operating costs for users and also substantially benefit the local environment.

At the time of this study, the developer Multiplex had managed to pre-let 68 % of the floor area of the tower to the State Government's Department of Justice, State Revenue Office and Department of Innovation, Industry and Regional Development.

Architect's Input[75]

The approach to the façade design reflects a strong commitment to addressing environmentally sustainable design (ESD) objectives. Performance of these façades is achieved through the use of glass technology, controlling both solar light and thermal heat, based on their orientation. For example, a significant emphasis has been placed on both Northern and Western façades through the implementation of a 'double façade' concept. This involves the use of two façades separated by a distance of 900 millimetres. The outer façade partly absorbs and reflects the initial solar light, and allows the warm air to move vertically within the 'double façade'. The performance of this system is further enhanced by perforated metal walkways between the two façades providing the concept of horizontal shading.

In essence the Southern Cross commercial project reflects the opportunity of integrating ESD design opportunities in particular through a large-scale urban project.

In terms of the building design, the architects tested a series of forms and plans with different arrangements of massing, servicing and circulation. The team refined a proposal based on a single 'offset' core that groups necessary support services along the western side of the building. This arrangement suited commercial planning requirements and created varied elevations specific to their orientation and context. A more solid presentation to the west elevation creates a logical solution to solar and heat control, while a twin skin curtain wall system to the balance of the west and north façades improves the building quality and performance markedly.

Unlike the typical high-rise office arrangement with its central core surrounded by a shallow ribbon of floor space, the offset core creates expansive, flexible working areas. While these deep plan floors suit the requirements of current city occupiers, the opportunity to introduce enclosed perimeter atrium spaces further enhances the light and amenity afforded to all areas of individual floor plates.

In both the podium and tower, the design allows for the atria to be naturally lit. A tenant can use the atrium as the focus of their operations, as a trading floor, library, exhibition space or casual meeting area. Tenants have the opportunity to add staircases to interconnect their floors and further animate the building.

The two- or three-storey atria scale and articulate the building's exterior. The vibrant and interactive organisation is reinforced by the rhythm of the highly visible atria structure to the east elevation. This structure, plan, organisation and form all come together to create a building bold in conception, rich in detail and elegant in form.

Summary

Although the building is not due for completion until July 2006, 68 % of the net lettable area has been pre-let, with the Government of Victoria being a major tenant.[76] The project was designed as twin towers; the second tower will be constructed under Stage 2 of the project.

The Custom House, Redcliffe Backs, Bristol

Project: 36 apartments in dockside location
Employer: Countryside Properties Ltd
Employer's agent: Woodeson Drury
Architect: Architecture and Planning Group
Engineer: Hyder Consulting
M&E engineer: Hyder Consulting
Contractor: Moss Construction
Contract value: £7.5 million + £3.5 million fit-out
Contract type: JCT 98 WCD
Contract period: 59 weeks + 42 weeks (fit-out) –
completion 2001

Introduction

The Custom House in the Redcliffe Backs area of
Bristol is an eight-storey steel framed apartment
block built on a city centre harbour-side site, close
to St Mary Redcliffe Church, and within the
conservation area. The project comprised the design
and construction of two elements of residential
accommodation on the harbour side in Bristol. The
intent was to provide high-quality living
accommodation within the shadow of St Mary
Redcliffe Church, but use the reflections from docks
to enhance the elevations.

Countryside Properties Ltd, the developer, had
always intended to sell the smaller first element to a
housing association and market the harbour side
block themselves. The second element, 'The
Custom House', has an exterior that is a
combination of brick panels and curtain walling
with steel balconies.

General

The employer and his team set this project up in
three phases, not necessarily using the same
contractor for each phase.

The first phase was to be an enabling works
package. This would clear the site for the main
contract. It was to be a traditional JCT 80 type
arrangement with the employer carrying the risks.

The second phase was the construction of the
shells. This included both the three-storey masonry
construction offering 20 apartments, with a
basement car park, as well as the eight-storey steel-
framed construction creating a significant harbour
side landmark. The eight-storey building includes
six penthouses with superb views over Bristol and
basement car parking.

The final phase was to be the fit-out of both
blocks. The three-storey block was to be sold as a
whole. Countryside Properties Ltd were going to sell
each of the apartments individually, which meant
that customer choice for finishing materials would
need to be integrated into the project.

Although the three phases could have been
undertaken by different parties, on this project the
same design team and contractor undertook all
three phases.

Architect's Input

The existing site consisted of two parcels of land
separated by an access road primarily used for
daytime office parking. In discussion with the
Planning and Highway Authority it was agreed that
the roadway should be pedestrianised on its original

Elevation of corner showing
cladding and different colours
of brick and stone

Detail at balconied corner

route, maintaining the site separation with the building along the waterfront responding to the warehouse character of the adjoining listed buildings and the building along the street frontage retaining the domestic scale and character of what would have been the original domestic street frontage.

The overall design intent was to develop buildings of unique character paying homage to their historic neighbours, but being very much of their own time to create landmark buildings on a unique intersection of the harbour side and busy roadway. The harbour side buildings were to take maximum advantage of their views over the waterside and look back across to the tall spire of St Mary Redcliff Church.

The initial design was worked up with the developer client, with the design-build contractor brought in at an early stage to provide expertise in buildability and construction programming.

The land purchase agreement was such that upon granting of planning permission, the full purchase price of the land was payable. However, full construction could not commence until the road closure was completed, a process that could not start until planning consent was granted. A construction programme was established to allow site preparation (including a substantial archaeological dig, which became a civil engineering exercise in its own right) and the main apartment block to commence without the road closure.

Each phase of the project was developed in detail before a fixed price was agreed, allowing all members of the team to contribute to the selection and specification of materials and to give the contractor the comfort of pricing a fully developed

scheme and subsequently reducing the risk element. It further meant that the 'client' was able to maintain a balance between design, buildability and cost, in particular avoiding the sacrifice of design for ease of build.

Tony Coles[77] of A&PG noted: 'The relationship with the design team remained amicable throughout, although as with all construction teams, there were points of debate during the on-site works but these were always resolved without loss of blood! Our difficulty was remaining impartial where we appeared to have two clients.'

Structural Engineer's Input
Although the steel frame was relatively simple, the bracing had to be carefully considered. The architect and engineer had to coordinate to ensure that the bracing did not obstruct a door or appear in a window opening.

M&E Engineer's Input
To maximise space within the flats, underfloor heating was used. Once the lining sheet, pipe work and pipe spacers were in position, a self-levelling screed was applied to complete the construction. Detailed design was left to the subcontractors. The electrical subcontractor, AR Daniels & Co (Chelt) Ltd, ensured full coordination between the electrical and mechanical services installation by producing computer aided design (CAD) layouts of each highly serviced apartment.

Contractor's Input
Within a short time of commencing work, the contractor discovered an obstacle. The previous

building, a warehouse demolished many years before the current project commenced, had been demolished but the existing foundations had been left in place. This had not been identified on any survey. The existing foundations consisted of a series of timber piles, driven into the clay. The contractor advised the most efficient way to remove the obstacles, pulling them out individually.

This element was in the first phase of the project, which was set up as a traditional JCT 80 type arrangement, the risk remaining with the client. The steel frame was designed such that small metal loops were added. These allow scaffold poles to be threaded through, providing instant edge protection. This is an example of the contractor inputting into the design, resulting in a small programme advantage for negligible cost.

The project had suffered a series of delays and as completion approached the construction was several weeks behind programme. Moss successfully negotiated the fit-out phase, although this phase suffered a delayed start. Through acceleration the overall project finished on programme.

The fit-out of the apartments was a very complex issue, since the fit-out elements are not determined until the apartments had been sold. The contractor liaised closely with the selling agent. When the fit-out options were determined, these were transferred to the subcontractor's work orders. Countryside Properties Ltd. later adopted the management method that the contractor developed to deliver this phase for use on other projects.

Tony Coles[77] of A&PG noted:

The key contribution of the Moss team was the ability to discuss problems as a shared responsibility and resolve them jointly, avoiding conflict. The contractor's team when putting together construction programmes was able to directly input the architect's information release programme identifying important issues and resolving them before they become a problem.

Summary

Tony Coles,[77] of A&PG commented:

I believe the final finished building to be a resounding success both in its design and quality of construction. The building has been well received as a contribution to the city landscape and was fundamental in kick starting the urban regeneration of the Redcliffe area.

The building is featured in *Bristol's Modern Buildings C20/21*,[78] which is probably a reward for the aesthetic complexity. Design-build has delivered the building, containing the costs within budget and allowing the developer to market the building with the comfort of knowing the fixed construction costs.

The building is unquestionably a success. The developer set out to create a landmark building, which would help to market it, attracting a premium on the market value and selling quickly. The developer had accepted the risk on the enabling works. Unfortunately the discovery of the existing timber piles, which had to be removed, meant that this risk was converted into a significant cost.

The contractor managed to deliver on time and to the agreed quality.

The Stevenage Centre, Stevenage

Project: New college building
Employer: North Hertfordshire College
Architect: Dyer
Engineer: Faber Maunsell
M&E engineer: Hoare Lea & Partners
Project manager/quantity surveyor: Heery
International/Ridge & Partners
Contractor: Willmott Dixon
Contract value: £16 million
Contract type: JCT 98 WCD
Contract period: 56 weeks – completion December
2002

Introduction

In the mid to late 1990s, the town of Stevenage
had a mismatch of educational output. The North
Hertfordshire College saw that it was vital to
contribute to a new vision for the town by creating
a centre of educational excellence. In 1999 land
owned by the College was sold to a supermarket
chain in order to realise assets to fund a new
College building. The College site occupies a
strategic gateway to the town centre and originally
comprised over 20 1950s and 1960s buildings,
which were energy inefficient and largely
inaccessible for the disabled.

The College's property strategy is to improve the
quality of their accommodation while reducing costs
by removing surplus, expensive or inflexible
buildings. Construction commenced in November
2001 on a 'College for the 21st Century' – a
building that was to be equipped to meet the needs
of the community in a technological age.

The New Stevenage Centre was opened in 2003
as a pioneering, state-of-the-art learning
environment. When opened it was the biggest
capital build for post-16 year olds further education
in the UK. The Centre now has 3500 students
using its facilities each day. The project was sized
at 84 000 square feet.

General

North Hertfordshire College is a designated Centre
of Vocational Excellence. It runs over 800
programmes for post-16 year olds higher education
students, lifelong learners and adults with special
needs and is an Associate College of the University
of Hertfordshire.

The project is for a new state-of-the-art 8000
square metre three-storey College building along
with various environmental and infrastructure
improvements. The IT system included computer
white boards and video links to accommodate the
latest teaching methods.

The project was procured with a design and
build contract with Dyer,[79] Faber Maunsell and
Hoare Lea being novated to the contractor. Dyer
was subsequently retained by the college to act in
an 'audit architect' role.

Architect's Input

The brief for the Stevenage Centre was developed in
line with the College's 10-year progressive
accommodation strategy and established the
following criteria:

- A creatively designed building that is a landmark and thus helps to promote the College in the increasingly competitive further education 'market place'.
- A building to provide the college's students – of whom 80 % live locally – with the most up-to-date further education facilities in the country.
- A building with social spaces that promote informal shared learning and a sense of collective endeavour.
- A building that is homogeneous and easily navigable yet accommodates a range of disciplines, encouraging interfaculty interaction.
- A building that is accessible to all students and to the community at large.
- A building that can generate revenue.

The Stevenage Centre is one of the largest further education college developments of its kind in the UK to date. The design emphasises social space and visibility with careful attention given to circulation and orientation. There are two wings of flexible teaching accommodation, which are organised around and are linked by a central three-storey atrium expressed externally by a smooth, sinuous wall that encompasses the whole approach façade. The gross internal area is 7428 square metres.

The atrium is a vibrant and dynamic space and the building's social focus. It houses a Learner services reception, a Careers Advice point, a drop-in community use IT Learning shop, and a range of commercial and dining outlets, including an internet café. At its centre is the building's visual focus – a

free-form suspended pod, clad in a mixture of clear and translucent glass facetted into a specially adapted curved aluminium frame. The pod houses the centre's administration functions and a Key Skills Development Centre.

From the atrium, the main staircase leads up to an open walkway enlivened by cantilevering balconies. This walkway links the three-storey Learning Resource Centre (which defines the 'hinge' of the building) with the two wings of teaching accommodation and meeting rooms to either side. The provision of large areas of fenestration to the teaching spaces fronting on to the atrium means that, although they are wholly internal, they still benefit from natural daylight. The teaching spaces are all equipped with 'smart' wall technology and have a fully integrated computer network system linking staff and learners. Lighting and acoustics systems support learners with visual or hearing impairments. There is a multiuse community hall on the ground floor.

The elevations were designed in response to the layout of the site. Those opening on to landscaped public space are a visually dynamic interplay of smooth white Sto render, glazing and sustainability sourced cedar timber cladding (pressure treated for resistance to water and fire). There is an appreciable gap between the sinuous screen façade and the timber and glass cladding of the atrium, the connection between the two being expressed by an exposed section of steel frame. By contrast, the elevation on to the main road is articulated almost solely in brick and metal panelling, thereby

External curved elevation

producing a solid acoustic barrier to the traffic noise.

As with most education buildings, the project was subject to a finite budget (£16 million). It was predominantly funded by the College who, in order to raise the money, had sold the land on which their existing facilities were built to the supermarket chain Asda.

Structural Engineer's Input[80]

The structure for the new College was formed in braced structural steelwork and supported on piled foundations. An option review was undertaken at an early stage to assess which structural solution best suited the layout, cost and programme aspirations of the project. The structural steelwork option with profiled metal deck concrete floors was adopted for various reasons, which included:

- Accommodation of the long span roof over the atrium and the regular general arrangement of the main teaching blocks within the College.
- Speed of construction to suit a tight programme reflecting academic calendar requirements. As the substructure involved bored pile foundations and a suspended ground floor slab it was anticipated that the steelwork procurement could run in parallel with the substructure works.
- The requirement for service penetrations required extensive risers and builders work trimming. This was readily achieved within the steelwork framing and metal deck concrete floor system.
- Cost assessment of the various structural options identified the steel frame solution as an economic basis for the new structure.

The steel erection site works was approached on two work fronts, starting simultaneously at opposite ends of the two regular teaching accommodation wings. As a consequence the project was two weeks ahead of programme when the principal structural works had been completed.

The length and shape of the new building required careful consideration of the anticipated thermal behaviour of the structure. As a result two movement joints were introduced into the building at the interfaces of the two wings with the more irregular central portion of the building. The movement joints created additional design complexity in terms of the support to the relatively long span atrium. The atrium beams were finally supported on the two wings via sliding bearings that simultaneously provided restraint to the front elevation, tall, curved wall. Further complexity to the design and construction of the atrium was created by the architectural requirement for the beams to pass below the peripheral and radial roof lights orthogonal to the window panels.

The stormwater drainage of the site required an innovative approach to the design. Stevenage Brook, a small stream behind the College and outfall for the stormwater was known to flood extensively downstream. As a consequence a very tight limit on the discharge of stormwater was imposed on the design. Various options to achieve stormwater attenuation were considered and discounted. The final solution adopted was 'Formpave', which utilises blocks with small recesses that allow water to drain into the sub-base. This sub-base was

Right
Interior view of double height space

Opposite
External curved elevation

selected to provide storage capacity and to attenuate flows to the Brook significantly.

M&E Engineer's Input

Hoare Lea adopted a flexible but pragmatic approach to the services design to allow differentiation between general teaching areas and IT intensive learning areas. The use of passive techniques and low energy systems was maximised. These include comfort cooling to all IT learning spaces and a combined perimeter heating/displacement ventilation unit for the general teaching areas. The atrium features displacement ventilation in conjunction with openable rooflights and a secondary reflector lighting system for uniform light and ease of maintenance.

Contractor's Input

The academic timetable placed large demands on the project planning. The new building had to be constructed while the existing ad hoc collection of 1960s buildings was retained in use. Completion was programmed for the Christmas break (2002–3) to facilitate the College's seamless relocation from existing to new premises.

The programme was rigorously adhered to. Construction started in November 2001 and finished 13 months later. This was challenging from a Health and Safety perspective, as the site only had one main point of access from the main road and so students had to share an entrance with heavy construction traffic. Considerate strategising and forward planning during the design development and construction phases minimised disruption, and pedestrian and cycle routes linking the site with the town centre were improved.

Summary

This is a very successful project, satisfying criteria from many viewpoints, completed on time and to budget. The building has been heralded by the Learning and Skills Council as the quality benchmark for further education projects in the future. Since its completion and occupation, the client's enrolments have increased by 27 %.

Her Majesty the Queen officially opened the college building on 14th March 2003. The building was funded by the sale of part of the existing site to Asda.

The design-build environment allowed the project to be managed to both cost and programme. Because of the close links with the contractor, the architect was able to produce extemporary architecture in the knowledge that it was buildable.

The atrium was reconfigured in December 2004 and is now a spectacular fresh new area with contemporary seating, screens and a stage area.

Wellington E Webb Municipal Office Building, Denver, Colorado, USA

Project: Office complex
Employer: Mosher Sullivan Development Partners
Architect: David Owen Tryba architects with RNL Design
Engineer: Martin/Martin
M&E engineer: BCER Engineering
Contractor: Hensel Phelps Construction Company
Contract value: $131 million (tower 85 %, annex 15 %)
Contract type: guaranteed maximum price
Contract period: 24 months – completion July 2002

Introduction

Wellington E Webb was elected the 21st Denver City Auditor in May of 1987. He served as City Auditor from 1 July 1987 until 1 July 1991, when he was sworn in as Mayor of Denver. In tribute to the Mayor, the Civic Center Office Building was renamed the Wellington E Webb Municipal Office Building upon its completion in July 2002.

'Annex One' was originally constructed in 1948–49 as a classroom building for the University of Denver School of Commerce, with the University occupying the building until January 1950. The building was listed on the National Register of Historic Places on 6 December 1990. At the time of its listing, Annex One was not yet 50 years old. It is important to note that National Register nomination documentation for properties of recent significance must contain deliberate, distinct justification for the exceptional importance of the resource. The clarity and persuasiveness of the justification is critical for registering properties that have gained importance in the past 50 years.' The National Register listing of Annex One in 1990 is important recognition of its exceptional importance as a significant example of International Style architecture in the United States. For this reason the original Annex One building was totally integrated into the new design, fully recognising the significance of the listed building.

The Wellington E Webb Municipal Office Building complex consists of the remodel of the existing 4-storey court annex building, a 4-storey atrium that bridges the annex building to a new 600 000 square feet, 12-storey tower and a 3-storey below-ground parking garage. The Wellington E Webb Municipal Office Building brings together nearly 2000 employees in 46 city departments previously scattered throughout two city districts. Located on the border of Denver's central business district and Civic Centre Park, the building creates a physical and symbolic link between the city's business and government interests.

The 12 office floors have a democratically designed space to plan with the most unique spaces in the building allocated to public areas, circulation along the glass and office spaces located within the building's core. The exterior curtain wall is designed to purposely allow a flood of natural light deep into centre of the building, with the first four floors open to the atrium to welcome this light and encourage interaction. There are about 46 government agencies consolidated under one roof, saving considerable lease payments by the agencies

Right
Cityscape featuring new
building

Below
Building elevation with flags
in the foreground

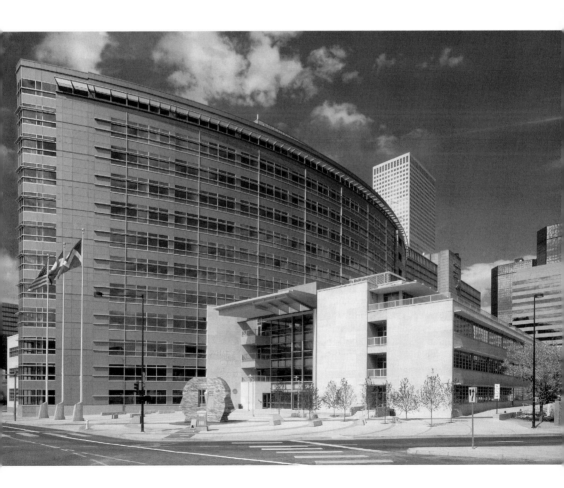

and providing convenience to the customers using these agencies.

The fast-track design-build process that Hensel Phelps used for this project allowed the team to finish one month ahead of schedule and the proactive management and coordination of design in conjunction with the owner's needs allowed for a $5.5 million added value for a cost of $1.9 million, primarily due to the success of the design-build process.

General
Following an extensive three-stage design competition, the design-build team of David Owen Tryba Architects and RNL with Hensel Phelps Construction Company was selected for the landmark Wellington E Webb Municipal Office Building project in Denver, Colorado.

Encompassing over 680 000 square feet of new offices (600 000 in the tower and 80 000 in Annexe One), the complex also accommodates 600 vehicles on three levels and 200 000 square feet of underground parking levels. In addition, the project included the renovation of over 80 000 square feet of an existing building (Annexe One), which was incorporated into the final design.

The procurement/selection process involved an assessment of best value (technical and price) and followed a series of design, technical, construction and budget workshops with the selection committee.

Additional challenges were authoritatively resolved when the security requirements of this design-build project changed dramatically as a result of 11 September 2001. Significant changes resulted in $5 million of change orders directly attributable to the enhanced security requirements, including upgrading the parking garage and loading docks to blast resistance and installation of state-of-the-art security and monitoring systems. The design-build process allowed the team to successfully incorporate these mandated security upgrades with less than five months added to the scheduled completion date.

Architect's Input
The client insisted that this should be a landmark 'green' building, one that is energy efficient and environmentally responsible. Before designing the building, architect David Tryba stood on the site at noon on 21 December – the winter solstice. He watched the sun rolling across the sky and then used a computer to plot the sun's path through the rest of the year.

Those measurements inspired David Owen Tryba Architects and RNL Design of Denver to create a building that minimizes the amount of sun that shines directly into the building, heating up the space. The building includes sunshades outside that extend about 20 inches from the windows. Those shades bounce light into the building and block some rays from penetrating the windows. 'It's like wearing a baseball cap,' David Tryba said.

The design made use of natural light to decrease the amount of electricity required. Private offices are located in the centre of the building and workstations are located around the exterior, allowing natural light

to penetrate into the building's core. Additionally, various components of the interior design, such as ceiling tiles and carpeting, are made from recycled materials. Other components were made using manufacturing methods that have a low impact on the environment.

The interior design team consisted of a joint venture of RNL Design and David Owen Tryba Architects. They determined that the interior design would be 'themed' and would follow the 'seasons', using three seasons on alternating floors. Tones and colour palettes would reflect nature and would be applied to the furniture, fabric, paint, interior detail and carpeting

A primary driver throughout the project has been to provide natural light throughout the building. To that end, the shape of the building provides good access to exterior windows. Materials were selected that utilise recycled content as well as manufacturing methods that have a low impact on the environment, like carpet and ceiling tiles.

The public art component of Wellington E Webb Municipal Office Building is visible throughout the building, as well as in its exterior park and plazas. Lead artist Larry Kirkland from Washington DC and Robert Murase, a landscape architect from Portland, Oregon, were selected to lead the public art design.

The Webb Municipal Office Building design incorporates 80 000 square feet of one of Denver's best examples of International Style architecture, Annex One. Built in 1949 it was totally refurbished and incorporated into the new building. Its north exterior wall is now part of the inside four-storey,

light-filled atrium. MacIntosh Park greens up the south side of the revitalised Annex One, where a bust on an engraved pedestal honours Denver City Councilman Kenneth Mackenzie MacIntosh. Plazas at both entrances of the Webb Municipal Office Building along Colfax Avenue feature large-scale public art displays. At the main entrance is located a symbolic large granite sculpture of a Janus head. Within this sculpture a plumb-bob points down to the city's history engraved in the granite paving.

The building achieved a merit award, with the jury commenting: 'The design is a strong example of Civic Modernism. The strong play between the existing building and the new structure creates a seamless composition. The building sports an elegant entry volume and an interesting upper curtain wall that creates a nice dialog with the solid base.'

Structural Engineer's Input

The foundations consisted of augured piles. The stair cores were *in situ* concrete and provided the necessary rigidity. The lower level parking areas were constructed from precast concrete. The Office Tower was constructed from structural steel with concrete on metal decks. The exterior wall comprises a curtain wall of precast concrete and stone.

M&E Engineer's Input

Innovative digital heating and air conditioning systems programmable for three office zones are included, together with a four-zone smoke control and fire alarm life safety system with state-of-the-art vertical pressurization. Southland provided design-

build heating, ventilation and air conditioning (HVAC) and plumbing services for this fast-tracked project.

One of the most successful attributes of the overall project was the startup and commissioning plan. Having a plan proved vital, for example, when the pressurisation in the stairwell during the period scheduled for balancing did not meet new code procedures implemented by the fire department and city inspectors. Southland resolved the issues by adding three pressurisation fans. Typically, a last minute change such as this could have taken two months to design, fabricate and install. Southland implemented the necessary measures in five days.

Contractor's Input

Awarded for design-build acumen, construction excellence and design excellence, this project was designed to meet an environmental target and criteria for design. Material selection and system analysis were constantly assessed against the environment performance standards.

Innovative ideas were the rule rather that the exception, including the Hensel Phelps custom limestone panel truss system allowing 33 trusses to be hung, similar to architectural precast panels. These innovative ideas led to 14 patents pending and energy savings to the city.

Summary

Michael Sullivan stated:[81]

I wanted to write this letter to express my sincere appreciation for the outstanding performance put forth by Hensel Phelps on this very high profile project. I cannot overemphasize how pleased I am with the results of every aspect of the job. From Hensel Phelps' initial proposals, its detailed estimates, all of the cost effective value enhancement suggestions, the hard-nosed approach to the subcontract buyout process, and overall quality of its self performed work, Hensel Phelps has exceeded my expectations every step of the way. I honestly trust Hensel Phelps 100 %. I cannot say this about any other general contractor I have worked with.

The building was selected for an award in the 2003 Architects Institute of America, Denver Chapter Design Awards.

Jack Mincher People's Choice Award, Project of the Year (over $40 million) – General Contractor, Bronze Award:[82]

Hensel Phelps Construction Co. directed a large community of designers and architects, engineers, construction workers, subcontractors, and other specialists for fast-track creation of the Wellington E Webb Municipal Office Building.

Despite the fast-tracking and budget restrictions, nothing was sacrificed – not quality, amenities or space. At more than 700 000 sq ft, the Webb Building at 14th and Court Place is the largest construction undertaking in Denver since 1932. Bridging to the original City and County Annex Building, the dramatic 12-story structure physically spans history and progress

Sun reflecting off the cladding
in the evening

by way of a stylised four-story atrium.

Housing more than 2200 city employees, the interior space creatively serves up curved walls, a maximum distribution of daylight through floor plates, 3.1 m ceilings and public spaces for art displays and civic exhibitions. The atrium space allows for easy access to high-traffic agencies such as Permit, Planning and Building Inspection divisions.

The Hensel Phelps team – which also included design-build partners JA Walker, David Owen Tryba Architects and RNL Design – controlled the budget, centralised coordination, fostered cooperation versus competition, expedited scheduling, provided systematic quality control and solved design/construction concerns to avert unexpected costs or lost time.

Choreography of all entities demanded tactical communication. For instance, during the intense six-month design phase, Hensel Phelps partnered with as many as 40 design team members. The compression of the schedule to a 24-month construction phase required as many as 600 construction workers and technicians to apply expertise, fat thinking and straight talk. Each entity was electronically connected to construction management for instant status checks, collaboration, and problem solving.

Substantial completion of the Webb Building came after only 24 months of construction. The project was brought in under budget and four weeks ahead of the compressed deadline.

Design Management

DESIGN MANAGEMENT IS THE PROCESS OF MONITORING THE DESIGN DEVELOPMENT OF THE PROJECT, ENSURING THAT IT IS CONSISTENT WITH AND CONSTRAINED BY THE EMPLOYER'S REQUIREMENTS AND THE CONTRACTOR'S PROPOSALS, FACILITATING THE PRODUCTION OF THE CONSTRUCTION INFORMATION AND ENSURING THAT IT IS OF ACCEPTABLE QUALITY AND DELIVERED TO THE AGREED PROGRAMME AND RELEASE SCHEDULE.

Introduction

This section is written from experience, although it does make reference to BS 7000,[83] which is the British Standard for design management systems, Part 4 being for construction. The basic design management process is similar regardless of the method of design or procurement route, but some of the terminology will change. This section is written for design-build type procurement routes, which include PFI.

The similarity of the format and terminology to ISO 9001 should be noted, although ISO 9001:2000 has been issued since the issue of BS 7000: Part 4. The British Standards Institute has worked hard to establish a common core through all design activities, regardless of whether design output is for a product, building or service.

Framework for Design Management

As the project starts, the project responsibilities and reporting routes need to be established. These will normally be recorded in a Design Management Plan (DMP).

The design manager (normally from the contractor) is responsible for establishing the reporting framework and coordinating the work of the design consultants. Initially he will contribute to the overall planning of the project and be directly responsible for planning, programming, controlling and delivering the design and design deliverables.

The design manager's detailed responsibilities at this stage include:

- Establishing the project brief, which should include the design-related client requirements.
- Participating in the overall development and monitoring of the design-related elements of the DMP.
- Preparing the DMP.
- Formulating overall targets for all the design team that are consistent with the DMP.
- Collating individual consultant design programmes and establishing a consolidated programme.
- Coordinating activities of the design team.
- Monitoring and controlling progress.
- Establishing compatible design information interfaces and a verification strategy.
- Determining the form and content of the design output.

Establishing the Brief

The project needs to address a set of parameters or a brief. Developing the brief involves input from both the client (employer) and the design team. It could also include other parties such as the planning authority and local utilities.

The brief development continues through the early design phases, being complete only when the client approves the consolidated brief. At this stage it needs to be tied back to the contract documents, since it represents both the Employer's Requirements and the Contractor's Proposals.

The client provides information, including the following:

- The purpose and proposed life of the construction.
- Functional requirements, activities that will occur within the envelope.
- Special, innovative or unusual features either required or to be considered.
- Health, safety and environmental constraints or requirements.
- Financial constraints.
- Time constraints.
- Quality constraints, life cycle costing.
- Aesthetic considerations including 'house style' and landscaping requirements.

The following work might need to be undertaken by the contractor and design team to clarify and to develop the brief:

- Technical and economic feasibility study testing the whole or part of the design.
- Prototype or model evaluation.
- Preliminary design.
- Site survey and investigation.
- Environmental impact assessments (EIA).
- Planning submissions and feedback.

Planning

It is essential that the deliver of the design deliverables is programmed, planning the design deliverables will involve:

- Establishing the required design team, which will include any specialist consultants or suppliers and manufacturers who have a design input.
- Identifying the need for other resources, either from the contracting or consulting environments.
- Establishing key dates for specific objectives and start and finish dates for identified tasks. This will enable progress to be monitored. These dates will form the basis of the Information Release Schedule (IRS).
- Determining intervals for reporting on progress, time and cost, both from the design team to the contractor and from the contractor to the client.

Design Management Plan (DMP)

The Design Management Plan is produced by the design manager and will normally contain management procedures for most of the design elements of the project. As well as general reporting, drawing issue and change control procedures and flow charts, it will typically include: a project directory, list of contract documentation, the design programme and Information Release Schedule (IRS), a detailed scope of each consultant's duties and details of any specific project controls.

The DMP is often based on a plan of work, the RIBA has a 'model plan of work' and most contractors will have based their own plan of work on this format. However, I particularly like a plan of work that includes the following stages:[84]

- Feasibility
- Concept
- Outline
- Consolidated outline
- Detailed design
- Construction information

However, the DMP needs to be fully coordinated with the consultant's appointment, as such, the best that I have seen is actually a generic DMP with the project specific information contained within schedules to the appointment itself.

Programming

At the project outset, the project planner will produce a construction programme. From this construction programme is derived a procurement programme to meet the construction requirements. The design manager then prepares the outline design programme, which feeds the procurement programme; the individual consultants produce their own design programmes. The design manager consolidates the programmes, updating the original outline design programme into the consolidated design programme.

From the consolidated design programme is produced the Information Release Schedule (IRS). This will normally be a schedule of dates for the design deliverables. It is normal for the IRS and consultant design programme to be included in the specific consultant appointment documentation. Although this then ties the consultant to feeding the project requirements, it does rely on the accuracy of predictions included in the outline programme. As information changes the consolidated programme may need to be updated. This could then distance the original consultant appointment from the current project requirements.

Consultant

The consultant should select the person who will represent the practice within the project. This will need to be a senior personnel. In line with ISO 9001, a precommission review should be undertaken, generally confirming that the practice has the ability and technically qualified resources to complete the project.

The project architect or engineer may have the following responsibilities:

- Establishing a rapport with and between design unit personnel.
- Liaising with the design manager, client and specialist advisers and obtaining the necessary approvals.
- Participating in the development of the design brief.
- Advising on the selection of the necessary resources for the design activity.
- Establishing channels of communication with other consultants, and arrangements for the distribution of information.
- Identifying the need for subconsultancies and specialists.
- Identifying relevant design procedures and sources of design data.
- Ensuring that all aspects of the commission are designed professionally and competently.
- Managing the overall design function for the commission including applying cost and design control procedures and ensuring that the outcome is of an acceptable quality.

- Obtaining planning and other essential approvals at predetermined stages.
- Monitoring the production and issue of design information in compliance with the IRS and design programme.
- Appraising designs from contractors, subcontractors and others according to relevant tender drawings, specifications and contractual requirements.

Consolidated brief

The project brief is rarely sufficient to meet detailed design requirements, and needs to be developed and refined as the design process proceeds. This development may include:

- Assemble all relevant information.
- Initiate studies, if appropriate.
- Try out various solutions.
- Prepare an outline scheme.
- Prepare an outline cost plan covering design and construction costs.

When the design brief has been developed to the point where it can be used for detailed design, it should be presented to the client as the consolidated brief.

The brief will form a report, which should be submitted to the client for comment and approval. A typical report will include:

- Introduction including purpose and significance of the report to the client.
- List of principle participants, including client, architect, engineer, planning supervisor and any other consultants.
- Identification of design personnel and other significant resources, such as a project directory.
- Research undertaken and outcome.
- Discussion of options, constraints and conclusions.
- Description of proposed design solution, including meeting/interpreting client's requirements, assumptions, legislative aspects, limitations, technical risk, construction problems and operational aspects.
- Cost plan.
- Ongoing design programme.
- Drawings.
- Supporting calculations.

As mentioned before, the consolidated brief represents the Employer's Requirements and Contractor's Proposals, and needs to be tied into the contract. Of course in the American 'bridging' system or the UK 'novation' the design is already adequately advanced to be at this 'consolidated brief' stage. Changes after this point will result in abortive work and additional costs.

Design Stages

The following stages represent the design 'steps' in completing the project design; these steps are identified in the plan of work:

1. *Feasibility.* Comment on scope/brief, selected options and management appraisal.
2. *Concept.* Selected concept proposals including business case and construction analysis.
3. *Outline.* Outline proposals including construction schematics to scales of 1:500, 1:200 and 1:100.
4. *Consolidated outline.* Updated design programme, developed brief, room data sheets, dimensioned location drawings from all disciplines, preliminary calculations. Interior design, landscape proposals, specification, identification of critical interfaces. Should comment on statutory compliance, whole life costing, project risk profile.
5. *Detailed design.* Updated design programme, developed brief, room data sheets, dimensioned location and assembly drawings from all disciplines, confirmed calculations. Confirmed interior design, landscape proposals, developed specification, identification of critical interfaces with solutions. Updated comment on statutory compliance, whole life costing, project risk profile.
6. *Construction information.* The required construction information and fabrication drawings should be prepared during this stage, together with relevant specifications. Tender action to select the various suppliers and other subcontractors may be completed using the information provided. All remaining design activities should be completed, including those occurring during the construction period and those that are necessary for completion of all site works and handover to the client.

Design input

Design input is more than the consolidated brief and includes all of the information that the designer will need to develop the design for the various design stages. Such design information may include the following:

*   The design brief.
*   Information from previous stages.
*   Output from other design disciplines or specialist advisers.
*   Design methodology and data.
*   Product information from manufacturers and suppliers.
*   Codes, standards and legislation.
*   Staff expertise and knowledge.

Design process

Various forms of design input need to be manipulated and coordinated to produce the design output. Significant design assumptions and decisions should be recorded as the design proceeds. This will allow traceability and provide evidence for more formal design reviews.

Design output

The form of the design output will be determined by the design approach adopted for each project and will vary according to the design stage. The exact form of the output will be agreed between the design manager and the various consultants. Such agreement could not only include the type of information but also how it is delivered, ie electronically in AutoCAD format.

The construction information phase should consist of a precisely defined collection of documents, possibly tailored to suit package procurement.

Monitoring

Having established the design deliverables required and a programme for their issue, the design manager now monitors the delivery. This monitoring is more likely to be a day-to-day activity but also at the end of each stage, the following should be undertaken:

- Check that the stage or overall objectives have been met.
- Prepare for the next stage by reassessing resources and the programme.
- Check that all authorisations have been obtained.
- Check that the design deliverables issued comply with the IRS, are of acceptable quality and comply with the brief requirements, including the ER/CP.

Design change control

It is essential that procedures for monitoring and recording changes are established at the project outset. Change can be highly disruptive and should always include an auditable process. This applies to both client and contractor instigated changes. The procedure for design change control should be recorded in the DMP.

Client initiated change will normally be carried out at cost and the contractor would normally receive some form of compensation from disruption. However, the responsibility for the implementation rests with the contractor.

Contractor initiated change will normally be for financial or buildability reasons; either way the employing organisation will want to benefit from the change. This benefit is normally in the form of a financial saving although increased quality or time recovery are also reasons to be considered.

Design validation and verification

Validation and verification are terms used in ISO 9001; validation refers to the data or design information used in developing the design and verification refers to the global design and whether it meets all of the design input requirements.

All design methods and sources of data should be validated. This would normally be done through usage and familiarity with the data, but any new information may be considered in terms of the status of the source or using technical judgment. This will particularly apply to product information. It is quite acceptable for a design architect to validate a product or detail by demonstrating that 'we have used this detail for many years without any problems ....'

Verification is checking that the design output complies with the design input, and should be carried out at predetermined points. This may be done through:

- Design reviews.
- Checking, approving, authorising.
- Testing repetition.
- Comparison.

Design review

A design review is the primary method of verifying the design and should establish:

- The requirements of the brief and any inadequacies have been recognised.
- The special features of the project have been addressed.
- Acceptance criteria have been met.
- The design follows good practice.
- All relevant statutory and planning requirements have been met.
- All relevant standards have been met.
- Due regard has been given to health and safety, fire prevention, safety, security and environmental impact.
- Validate/approved data, guides and other references have been used.
- Correct design criteria and conditions have been assumed.
- All calculations have followed approved procedures.
- All project documentation is coordinated and cross-referencing is satisfactory.

Completion

On completion of the project, the UK design team still have information to provide, particularly:

- Assemble 'as built' information and contribute to the health and safety file.
- Assemble operational and maintenance procedures.

If a particular defect has been found, the design team may be requested to inspect the works, identify nonconformity and suggest corrective action.

Design Manager

A design manager is a person, and will have his own feelings about different architectural techniques and construction methods. He may consider that some particular construction techniques, details or products carry too much risk of failure for the contractor to allow these to be used on a project. Such a consideration normally comes from experience; ie the same product or detail has failed on a previous project.

This experience is used when checking consultant's information, in simplistic terms. There are three 'hats' to wear when checking design information:

1. *Basic*. Checking that design deliverables are delivered on time and that the content is coordinated with both the Employer's Requirements and the Contractor's Proposals.
2. *Middle*. As for the basic elements, but also considering the design/construction information in terms of construction techniques, ie buildability. Also a consideration of how friendly the design will be to construction tolerances, if all allowable tolerances conspired against the construction. Would it still work?
3. *Advanced*. This includes the two previous categories but then questions the design. Is there a better or more economic way of doing that?

Value Engineering

'VALUE ENGINEERING (VE)' IS A TERM THAT WILL CAUSE DESPAIR WITH MANY CONSULTANTS, INTERPRETING IT TO MEAN SIMPLY A COST-CUTTING MECHANISM, AND COST-CUTTING NORMALLY MEANS REMOVING THE FEATURES THAT GAVE THE PROJECT ITS INDIVIDUAL IDENTITY IN THE FIRST PLACE.

I PREFER THE DEFINITION FROM THE AMERICAN GENERAL SERVICES ADMINISTRATION:[85] 'AN ORGANISED EFFORT DIRECTED AT ANALYSING THE FUNCTIONS OF SYSTEMS, EQUIPMENT, FACILITIES, SERVICES AND SUPPLIES FOR THE PURPOSE OF ACHIEVING THE ESSENTIAL FUNCTIONS AT THE LOWEST LIFE CYCLE COST CONSISTENT WITH THE REQUIRED PERFORMANCE, RELIABILITY, QUALITY AND SAFETY.'

There are several terms used to describe the process, 'value engineering' and 'value management' being just two. VE can be applied to the design-build project delivery system at several stages, although the earlier in the process that the alternatives can be considered, the larger the potential savings.

Alternative engineering is most efficiently used by the contractor during the initial stages of project design and development. The greatest cost reductions are generally accomplished early on in design when the project programme, function, quality and cost information can be used at the conceptual stage to achieve the very important balance between owner need/desire and cost of construction.

However, there are many forms of design-build procurement that will not allow a contractor to be involved at this early stage. Both 'novated' design teams in the UK and 'bridging' in America develop the design to a relatively advanced stage, a stage where the contractor offering alternatives may be disruptive to the project.

The employer needs to determine what represents 'value' and how welcome cost savings would be. If cost savings are required, it will be necessary to engage the contractor at an earlier stage.

The history of value engineering can be traced back to manufacturing in 1930s America. General Electric (GE) began using the process by identifying unnecessary cost, or cost that contributed nothing to quality, use, life-cycle, appearance or desired customer features. Although the process was aimed at analysing the overall value of an item, it soon became known for its ability to reduce cost.

What began as a small division soon grew to become an integral part of the entire organisation. The savings that GE realised prompted other American corporations to embrace the concept and develop techniques that are the basis for current value engineering.

The American Navy's Bureau of Ships called the process 'value engineering' to reflect its emphasis and relation to engineering design application. The practice was extended to docks, yards and supply facilities. Soon, all armed forces made value engineering standard practice in all facility developments. By the 1960s, private sector designers and constructors incorporated value engineering into their processes.

The development has continued into the construction industry. Together with the realisation that value engineering works best as a collaborative, integrated process, not a set of singular examinations. The VE programme is an integral part of the overall project delivery process, not a separate entity for checking design decisions. For maximum effect without undue impact on project design deliverables, value engineering should begin early in the design process (concept design) and then continue through the scheme design and detailed design.

Primary emphasis is placed on obtaining maximum life-cycle value for money expended within project budgets. Improved value can be represented in a number of different ways depending upon specific project needs. This would include improved function, flexibility, expandability, maintainability and/or aesthetics, as well as reduced life cycle costs.

Secondary emphasis is placed on cost reductions derived from the programme. Reductions achieved to bring a project within approved budget or programme are not 'savings'. Savings only occur when required project functions and features can be delivered at a reduced project budget. VE is not to be applied as a simple cost cutting mechanism at the expense of required functions or features.

Where consultant's fees are based on a percentage of the construction costs, there may be resistance to VE. After all, if successful then the engineering will reduce the construction cost, and consequently their fees. This will need to be addressed for the process to function properly.

The VE team will provide the technical input, and should have experience of the following:

- Programming
- Architecture
- Engineering
- Cost estimating
- Specifications
- Special areas (environmental, asbestos, building automation etc)

The first VE study, at the concept design stage, is intended to review the basis of design decisions and could cover:

- Siting and building orientation
- Building form, shape and massing
- Layout
- Net to gross area relationship
- Design criteria
- Building systems selection options
- Building space/volume parameters
- Vertical and horizontal circulation
- Major mechanical, electrical, plumbing considerations
- Overall energy considerations
- Site access/egress
- Overall programming and phasing
- Subsoil conditions and geographical data
- Utility availability

The success or otherwise of a VE study is dependent on several factors, one of which is design 'quality'. 'Quality' in this context is a measure of the value and appropriateness of design decisions and the clarity of the design requirements. Good 'quality' design tends to yield less significant results in the VE study.

Design-Build

Prior to the VE study, it is helpful to assess the 'quality' of the original design. The following techniques could be used:

- Assess the quality of the design calculations and supporting documentation. Calculations and design rationale statements should be clear, well conceived and complete.
- Compare the estimated cost with other similar projects. A high cost might indicate extreme requirements or excessive design. A low cost might indicate inadequate consideration of life cycle costing.
- Consider the track record of the architect and engineer.
- Solicit the opinion of the contractor.

All construction projects have associated risks. A significant risk is always the ground. Contractors try to leave this risk with the employer by qualifying their proposals. It is possible that value could be added to the project by engaging a specialist geologist to reduce this risk.

VE is much more than just cost cutting. The VE study normally follows a VE workshop with all interested parties represented. The study should serve to confirm to the employer that the design is correct for his requirements and that the correct decisions have been made.

The Way Forward

IF DESIGN-BUILD CAN PRODUCE GOOD BUILDINGS, WHAT CAN WE DO DIFFERENTLY THAT WOULD IMPROVE THE PROBABILITY OF THE OUTCOME OF ALL OF OUR PROJECTS AND NOT JUST THE LANDMARK BUILDINGS?

Previous text has suggested that there is nothing inherent in a design-build procurement route, which will prevent good design and the construction of landmark buildings. The same assumption applies to projects procured through PFI. There is nothing inherent in the procurement that suggests that 'good value' is preventing the construction of excellence.

The case studies provide a global snapshot of the high standards that are being achieved, but if good examples are not the mean, what is the problem with design-build? Design-build procurement is different to traditional procurement. For success the client must get involved. Post-contract, the design team is employed by the contractor. Their brief is defined in the contract documents.

The client has to think at all times about what a new or restored building will contribute to the activities that will take place within it. This is true whatever the building type – a hospital, a school, arts or community building, shop or office. The real costs and benefits of a building are in its occupation and the client should be striving from the outset for a building that will maximise whole-life benefits.

It is now generally accepted, and Treasury guidance[86] makes clear, that selecting project partners purely on the basis of lowest cost rarely provides the best value. The costs of running and managing buildings over their whole life are proportionately much higher than the initial capital cost. Extra resources spent on design or construction to achieve high quality can pay for themselves many times over during the life of a building. The result will be better internal and external planning and a building that fits well into the neighbourhood, is more adaptable, has low maintenance, has sustainable and attractive materials and finishes and well-planned, cost-effective systems.

CABE (Commission for Architecture and the Built Environment) have produced a series of 10 key success factors. Following these should allow the client to be able to achieve the desired building. The keys to being a successful client:[87]

1. *Provide strong client leadership*. Effective decision making is only possible if you have a clear view of what you want to achieve at each stage and are able to give and receive the necessary information at the right moments.
2. *Give enough time at the right time*. A successful building will last many, many

years. The value of putting in time when it is needed cannot be overestimated. The client must take time to explore options, to get data on which to base decisions, to communicate carefully to all concerned and to decide what help to seek.

3. *Learn from your own and other successful projects.* The most effective decisions are based on thorough knowledge. To know what you could achieve, the client needs to understand what others have been able to achieve.

4. *Develop and communicate a clear brief.* A good brief must be allowed to evolve during the early part of the project. In its final form when detailed design is carried out, the brief captures all the necessary information:
   - Both the wider vision and the specific activities and operational requirements.
   - The desired image.
   - Atmospheres and quality.

5. *Make a realistic financial commitment from the outset.* Costs need to be realistic from the outset. It will help to benchmark these against a comparable project.

6. *Adopt integrated processes.* The client team is one of three major players, the others being the design and construction teams. An integrated team and work processes will help see that good design is the result, that the project is carried out efficiently and does not waste time and that the costs are contained to meet the budget.

7. *Find the right people for the job.* The client's in-house team requires people who understand your needs and someone to act as an internal project manager. If the client has little construction experience, they may want to include an external consultant, somebody with experience of designing buildings.

8. *Respond and contribute to the context.* The urban fabric or open landscape setting for the site is not a constraint, but represents an opportunity to develop a solution that adds value to the neighbourhood by enhancing the physical, economic and social situation surrounding the project.

9. *Commit to sustainability.* A design that takes a holistic approach will save money in the long run by considering the costs of the building over its lifetime.

10. *Sign off all key stages.* Every project has key stages or milestones, when agreement must be reached to allow the next stage to progress. Formal agreement, or 'sign off', is the clearest way to achieve this.

The above text is suggesting that the key to a successful project is not down to the contractor and design team alone. A client who is not prepared to invest in the initial brief is unlikely to reap the reward from the finished project.

Perhaps the real way forward is not the refinement of a particular procurement route but the education of our clients.

NOTES

NOTES

1. Sir Michael Latham, feature in *Building* magazine, Friday 10 May 2005.
2. David Hutchison of DHP Architects, Bath, provided the information directly for this publication.
3. Will Hughes, University of Reading, 'Comparative costs of the commercial process in different construction procurement methods', paper to the Joint International Symposium of CIB Working Commissions W55, W65 and W107, Singapore, October 2003.
4. Figures provided for this publication by Robin Butler, managing director, Moss Construction.
5. Figures provided by RG Carter on their internet site, www.rgcarter-construction.co.uk.
6. Quotation provided for this publication by John Turner, technical services director, Moss Construction.
7. *Constructing the Team: Final Report of the Government/Industry Review of Procurement and Contractual Arrangements in the UK Construction Industry*, by Sir Michael Latham, 30 July 1994.
8. *Rethinking Construction: Procurement and Partnering (Report of the Construction Task Force on the Scope for Improving Quality and Efficiency in UK Construction)*, by Sir John Egan, 1 January 1998.
9. Brian Wilson MP, Minister for Construction, writing the foreword for *Accelerating Change, A Report by the Strategic Forum for Construction*, chaired by Sir John Egan.
10. *Constructive Change*, report produced by the RIBA Practice Department, 1999.
11. Design Quality Indicators are available online through www.dqi.org.uk.
12. Quotation provided directly for this publication by Richard Brindley, director of practice, RIBA.
13. Quotation provided directly for this publication by Kevin Merris, employer's agent/QS, Faithful & Gould, Birmingham.
14. Quotation provided directly for this publication by John Cristophers, principal design architect, Associated Architects, Birmingham.
15. Quotation provided directly for this publication by Steve Andrews, principal architect, Gensler, London.
16. Quotation provided directly for this publication by Ed Badke, director of RICS.
17. Quotation provided directly for this publication by Jo Wright, Project architect, Feilden Clegg Bradley, Bath.
18. Attributed to the National Audit Office and published in the OGC document, *Achieving Excellence in Construction Guide 06, Procurement and Contract Strategies*, 2003.
19. Quotation provided directly for this publication by Chris Johnson, managing director, Gensler, London.
20. *Which Contract?* third edition by Stanley Cox and Hugh Clamp, RIBA Enterprises, 2003.
21. *Risk and Value for Money Management in the UK PPP/PFI Projects* by Professor Akintola Akintoye of Glasgow Caledonian University School for the Natural and Built Environment.
22. Rt Hon Gordon Brown MP, Chancellor of the Exchequer, excerpt from his Budget Speech 2005.
23. PPP Forum database, March 2005.
24. National Audit Office, *PFI: Construction Performance*, February 2003.
25. HM Treasury, *PFI: Meeting the Investment Challenge*, July 2003.
26. HM Treasury, *Treasury Taskforce – Step-by-Step Guide to the PFI Procurement Process*, available from www.hm-treasury.gov.uk.
27. Taken from Woods Bagot marketing information and further details provided specifically for this publication.
28. Taken from the Bovis Lend lease website www.bovislendlease.com.
29. Taken from the Australian Bureau of Statistics website www.abs.gov.au.
30. Taken from the article 'Designing outside the comfort zone' on the website www.propertyoz.com.au.
31. Information taken from the Argent website, www.brindleyplace.com.
32. Roger Madelin is Chief Executive of the Argent Group; the quote is taken from the RIBA website, www.riba.org.
33. Quotation taken from a *Birmingham Post* article by Neil Connor, dated 22 October 2003. Full text is available on www.icbirmingham.co.uk.
34. *Better Civic Buildings and Spaces*, produced by CABE, www.cabe.org.uk.
35. Taken from www.lookingatbuildings.org, an education resource created by the Pevsner Architectural Guides.
36. Taken from a review by CABE, www.cabe.org.uk.
37. Most information was taken from the project website, www.eastend.dgs.ca.gov.
38. Taken from a paper by Jim Avant and Jim Ogden, 3D/International Inc, 23 February 2005.
39. Jonathan Lancashire, Bursar of Dean Close School, provided quotation directly for this publication.
40. John Christophers, design architect, Associated Architects provided quotation directly for this publication.
41. Kevin Merris, Employer's Agent, Faithful & Gould, provided quotation directly for this publication.
42. Chris Johnson is managing director of Gensler, London; quotation was provided directly for this publication.
43. Darius Aibara is principle engineer for TPS Consult; quotation was provided directly for this publication.
44. Taken from a press release by Carillion plc.
45. Taken from a press release 'GCHQ is "refreshingly different", 2 November 2004' on the GCHQ website, www.gchq.gov.uk.
46. Taken from a press release 'Doughnut scoops another award, 26 October 2004' on the GCHQ website, www.gchq.gov.uk.
47. Taken from a press release "Doughnut gets Royal seal of approval, 25 March 2004" on the GCHQ website, www.gchq.gov.uk.
48. Taken from a press release 'Foreign Secretary impressed by the Doughnut, 19 January 2004' on the GCHQ website, www.gchq.gov.uk.
49. Gandhi's quotation is taken from the Carillion plc promotional material for the Great Western Hospital project.
50. Les Meaton, technical project manager of Swindon and Marlborough NHS Trust, quoted in the Carillion plc promotional material for the Great Western Hospital project.
51. Paul Dempster, construction project manager, quoted in the

PHOTOCREDITS

Carillion plc promotional material for the Great Western Hospital project.

52 Carillion plc promotional material for the Great Western Hospital project.

53 Quotation contained in Carillion plc promotional material for the Great Western Hospital project.

54 Trevor Payne, director of estates and facilities at Great Western Hospital, quoted in the Carillion plc promotional material for the Great Western Hospital project.

55 Presentation to RIBA Healthcare Forum on 14 February 2005, by Les Meaton, Technical and Commissioning Project Manager of Inventures and Trevor Payne, Director of Estates and Facilities, Swindon and Marlborough NHS Trust. Full text is available from www.architecture.com.

56 From the original submission of April 1995 produced by the Mile End Park Partnership.

57 Taken from the National Playing Fields association website, www.npfa.org.

58 Ray Gerlach, acting corporate director of Environment and Culture at Tower Hamlets Council; quotation taken from the website, www.towerhamlets.gov.uk.

59 Roger Draper, chief executive of Sport England; quotation taken from the website, www.towerhamlets.gov.uk.

60 Councillor Rahman of Tower Hamlets Council; quotation taken from the website, www.towerhamlets.gov.uk.

61 David Hutchison, DHP Architects, Bath, provided the information directly for this publication.

62 Provided by Sue Hayward, Principal Museums Officer.

63 Taken from the www.kier.co.uk website.

64 Taken from the 'This is Wiltshire.co.uk' archive, 6 November 2002.

65 Iain Roberts, project director for Buro Four, provided the quotation directly for this publication.

66 From the National Trust Trustee's Statement 2003.

67 BBC News/Wiltshire, Thursday 10 April 2003.

68 Taken from the EuroPower.com website.

69 Press release from the office of Governor Frank Keating, 25 July 2000.

70 Press release from the office of Governor Frank Keating, 14 August 2000.

71 The website, www.oklahomadome.com, provided much of the information for this case study.

72 Craig Bennett of CODA was the project architect and provided the quotation directly for this publication.

73 Geoff Shutt of Waterman Partnership Ltd was project engineer (structure) and provided the quotation directly for this publication.

74 Steve Pardy of Zisman Bowyer & Partners LLP was project engineer (M&E) and provided the quotation directly for this publication.

75 Taken from Woods Bagot marketing information and further details provided specifically for this publication.

76 Taken from the developer Multiplex's website, www.multiplexpropertytrust.com.

77 Tony Coles, director and design architect of the Architecture and Planning Group, provided the information directly for this publication.

78 *Bristol's Modern Buildings* by Tony Aldous, a survey of architecture by the noted architectural writer of 100 years of Bristol architecture.

79 Dyer provided the information and images directly for this publication.

80 Faber Maunsell provided the information directly for this publication.

81 From the unsolicited 12 November 2002 letter by Executive Vice President Michael Sullivan of Mosher Sullivan Development Partners.

82 Taken from the explanatory award text shown on www.colorado.construction.com.

83 BS 7000 Part 4:1996, *Design Management Systems: Part 4. Guide to Managing Design in Construction.*

84 This particular plan of work is based on 'Project Life', developed for Carillion by Paul Hartmann.

85 *Value Engineering Programme Guide for Design and Construction*, Volume 1, *Internal Operations and Management*, produced by the US General Services Administration Public Buildings Service.

86 HM Treasury, 'Draft value for money assessment guide' and 'PFI: meeting the investment challenge.'

87 *Creating Excellent Buildings – A Guide for Clients*, produced by CABE; available from www.cabe.org.uk.

PHOTOCREDITS

Cover, pp 167, 223–25, 227, 247–50, 253, 254, 256–59 277–78 © Moss Construction, photographs by Martin Cleveland Photography; pp 5, 69, 89–91 images courtesy of Lend Lease; p 7, photography © Edmund Sumner; pp 31, 109, 111, 116, 123–27, 129, 141, 165, 191, 229, 230, 233–35, 237, 238, 241 photographs provided by Carillion plc; pp 33, 36, 45 Aaron Evans Architects; pp 47, 55, 57–9 images courtesy of Atkins Walter Webster; pp 61, 67 images courtesy of Parsons Brinkerhoff; pp 93, 103 images courtesy of Faber Maunsell; p 101 images courtesy of Laing O'Rourke; pp 143, 163 images courtesy of Alsop Architects/Blue Skies; p 177, images courtesy of Panos Pictures; pp 179, 281, 282, 284, 305 © Dyer, photography: David Barbour; pp 193, 287, 288, 290–91 photography copyrighted by Frank Ooms; pp 197, 201, 273, 275 photography: Woods Bagot; pp 203–11 images courtesy of Argent Group PLC; pp 213–14 © Birmingham Picture Library, photography: Jonathan Berg / www.bplphoto.co.uk; pp 217–21 © Fentress Bradburn Architects, photography: Erhard Pfeifer 2003; pp 243–45, © Limbrick Ltd; p 251 © David Hutchison; pp 261, 263, 264 © Ken Sharpe; pp 267–71, © CODA Architects.

TERMINOLOGY
BIBLIOGRAPHY
GENERAL INFORMATION

TERMINOLOGY

There are some terms, appearing in the text where further explanation would help understanding.

Novation. This is a term used in the UK to describe the situation when the client or owner engages the design team. The design is developed to an adequate extent to allow the project to be tendered or bid. When the successful contractor is identified, part of the contract documentation is the requirement to engage the specified members of the design team. It is often felt by the client that this reduces the risk of the contractor changing the design or downgrading the quality.

Bridging. This is an American term, although the process is used in Japan and the French system is very similar. The client or owner engages the design team who take the design to the detailed design stage. This detailed design will contain sufficient information to define the project and specify the quality of materials etc.This detailed design is then used for the tender or bid and is included in the contract documents as the Employer's Requirements (ER). In the UK, a two-stage approach is very similar, with most design decisions being made before the engagement of the contractor.

Architect of Record. This is an American term for the complete responsibility for design, production of construction documents and construction observation. The 'Architect of Record' is the legal entity that has contracted for and completed the work in question.

Design/build prime. This is the contractor who has a direct contractual relationship with the owner for the work, as distinguished from a subcontractor whose contractual relationship is not with the owner but with a general or prime contractor.

BREEAM. This is a UK sustainability assessment – the Building Research Establishment Environmental Assessment Method. Each project assessment is compiled by the BRE, usually for an accredited consultant engaged by the project. The assessment will cover the categories: Management, Energy, Water, Land use and ecology, Health and wellbeing, Transport, Materials, Pollution. The assessment calculates a percentage score; the highest score is 'excellent' which is awarded for scores over 70 %.

LEED. This is the American sustainability assessment, administered by the United States Green Building Council. The Leadership in Energy and Environmental Design rating has a metallic grading, gold being the highest. The standard was established with the aim to:

- Define 'green building' by establishing a common standard of measurement.
- Promote integrated, whole-building design practices.
- Recognise environmental leadership in the building industry.
- Stimulate green competition.
- Raise consumer awareness of green building benefits.
- Transform the building market.

BIBLIOGRAPHY

Jeffrey L Beard, *Design-Build: Planning through Development* (ISBN 0 070 06311 7)
David Chappell, Vincent Powell-Smith, *The JCT Design and Build Contract*
Design-Build Manual of Practice, available through Design Build Institute of America
Michael C Loulakis, *Design-Build Lessons Learned*, 2001 Edition
G William Quatman, Ranjit Dhar, *The Architect's Guide to Design-Build Services* (ISBN 0 471 47283 2)
SFA Design and Build Guide, A guide to the standard form of agreement for the appointment of architects for Design and Build (ISBN 0 947 87792 4)

GENERAL INFORMATION

BS 7000 Part 4:1996, *Design Management Systems*: Part 4, *Guide to Managing Design in Construction*, British Standards Institution (London), 1996.
Sir John Egan, *Rethinking Construction: Procurement and Partnering (Report of the Construction Task Force on the Scope for Improving Quality and Efficiency in UK Construction)*, 1 January 1998.
Sir John Egan (Chairman), *Accelerating Change – A report by the Strategic Forum for Construction*; www.strategicforum.org.uk.
Sir Michael Latham, *Constructing the Team: Final Report of the Government/Industry Review of Procurement and Contractural Arrangements in the UK Construction Industry*, 30 July 1994.
Better Public Building – Prime Minister's Award; www.betterpublicbuilding.org.uk.
The Great Buildings Collection; www.greatbuildings.com.

GOVERNMENT

'Achieving Excellence' Procurement Guides, National Audit Office; www.constructingexcellence.org.uk.
Creating Excellent Buildings – A Guide for Clients, Commission for Architecture and the Built Environment; www.cabe.org.uk.
Treasury Taskforce – Step by Step Guide to the PFI Procurement Process, HM Treasury; www.hm-treasury.gov.uk.

INSTITUTIONS

Architects Institute of America; www.aia.org
American Society of Civil Engineers; www.asce.org
Chartered Institute of Building; www.ciob.org.uk
Design Build Institute of America; www.dbia.org
National Society of Professional Engineers; www.nspe.org
Royal Australian Institute of Architects; www.architecture.com.au
Royal Institute of British Architects; www.architecture.com
Royal Institute of Chartered Surveyors; www.rics.org.uk